THACKERAY'S UNIVERSE

William Makepeace Thackeray: Self-portrait 1834

THACKERAY'S UNIVERSE

Shifting Worlds of Imagination and Reality

Catherine Peters

Oxford University Press
New York
1987

© 1987 by Catherine Peters

Published in 1987 by
Faber and Faber Limited
3 Queen Square London WC1N 3AU

Published in 1987 in the United States by
Oxford University Press, Inc.
200 Madison Avenue, New York, New York 10016

Oxford is a registered trademark of Oxford University Press

ISBN (U.S.) 0 19 504855-5

Printing (last digit): 9 8 7 6 5 4 3 2 1

Photoset by Wilmaset Birkenhead Wirral
Printed in Great Britain by
Butler and Tanner Ltd Frome Somerset

Contents

FOR ANTHONY

Preface

Ah sir – a distinct universe walks about under your hat
and under mine – all things in nature are different to each – the woman
we look at has not the same features, the dish we eat from has not
the same taste to the one and the other – you and I are but a pair of
infinite isolations, with some fellow-islands
a little more or less near to us.

Pendennis Chapter 15.

When Thackeray was a little boy, his favourite aunt Ritchie was alarmed
to discover that his uncle's hat exactly fitted the five-year-old. She took
him to the doctor, obviously fearing that the clever child had water on
the brain. She was reassured to be told that the child had indeed a large
head, but that there was a great deal in it.[1]

What there proved to be in it was, as he was to become increasingly
aware, a 'distinct universe'. Thackeray's way of looking at the world
was, at its best, to disturb nineteenth-century readers, forcing them to
re-examine their preconceptions; challenging assumptions about perfec-
tibility. His art takes an essentially moral view of the world. He
satirized his own society, but, unlike many Victorians, he had no
illusions about a golden age in the past, or a better time to come in the
future. The mixture of motives in the human mind, and the stratagems
that men and women adopted to get their own way in the world, were
his themes. He said of *Vanity Fair* that his aim had been to show a
society of people 'living without God in the world'[2] – the Biblical
phrase was also used as the title of a poem by Lamb, one of Thackeray's
moral heroes. In this he was in some ways similar to his contemporary
and rival, Dickens, but his methods were very different.

Thackeray's novels are not so much loose baggy monsters as parcels
that have come untied in the post, on their way from author to reader.
Characters escape, to turn up in other parcels, with different labels. It is
impossible to imagine Mr Micawber popping up in *Bleak House*, or
having an ancestor who plays a part in the plot of *A Tale of Two Cities*.
The world of a Dickens novel is self-sufficient, hermetically sealed; it
does not spill over into our world. Thackeray's writing, by contrast,

seems often process rather than product. He offers a shifting, kaleidoscopic view of a changing world which reaches out to the reader, but which he is continually prevented from entering by a number of deliberately used distancing devices. The frequent interruptions of a narrative voice which repeatedly shifts its ground creates a sense of contingent, provisional judgement aimed at the reader as well as the characters, forcing the final responsibility on to the audience.

Unlike Dickens, Thackeray does not work through exaggeration of character or incident. The grotesque is rare in his mature work, in spite of an early fascination with the caricatures of Hogarth and Cruickshank. 'I quarrel with his Art,' he wrote of Dickens, 'wh. I don't think represents Nature duly; for instance Micawber appears to me an exaggeration of a man, as his name is of a name. [I hold that] the Art of Novels *is* to represent Nature: to convey as strongly as possible the sentiment of reality . . . in a drawing-room drama a coat is a coat and a poker a poker; and must be nothing else according to my ethics, not an embroidered tunic, nor a great red-hot instrument like the Pantomime weapon.'[3] The establishment of the truth that may lie in the gap between one person's 'distinct universe' and another's, without ever losing interest in, and respect for, differences of vision, or taking refuge in a world of fantasy where exceptional sorrows are, on the last page, resolved into exceptional joy, was the task that Thackeray set himself as a novelist.

He was eventually to feel that it was a thankless task. He was branded a cynic, and a woman hater who saw all women as either stupid or wicked. His attacks on society, and the distortions it forced on individuals, were seen as attacks on the results, rather than the causes. His attacks on religious hypocrisy, especially of the evangelical variety, were seen as attacks on the Christian religion. He became so disillusioned and weary with what he called the 'novelist business'[4] that he would have given up writing fiction altogether if he could have afforded to, as Hardy was to do. The irony was that the first misrepresentation gave place, after his death, to another, equally mistaken view, based on a reading of his later work. He became revered as the typical exponent of Victorian middle-class values, and when these values were discarded Thackeray's reputation suffered a decline from which it has never really recovered.

One day in 1900, thirty-seven years after Thackeray's death, a faintly comic event took place which could be seen as symbolizing the problems for anyone attempting to adjust these persistent misrepresentations. A cab drew up to the door of the office of the Clerk of the Works of Westminster Abbey, in Dean's Yard. A small, determined, elderly lady got out, followed by a more hesitant younger one, and was greeted by the Clerk. The two were Lady Ritchie, Thackeray's eldest daughter, and her niece Molly MacCarthy. Anne Thackeray Ritchie had come to supervise a belated act of justice to her father's memory. Thackeray is not buried in the Abbey; he chose to lie in Kensal Green cemetery, beside his infant daughter Jane, but a bust had been erected to his memory in the Abbey, a heavy, not very well-sculpted piece by his friend Marochetti, wreathed in an abundance of Victorian whisker. Except for a short period when he sported a rather dashing little moustache, which he shaved off because it made his youngest daughter cry, Thackeray had always been clean-shaven, and Lady Ritchie had finally managed to get permission to have the bust modified. Under her keen eye, the stone was chipped away at until she was satisfied, and the great face appeared naked before its public once more.[5]

To remove the whiskers from Thackeray's literary reputation is a harder task. To Thackeray himself, the modern idea that a text should, or even could, be studied without reference to its author would have been inconceivable. He loved Lamb, 'St Charles', for his sweetness of temper and goodness to his mad sister, Fielding for his courage and kindliness; and he loved the *Essays of Elia* and *Amelia* for what they revealed of their authors, as well as for the qualities of the works themselves. 'Our object in these lectures is rather to describe the men than their works; or to deal with the latter only in as far as they seem to illustrate the character of their writers,' he wrote of his subjects in *The English Humourists of the Eighteenth Century*. It is, of course, a limiting view of literature, and his own literary and art criticism is bedevilled by the search for the personality behind the work, which often leads to a neglect or distortion of the work itself. Thackeray's judgement of Swift, of Sterne, of George Sand and Balzac, among others, is warped by his determination to see literature as a by-product of life, rather than an alternative vision of it. However, the twentieth-century critical theories that have proposed a complete schism between writer and work are hard to apply to a novelist who quarried his own life for the impressive edifices of the novels; they lead to other kinds of distortion. The problem is to keep a balance; to identify the raw materials, but to be aware that the finished work is a work of art, and not a covert autobiography. This study attempts such a balance, seeking to chip away at the view of Thackeray as one of the great, unread, unreadable, monuments of nineteenth-century fiction – a view still widely held, in spite of the scholarly rescue work of Gordon Ray, Robert Colby and John Sutherland, among others, and the lively studies of such distinguished literary critics as Barbara Hardy and John Carey.

A book of this length cannot include all the detailed facts of Thackeray's life. Those who wish to learn more can turn to Dr Gordon Ray's magnificent two-volume *Life*, and the four volumes of *Letters and Private Papers* edited by him. There is still no complete modern edition of Thackeray's works. The 1908 Oxford *Works of W. M. Thackeray*, in 17 volumes, edited by George Saintsbury, though unsatisfactory by modern standards of bibliography, has the advantage of Saintsbury's perceptive introductions to each volume, and the original illustrations. A new collected Riverside edition is in preparation, but so far only the *Vanity Fair* volume, edited by Geoffrey and Kathleen Tillotson, has appeared. The Oxford edition seems likely to remain the standard edition for some years to come. Many of the novels have been out of print for years, while the works of minor Victorian novelists are reprinted in paperback. *The Newcomes* at least should be made available again to the general reader.

Acknowledgements

I am most grateful to the institutions and individuals who have helped in various ways with the writing of this book. The first debt is to the work of Dr Gordon Ray, greatest of Thackeray scholars. Mrs Belinda Norman-Butler, Thackeray's great-granddaughter, has been unfailingly helpful and kind, and has given me permission to quote extensively from Thackeray's letters and private papers. Professor John Carey gave much needed encouragement and advice, particularly in the early stages of research. Dr K. R. Jamison, Dr Irvine Loudon and Dr Ray Ockenden gave me expert advice on, respectively, manic-depressive illness, nineteenth-century medicine, and Weimar at the time of Goethe. I should also like to thank the librarians and staff of the Bodleian Library, the British Library, the Print Room of the British Museum, the Victoria and Albert Museum, *Punch*, the Berg Collection at New York Public Library, the Pierpont Morgan Library, New York, and the Parrish Collection at the Library of Princeton University. I am particularly grateful for the personal help given me by Frank Walker, Fales Librarian at New York University, and Dr Patricia Willis, Curator of Literature, Rosenbach Museum and Library, Philadelphia. In addition to permissions granted by the above institutions for the use of unpublished material, I am grateful to the Oxford University Press and the Board of Trustees of the Leland Stanford Junior University for allowing me to use copyright material in print. Finally I should like to thank Giles de la Mare and Sarah Hardie of Faber and Faber for their helpfulness to a novice author, and my husband Anthony Storr for encouragement at times when it seemed the book would never be finished.

Chapter 1

The Passage from India

If we are to narrate the youthful history not only of the hero of
this tale, but of the hero's father, we shall never have
done with nursery biography.

The Newcomes, Chapter 4.

Thackeray is, of all the novelists of the first half of the nineteenth century, the most consistently realistic about marriage. In *The Newcomes*, which, with *Pendennis*, contains more material that can be directly related to his own life than any of his other fiction, Clive Newcome, surveying the wreck of his own first marriage, turns accusingly on his father:

> *You* had a wife: but that doesn't prevent other – other thoughts. Do you know you never spoke twice in your life about my mother? You didn't care for her. (*The Newcomes*, Chapter 68)

It is not only foolish first marriages that he scrutinizes without sentimentality, but the second ones that should put everything right. 'You must let Dobbin marry Amelia,' said Mrs Liddell, when *Vanity Fair* was coming out in numbers. 'Well,' said Thackeray, 'he shall; and when he has got her, he will not find her worth having.'[1] His refusal to allow 'good' characters a conventionally happy ending often distressed his Victorian readers; and he was forced, in a grudging half-page coda to *The Newcomes*, to allow Clive and his cousin Ethel to come together at last. 'We can hope they won't have any children,' he said to James Russell Lowell.[2] The story of Dickens surrendering the ending of *Great Expectations* to Bulwer's pressure is similar, but one senses that Dickens, who liked happy endings, gave way with less reluctance. In *Rebecca and Rowena*, Thackeray's affectionate comic sequel to *Ivanhoe*, the whole purpose of the story is to unite Ivanhoe and Rebecca, Rowena having been disposed of, and yet the marriage ends what had been a deliberately anachronistic romp on a melancholy note, and they, like Clive and Ethel, are denied offspring; their marriage is a sterile dead end:

> Married I am sure they were, and adopted little Cedric [Rowena's child by Athelstane]; but I don't think they had any other children or were subsequently very boisterously happy. Of some sort of happiness melancholy is a characteristic, and I think these were a solemn pair, and died rather early. (*Rebecca and Rowena*, Chapter 7)

The little boy, the only child of a previous marriage who is never supplanted by subsequent siblings, Clive's son, or little Cedric, is the person for whose benefit, one feels, the second marriage exists at all, even though it, and not the first marriage, is the real love match. Elsewhere in Thackeray's fiction the widow or widower, parent of an only son, is denied even this kind of devoted and implicitly asexual union. Helen Pendennis's first lover, Frank Bell, dies before her husband, and her only suitor in her widowhood is the ridiculous Mr Smirke, who is soon sent packing by her son. Colonel Newcome and Mme de Florac do meet again, but there is no question of their marriage. Helen Pendennis and Thomas Newcome are devoted, first and last, to the child who is, in each case, the centre of their lives.

In his presentation of these marriages and non-marriages in his fiction, Thackeray was combining reality with compensatory fantasy, paradoxically using the facts of his own early life and his mother's two marriages to create situations which are more soberly believable than the impossibly romantic facts of his own mother's past. The elements of drama and suspense in her story make it more like the plot of a novel by Wilkie Collins than anything Thackeray himself ever wrote. With marvellous material under his nose he steadfastly refused to use it in its entirety, or to grant his mother's happy ending to his characters; the little boy who felt ousted and was determined to be in some way the centre of the story ended by being more realistic than reality itself.

Three years before the birth of her only son, Anne Becher, then a girl of fifteen, went, like Catherine Morland, to a ball in Bath and there met the man she was to fall in love with. Lieutenant Henry Carmichael-Smyth was a handsome, gallant officer in the Bengali Engineers, home on leave. He was of good family, but a second son, with no immediate financial prospects, and Anne's family was not in favour of the match. Anne Becher had a turbulent ancestry. 'I have heard', her granddaughter wrote, 'that the Bechers were adventurous and excitable people.'[3] Anne's father had died a bankrupt, in spite of holding potentially lucrative posts in the East India Company at a time when such employment was considered a passport to riches. Her mother had left her husband and run off with a Captain Christie who also died penniless. She finally married a Major Butler, who, although he also died insolvent, had at least taken out two insurance policies on his life.

While their mother dashed round India in pursuit of men, her three daughters were brought up in Fareham by their grandmother, old Mrs Becher, and her unmarried daughter. Fareham, like Cranford, was a town given over to the Amazons, mostly the widows and daughters of naval officers, and the girls had a strict, old-fashioned upbringing. But the family strain of extremism came out in Mrs Becher's handling of her granddaughter's love affair. She was determined to part the two, by whatever means seemed necessary.

> Their secret trysting place was a terrace at the end of the Bechers' garden, past which flowed the broad tidal river which skirts the town. Here Anne was accustomed to wait for the boat which brought her lover. But their meetings were discovered, and Anne was ordered to her room, where she was kept under lock and key until she should give her word of honour that she would not again meet Ensign Carmichael-Smyth. With this order she refused to comply, and she was supported in her confinement by the letters which the Ensign managed to smuggle to her by a maid, and to which she replied by the same agent.
>
> Then suddenly the letters ceased, and one day old Mrs Becher hobbled into her granddaughter's room and told her to muster all her courage to bear a great blow; the Ensign had died of a sudden fever and on his death-bed had sent her messages of his undying love.[4]

This outrageous lie was compounded by telling Carmichael-Smyth that Anne no longer wished to see him. Anne, pining for her lost lover, was quickly dispatched to India to get over the affair; an odd move, characteristic of this eccentric family: Carmichael-Smyth had already rejoined his regiment. The subcontinent was vast, but Anglo-Indian society was small, and the chances of their meeting in Calcutta must have been high.

Even as a young girl Anne Becher seems to have had her share of the family taste for flamboyant behaviour. She embarked on the six-month voyage to India, in the company of her mother, stepfather and older sister Harriet, wearing a green riding-habit; hardly suitable tropical wear. Perhaps it was the closest she could get to mourning. This odd taste in clothes persisted; her granddaughter Anny remembered that she 'used to walk out in a red merino cloak trimmed with ermine, which gave her the air of a retired empress wearing out her robes'.[5] She was tall and extremely beautiful, with an imperious manner which impressed itself on all who met her. Thackeray remembered how, when he was a boy, she came to take him out to a concert 'splendidly dressed in a handsome carriage, and all suitable appurtenances',[6] and his cousin Richard Bedingfield described her as 'very tall, very graceful, and decidedly sarcastic'.[7]

Not surprisingly, she was a great success in Calcutta society, where there was a shortage of elegant and eligible young women. The suitable marriage her family was hoping for soon took place. Richmond Thackeray, so she told her granddaughters on the night she died, came courting her on a white horse, and she agreed to marry him without, so far as we know, any hesitation. He, like Carmichael-Smyth, was a second son, but in every way a more suitable *parti*. He had, at twenty-eight, already done very well for himself out of his East India Company appointments, and lived in the opulent style characteristic of Calcutta society, with his two unmarried sisters. In 1807 he gave 'a masqued ball of peculiar splendour'[8] – small, quiet parties were unknown in Calcutta – and a sale catalogue of some of his effects which were auctioned in 1806 gives an idea of the objects with which he surrounded himself. It is clear from this that many of his interests anticipated those of his son: 'an handsome Ebony Portable Desk, richly ornamented and mounted in solid silver; a large Mahogany Box of Reeve's colours, with silver mountings; an excellent Library of Books; Ackermann's Collection of beautiful Engravings for 1804–5 . . . a capital patent Saloon organ, with fine Barrels, of the lastest and most approved Tunes, having the Flageolet, Tabor, Drum, Triangle, Diapason Principal, Twelfth and Flute Stops . . .'[9] He also kept, in a separate establishment, a native or half-caste mistress, by whom he had a daughter; acceptable adjuncts to the life of an English nabob of the period. Richmond Thackeray was, without question, a gentleman, not in the spiritual and moral sense in which the Victorians came to redefine the term, but in the straightforward eighteenth-century style; a man of means and position.

Richmond Thackeray and Anne Becher were married in 1810, and their only child, William Makepeace Thackeray, named after his grandfather, was born on 18 July 1811. He was a premature baby, and his mother was told that, had he been a full-term child, the birth would have killed her. She must never have another. She never did; and Thackeray for the rest of his life was to have the advantages and difficulties of being the only son of a possessive and passionate mother only eighteen years older than himself.

In 1812 Richmond Thackeray brought an interesting young officer home to dinner, and Anne was faced with a revenant when the supposedly dead Carmichael-Smyth walked into her drawing-room. It is impossible to know what her feelings for Richmond Thackeray were at the time of her marriage, or to what extent she had got over the tragedy of her first love, but this sudden reappearance seems to have caused more than mere embarrassment. (In 1849 Thackeray still didn't like to hang up his father's portrait, feeling that his mother would not be 'over well pleased' to see the picture on the wall.) Eventually Richmond Thackeray had to be told. 'He listened gravely, said little, but was never the same to Anne again.'[10] Two years later he was dead of a fever. His son remembered him only as a very tall man, rising up out of a bath.

If the little boy imagined that he would now have his mother entirely to himself, he was soon to be disillusioned. She and Carmichael-Smyth decided to marry as soon as a decent period of mourning had been observed, and in the meantime the boy, like all well-to-do 'Indian children' of the period, had to be sent home to England. In the early part of the century there were no hill-stations to which children could go in the hot season, and they were often sent home to relatives at three, or even younger. Thackeray's mother kept her son as long as she dared, but in 1816, when he was five and a half, he and a younger cousin, Richmond Shakespear (later to be the rescuer of the European women and children from the siege of Kabul) parted from their mothers on the ghaut, or river-stair, at Calcutta. In *The Newcomes* Thackeray looks at the parting from the point of view of the parent, and makes light of the children's suffering; but that was after he had had many partings from his own children.

> Half-an-hour after the father left the boy, and in his grief and loneliness was rowing back to shore, Clive was at play with a dozen of other children on the sunny deck of the ship. When two bells rang for their dinner, they were all hurrying to the cuddy table, and busy over their meal. What a sad repast their parents had that day! How their hearts followed the careless young ones home across the great ocean! (*The Newcomes*, Chapter 5)

The voyage home, with a stop at St Helena where the boy was taken by his Indian servant to see Napoleon walking in his garden and told he was an ogre who ate little children, may have seemed an exciting holiday interlude, but the reality of life without his mother was soon to be brought home to him forcibly and unpleasantly. Thackeray was not to see his mother again for over three years, and to the trauma of being parted from her there were added almost unbearable experiences at school. The parting would not have been necessary at all if Mrs Thackeray had followed the path chosen by Mrs Pendennis, or Colonel

Newcome, who 'thought within himself, "no, I won't give Clive a stepmother. As Heaven has taken his own mother from him, why, I must try to be father and mother too to the lad." ' In real life, love for the man she had so cruelly been parted from took precedence over even her deep love for her son. She stayed in India; the boy was sent home to the grandmother who had once deceived her. 'In America it is from the breast of a poor slave that a child is taken; in India it is from the wife, and from under the palace, of a splendid proconsul.' (*The Newcomes*, Chapter 5)

The *Prince Regent* arrived in England just a month before Thackeray's sixth birthday. He was taken first to the London house of his father's married sister, Charlotte Ritchie, in Southampton Row. 'I think that Southampton Row was the only part of my youth wh. was decently cheerful, all the rest strikes me to have been as glum as an English Sunday,' Thackeray wrote to her in 1849.[11] The household was a relaxed and happy one; a grateful niece remembered Aunt Charlotte as 'the kindest of the kind, overflowing with the milk of human kindness . . . her elastic house was always ready to open its hospitable doors and take us all in. The house was true Holiday Hall to us, and seemed, at those times, to be quite delivered up to us.'[12] Thackeray's first glimpse of these jolly relatives, with whom he spent much time later, when he was a schoolboy at the Charterhouse, joining in amateur theatricals and drawing caricatures for the children, was relatively brief. He was taken from there to Fareham, where his great-aunt, always formally addressed by her mother as 'Miss Becher', took charge of him. His first surviving letter to his mother was written from Fareham. 'I hope Captain Smyth is well, give my love to him and tell him he must bring you home to your affectionate little Son' it ends wistfully.[13] Below the laboriously written letter there is a lively drawing of a man on horseback, and Aunt Becher's postscript tells her niece that 'William drew me your house in Calcutta not omitting his monkey looking out of the window & Black Betty at the top drying her Towells.' The father's talent for drawing, shown in the few sketches by him which survive, was already beginning to appear in his son.

Thackeray's drawings were treasured by his family and schoolfriends, and his talent recognized early. Drawing was to be a pleasure and a solace to him for the rest of his life. 'They are a great relief to my mind,' he said of his illustrations. 'I can *always* do *them*.'[14] At school his clever caricatures got him into trouble with his teachers, but were one of the ways in which he got by in an otherwise hostile environment. He was not physically active, being too short-sighted to be any good at sports and games, and was at first a small, timid, delicate boy.

A young Raphael.

The schoolboy caricaturist

He was sent first to a school in Southampton, with his cousins Richmond and George Shakespear, an experience which remained vivid for the rest of his life.

> We Indian children were consigned to a school of which our deluded parents had heard a favourable report, but which was governed by a horrible little tyrant, who made our young lives so miserable that I remember kneeling by my little bed of a night, and saying, 'Pray God, I may dream of my mother!' (*Roundabout Papers*, 'On Letts's Diary')

On one occasion the 'little tyrant', Mr Arthur, pulled all the boys out of their beds in the middle of the night and made them troop out to a shed, where each was made to put his hand in a sack of soot. Something had been stolen, and the master had the peculiar idea that this trial by ordeal would make the culprit reveal himself. This irrational petty tyranny, accompanied by frequent canings and semi-starvation, would have been hard for any child to endure, but must have been torture for a sensitive six-year-old who had been brought up in affluence, served, protected and spoiled by Indian servants; the adored only son of a widowed mother. The Arthurs' school must have been the first place where Thackeray had painfully to begin to construct the idea of a gentleman which continued to obsess him. A gentleman was not to be recognized by his material possessions, or his power over others, but by inner qualities of mind or heart. In one of the most bitter of the many passages about English schooling in his work, Thackeray wrote:

> I always had my doubts about the classics. When I saw a brute of a schoolmaster, whose mind was as cross-grained as any ploughboy's in Christendom; whose manners were those of the most insufferable of Heaven's creatures, the English snob, trying to turn gentleman; whose lips, when they were not mouthing Greek or grammar, were yelling out the most brutal abuse of poor little cowering gentlemen standing before him: when I saw this kind of man (and the instructors of our youth are selected very frequently indeed out of this favoured class) and heard him roar out praises of, and pump himself up into enthusiasm for, certain Greek poetry, – I say I had my doubts about the genuineness of the article. A man may well thump you or call you names because you won't learn – but I never could take to the proferred delicacy; the fingers that offered it were so dirty. Fancy the brutality of a man who began a Greek grammar with 'τυπτω, I thrash'! We were all made to begin it in that way. ('Punch in the East')

Schoolmasters and tutors in Thackeray's books are not always as brutal as this – often they are merely ludicrous – but, with the exception of Father Holt in *Esmond*, who is only incidentally a tutor, they are never gentlemen. Indeed the contrast between the pupil and the master set over him in terms of gentlemanliness is taken to ludicrous extremes in *Dr Birch and his Young Friends*, where Thackeray, after describing the idiot Plantagenet Gaunt, still kept out of the way at school though he is twenty-three, cannot resist making the comparison even between him and the schoolmaster and his family: 'And yet you see somehow that he is a gentleman. His manner is different to that of the owners of that coarse table and parlour at which he is a boarder.'[15]

His misery at the Arthurs' school must have been apparent to his relations, and he was transferred to a school at Chiswick kept by a Dr Turner, who was related by marriage to the Thackerays. This was an improvement, though he did once try to run away when he was in trouble for drawing a caricature of a master. While he was there his mother and her new husband returned from India. Her description of the meeting shows that it was a deeply emotional one on both sides.

> He had a perfect recollection of me; he could not speak, but kissed me and looked at me again and again. I could almost have said, 'Lord, now lettest thou thy servant depart in peace, for mine eyes have seen thy salvation.' He is the living image of his father, and God in Heaven send he may resemble him in all but his too short life. He is tall, stout and sturdy, his eyes are become darker, but there is still the same dear expression.[16]

What the meeting meant to her son may be gauged by the way he shies away from descriptions of similar meetings between parent and child: 'We forbear to describe the meeting between the Colonel and his son'; 'We will shut the door, if you please, upon that scene'; 'What passed between that lady and the boy is not of import. A veil should be thrown over those sacred emotions of love and grief. The maternal passion is a sacred mystery to me.' Partings are usually fully described in novels, sometimes with brilliant economy, but without shirking. Meetings after long separation never are.

Thackeray stayed at Dr Turner's until he was ten and a half. 'I do not think there could be a better school for young boys,' his mother enthused[17] but though he was, according to her report, sixth out of the twenty-six boys there in 1820, and younger than only four of them, he was inadequately prepared for the Charterhouse, which he entered in January 1822. His first interview with the headmaster, Dr Russell, set the pattern for his career there: 'the boy knows nothing and will just do for the lowest form' was the terrifying Doctor's verdict.[18]

English public schools at the beginning of the nineteenth century were notoriously in urgent need of reform, and 'The Slaughterhouse' as Thackeray called it, only partly in reference to its proximity to Smithfield, was one of the worst, in spite of having a good reputation. It was Carmichael-Smyth's old school; the Thackerays, including Richmond Thackeray, mostly went to Eton. Life at Eton under 'Flogger' Keate was no less barbarous than at the Charterhouse, but the education, within the narrow, exclusively classical limits universal in the public schools, was possibly better. It may be significant, too, from Thackeray's point of view, that he records, in *Philip*, that a group of Old Etonians discussing their schooldays all laid emphasis on the fact that the fearsome Keate was 'a gentleman'. Thackeray does not seem to have felt that Russell was.

9

The curriculum at Charterhouse was exceptionally narrow; the boys had to learn all the Odes and Epodes of Horace by heart, and did a couple of Greek plays very thoroughly, but little else. Russell had introduced, for reasons of economy, the 'Bell and Lancaster system', originally designed as a cut-price method of elementary education for the poor. Under this system junior boys were taught by seniors, and only examined on their work by masters. The 'praeposters', as the pupil-teachers were called, had a terrible time: 'to a boy who was not physically strong, the office was a sore burthen; and to those who were not mentally strong, it was a waste of time both to themselves and to their Form', Liddell, co-author of the *Greek Lexicon*, and a contemporary and friend of Thackeray's, commented.[19] Clever, well-prepared boys like Liddell managed to teach themselves something under this system; Thackeray, to whom such an education seemed totally irrelevant, gave up trying. He must have absorbed the Horace by a kind of osmosis. He was able to quote from him fairly extensively in later life, and one of his most elegant pieces of light verse is a 'version' of Horace's ode 'Persicos odi'. Yet Liddell said that Thackeray 'never attempted to learn the lesson, never exerted himself to grapple with the Horace. We spent our time mostly in drawing ... His handiwork was very superior to mine, and his taste for comic scenes at that time exhibited itself in burlesque representations of incidents in Shakespeare. I remember one – Macbeth as a butcher brandishing two blood-reeking knives, and Lady Macbeth as a butcher's wife clapping him on the shoulder to encourage him.'[20]

The poor quality of public school education is a frequent theme of Thackeray's journalism: examples can be found in *The Irish Sketch Book*, where he compares it adversely with the practical education given in the agricultural school he visited; and in 'Punch in the East', and *Cornhill to Cairo*. But it was not only the lessons, and the floggings, and worst of all the bullying sarcasm of Dr Russell, reproduced word for word in Chapter 2 of *Pendennis*, that Thackeray and other intelligent and sensitive boys found upsetting. 'Great schools suit best the sturdy and the rough,' Cowper wrote in 'Tirocinium', his attack on the public schools; and the vice, brutality and culpable lack of supervision which his poem castigated in 1784 had not been modified in any way forty years later.

Although Thackeray softened his descriptions of school life in his novels, designed for family readership, his letters and early journalism are full of bitterness at the total failure of the system to make boys tolerably happy. (He was still more outspoken in private. Henry Silver of *Punch* recorded in his diary that Thackeray said the first words ever addressed to him at the Charterhouse were: 'Come and frig me.')[21] The masters exercised little supervision out of class, and the physical violence of the boys to one another matched that of the masters towards them. Fagging turned the younger boys into little domestic slaves for the older ones, and left them little time for study, or even eating and sleeping. Bullying, and organized fighting with bare fists – Thackeray's nose was broken in a fight with his friend Venables – also contributed to the misery of an existence which seemed to many of the boys totally pointless. Martin Tupper, another contemporary of Thackeray's, who swore that if Dr Russell was ever made a bishop he would leave the Church of England, wrote of the evil effects on unsupervised boys of Smithfield, and the mean, prostitute-haunted streets round about: 'boys used to go . . . out of their way to see the wretches hanging at Newgate; . . . scenes of cruelty to animals at Smithfield were terrible . . . books of the vilest character were circulated in the long-room . . . both morality and religion were ignored by the seven clergymen who reaped fortunes by neglecting five hundred boys.'[22] Of course schoolboys have always read and passed round dirty books and used coarse language, and fagging and beating continued in public schools long after Thackeray's time; but the combination of brutality and sexual awareness in this exclusively male environment seems to have had a particularly deep and lasting effect on boys, who were often exposed to it very young. John Leech, Thackeray's lifelong friend, went to the Charterhouse at eight. Thackeray remembered the tiny boy being hoisted on a form and made to sing 'Home, Sweet Home', an incident he made use of in *Dr Birch and his Young Friends*.

Victorian society, in fact and fiction, was accepted as being divided into two parts: the gulf between rich and poor, Disraeli's 'Two Nations', was matched by the divide between the worlds of male and female, each with different customs, taboos and languages. When Pendennis comes home to his mother and cousin Laura, they cannot understand his slang, and this is symptomatic of a world they cannot and must not enter. 'You will not hear – it is best to know it – what moves in the real world, what passes in society, in the clubs, colleges, mess-rooms, – what is the life and talk of your sons,' Thackeray promises in the defensive Preface to *Pendennis*. 'The real world' is to be equated with the male world, permanently conditioned by school experiences of a barbarism and sexual explicitness that gentlewomen could never be allowed to know about, even though such a knowledge among mothers might have been the way to bring about reforms.

Thackeray's feelings about corporal punishment, and about physical brutality among schoolboys, were complex. He abhorred cruelty, and disapproved of power wielded by the strong over the weak. The hero in his passages about school life is the big boy who never initiates a fight, but will always fight in defence of a smaller boy who is being bullied. William Dobbin is a clumsy, physically unattractive grocer's son, but he establishes himself as a gentleman by fighting Cuff, the school bully, in defence of George Osborne. Champion, in *Dr Birch*, is none too bright, but his behaviour, like Dobbin's, is intended to ensure the reader's approval. A certain relish is apparent in these descriptions of justified violence; perhaps Thackeray, a short-sighted, gentle boy whose only fight at school seems to have been the one in which his nose was broken, got a vicarious satisfaction from depicting such events. As far as punishment by masters is concerned, the key factor seems to be that it must be carried out by an equal, not an inferior. In Thackeray's early writing the fact of the beating still matters.

> When, then, I came to Athens, and saw that it was a humbug, I hailed the fact with a sort of gloomy joy. I stood in the Royal square and cursed the country which has made thousands of little boys miserable. They have blue stripes on the new Greek flag; I thought bitterly of my own. I wished that my schoolmaster had been in the place, that we might have fought there for the right; and that I might have immolated him as a sacrifice to the manes of little boys flogged into premature Hades, or pining away and sickening under the destiny of that infernal Greek grammar. I have often thought that those little cherubs who are carved on tombstones and are represented as possessing a head and wings only, are designed to console little children – usher- and beadle-belaboured – and say 'there is no flogging where we are.' From their conformation, it is impossible. ('Punch in the East')

However, by the time *The Adventures of Philip* was begun, in 1860, the beating itself had become almost a matter of pride, part of the golden age which old gentlemen recall with pleasure. The opening paragraphs of Chapter 2 are only slightly ironic; the reader is left to take them quite straightforwardly if he (but not, I think, she) wishes. Three middle-aged men are discussing their schooldays at Eton:

> Each one, as he described how he had been flogged, mimicked to the best of his power the manner and the mode of operating of the famous Doctor. His little parenthetical remarks during the ceremony were recalled with great facetiousness: the very *hwish* of the rods was parodied with thrilling fidelity . . . All these mature men laughed, prattled, rejoiced, and became young again, as they recounted their stories; and each of them heartily and eagerly bade the stranger to understand how Keate was a thorough gentleman. (*The Adventures of Philip*, Chapter 2)

Thackeray never sent his own daughters to school, and dismissed a governess because the children were afraid of her, and her manners towards them were not those of a lady. Yet a letter to his mother about the necessity of whipping his adored Anny (aged six) makes distressing reading. He does not want to be present while she is beaten, but 'I wish indeed that for everything like brutality or violence or disobedience on the child's part, the rod should be applied to her: it is the only answer to such conduct, and you'll never keep up your authority without it.'[23] Perhaps he felt the straightforwardness of such punishment was preferable to the perpetual cloud of Christian disapproval which his Evangelical mother was inclined to spread around her in her later years. Certainly he felt corporal punishment a less terrible weapon than schoolmasterly sarcasm.

> Remember your own young days at school, my friend – the tingling cheeks, burning ears, bursting heart, the passion of desperate tears, with which you looked up, after having performed some blunder, whilst the Doctor held you to public scorn before the class, and cracked his great clumsy jokes upon you – helpless and a prisoner! Better the block itself, and the lictors, with their fasces of birch-twigs, than the maddening torture of those jokes! (*Roundabout Papers*, 'Thorns in the Cushion', *Works*, Vol. 17, p. 400)

When he was about thirteen Thackeray became a day-boy, lodging with a family who lived nearby. At the Charterhouse day-boys were a despised and bullied race, who had to be allowed out of school two

Asses' ears

minutes ahead of others to give them a chance to run for safety. Nevertheless the civilized atmosphere of the Boyes' household, in spite of some tiffs with Mrs Boyes, must have been a relief after the savagery of the 'Long Room' in Penney's House, where eighty boys ate, played, and studied together. When Mrs Boyes died in 1861 Thackeray wrote an affectionate letter to her son Frederick Boyes, recalling 'my illness at school and your Mother's dear kind face standing over me'.[24] After Thackeray's death, Boyes recorded his memories of him. His reminiscences are particularly interesting, because they are largely free from reverential hindsight about the great author. He remembered Thackeray as a stout, healthy boy, with a rosy face and dark curling hair, indolent physically, and avoiding schoolwork as far as possible. He was invariably good-humoured, and always kind and generous to younger boys.

> Instead of a blow or a threat, I can just hear him saying to one of them, . . . 'go up and fetch me a volume of *Ivanhoe* out of my drawer, that's a good fellow; in the same drawer you will, perhaps, find a penny, which you may take for yourself.' The penny was, indeed, rather problematical, but still realized sufficiently often to produce excitement in the mind of the youth, thus addressed, and to make the service a willing one.[25]

The general benevolence of Thackeray's heroes, when schoolboys, towards their juniors, which sometimes seems unrealistic, is based on his own behaviour at that age. Pen's care for young Clive in Chapter 4 of *The Newcomes*, and for Philip Firmin in *Philip*, is a reflection of Thackeray's own concern for Charley Smyth, a junior boy who was related to his stepfather. 'Shall I give Charley any tip I think half a crown would be acceptable to him & it would be no loss to me,' he wrote to his mother.[26] In adult life Thackeray said he could never see a schoolboy without wanting to tip him, and he was assiduous in providing young relations with the treats and outings that had helped to make school life bearable for him. His sensitivity to the sufferings of small boys was never blunted or frozen by his own experiences. But for public consumption he glossed over the misery. His middle-class readership needed to be reassured that such suffering was necessary for the proper formation of an English gentleman, particularly if, like so many of Thackeray's male characters, he was not a gentleman born, but the son of a *parvenu*. And so, when Thomas Newcome is sent to Grey Friars, he goes with delight, school food is transformed by a cliché into 'rough, plentiful fare', and fagging, flogging, fighting and gorging on tarts become the *rites de passage* which transform him from a hobbledehoy into an officer and a gentleman. When *The Newcomes* appeared in 1855 an article in *The Examiner* complained that the portrayal of the Charterhouse as 'Grey Friars' was false to the realities of the period.[27] It is ironic that Thackeray, one of the most unsuccessful and unhappy boys of his generation at the Charterhouse, should have done so much to publicize and perpetuate the myth of the English public school. 'There are but 370 in the school,' he wrote in one of his last letters from the Charterhouse, when the school was going through a particularly bad phase. 'I wish there were only 369.'[28]

However, though the official education provided there was useless to him, and, as Boyes wrote, 'no one could in those early days have believed that there was much work in him, or that he would ever get to the top of any tree by hard climbing',[29] Thackeray was educating himself after his own fashion. He spent much of his time drawing. He had a tendency to underestimate his own abilities, but he knew that he excelled at this one accomplishment, and achieved popularity through it, turning out, with astonishing facility, hundreds of caricatures and burlesque sketches on any subject which occurred to him or his friends. ' "I say, old boy, draw us Vivaldi tortured in the Inquisition", or "draw us Don Quixote and the windmills, you know" amateurs would say, to boys who had a love of drawing.'[30] Many of the surviving sketches are simply comic or descriptive; but some express a critical scepticism about received wisdom, or the excesses of romantic fiction, which seem prophetic. In his drawing of Clio, the muse of history is clearly an early version of Miss Tickletoby, whose lectures on English History were the first pieces Thackeray wrote for *Punch*. Umbrella and shopping basket in hand, Clio leans on a pile of 'histories' which include *Don Quixote, Orlando Furioso, Münchhausen*, and a school textbook, Rollin's *Ancient History*. A series of illustrations to *The Castle of Otranto* manages to make Walpole's gothic horrors irresistibly comic.

In an essay on Cruickshank written in 1840, Thackeray recalled how important his satirical prints were to him as a schoolboy.

> He is the friend of the young especially. Have we not read all the story-books that his wonderful pencil has illustrated? Did we not forego tarts, in order to buy his 'Breaking-up', or his 'Fashionable Monstrosities' of the year eighteen hundred and something? (*Works*, 2, p. 415)

He goes on to claim a jovial good-humour for Cruickshank, and a sympathy with his public: 'he pities and loves the poor, and jokes at the follies of the great, and . . . addresses all in a perfectly sincere and manly way.' This reduction of Cruickshank, one of the sharpest and most cruel satirists of his day, to a genial humourist, reflects what Thackeray

A Spanish Don

CLIO

Charterhouse drawings

saw in him as a boy; his innocent delight in parody, when he was still too immature and inexperienced to understand satire.

Parody – the affectionate attack on accepted norms – is a common form of adolescent self-expression, a bridge between imitation and originality, and a way of trying out one's powers without risking too much. It is difficult to ridicule, even though one may disapprove of, one who is himself ridiculing the status quo. Parody can also tame the terrifying, by making a schoolmaster a comic monster, or a Smithfield butcher an incompetent actor playing Macbeth. Usually it is a brief phase in an artist's development, but Thackeray, whose attempts at writing while at school also tended to parody, served an unusually long apprenticeship to it. His ability as a child to win popularity by drawing

A

LATIN GRAMMAR.

Sir William Wallace

FOR THE USE OF SCHOOLS.

Sir Aymer de Valence!

Thaddeus of Warsaw.

Charterhouse drawings

caricatures turned a private pleasure into a public performance; it was the only success of which he could be sure. In the end it was far from being a disadvantage that he took so long to gain self-confidence in his originality as a writer. The writing of parody entailed continued scepticism and careful observation, and this enabled him to evolve a narrative style which depended on perpetual self-monitoring, and often included self-parody. The performative nature of the drawing and writing he did at school also influenced his recurring vision of the artist as showman, a puppet-master at the service of his audience, and yet able to show the applauding circle that the stage it is watching has a mirror for a back-cloth.

Other consolations for school were reading, visits to the theatre, and eating. He read the eighteenth-century novelists and essayists, the gothic novels of Ann Radcliffe, Charles Maturin and others, the poems of Wordsworth, Southey, Byron, Keats and Shelley. He read, too, many of the now forgotten fashionable books of the period, such as Pierce Egan's *Life in London*, illustrated by Cruickshank, a badly written but frank account of the lives of Regency young men about town. He liked Shakespeare and Scott best of all. It is a fairly conventional list for a schoolboy of that date, but Thackeray spent more time reading English literature than more conscientious scholars, and he absorbed what he read so thoroughly that it stayed with him for the rest of his life. He and his fellow students in the Boyes' household also subscribed jointly to the most adventurous literary magazines of the day. Serious literature was at a low ebb in the late 1820s, and much of the liveliest writing appeared in these periodicals, in the form of short sketches and stories, and critical articles. Parodies were in fashion, not only with schoolboys, and *Blackwood's* and the *London Magazine* were merciless in exposing pretentious or inflated writing. The boys took both, and also the rabidly Tory *John Bull*, which Thackeray mischievously advised his radical mother to read.

Thackeray's lifelong love of the theatre also began at this time. Richmond Shakespear remembered him acting in amateur theatricals at the Ritchies, 'in a wig capitally got up as Dr Pangloss'.[31] But his great delight was to go to the play, whenever he could persuade an indulgent relative to take him. Theatre, for Thackeray as for Dickens, was an intense experience which bore little relationship to the intrinsic worth of the plays – apart from productions of Shakespeare, they were mostly rubbish – nor to the generally low standards of performance and production. 'Don't you like the play?' Thackeray once asked a fellow member of the Garrick Club. 'Well – yes – I like a *good* play.' 'Oh go along! You don't understand what I *mean*!'[32] He was unusually susceptible to the excitement of the physical experience; the heat and smell of the gas-lit theatre, the music, the illusion of the theatrical effects, which is no less enchanting because it is so palpably an illusion. He recalls this atmosphere vividly in 'De Juventute', and contrasts it ruefully with the sober realism of age, when he could only fully recapture the magic at second hand by taking schoolboys to enjoy the scene for him.

As for eating, Boyes remembered him as 'rather gustative, never greedy'; a nice distinction. Early-nineteenth-century children's books reveal that food played a far more important part in the lives of English children than it does now. No doubt this was because the food thought suitable for them was not only plain, but decidedly nasty. Vegetables were thought to be unhealthy unless they were thoroughly boiled; too much meat was over-heating, and 'sweet-stuff' was strictly rationed, and hence came to be used as a reward and the withholding of it as a punishment. Food became part of the parent's moral armoury in the fight against the evil which the Evangelical Movement saw as lurking in

Charterhouse drawings

every infant breast. Sweet things in particular came to be seen by writers, thus rationed in childhood, as symbols of pleasure, and often became, because of the prudery of the age, literary substitutes for the pleasures of sex. Thackeray continued to be decidedly 'gustative' for the rest of his life; but the emphasis on food in his writing is part of the literary tradition of his youth, rather than the unique expression of a self-indulgent man. However, unhappy children do tend to overeat, and he may have originally been encouraged in this by relatives anxious about his health when his prematurity at birth was still showing itself in his delicacy and small size. 'I have lost my Cough and am quite well, strong, saucy, & hearty; & can eat Granmamas Goosberry pyes famously', he writes in one of his happiest early letters to his mother in India.[33] His reminiscences of school, and his descriptions of his characters' school lives, almost always include some reference to 'the tart-woman', and his young men often confuse the pleasures of sex and eating, falling in love for the first time with the tart-woman's daughter. He considered the refusal of such goodies by a child mere affectation and childish snobbery.

Holidays were spent with his mother and stepfather, first at Addiscombe in Surrey, the army college where Major Carmichael-Smyth was for a time Superintendent, and then at Larkbeare, the house near Ottery St Mary in Devon which the family rented from 1824. Larkbeare, which is accurately described as 'Fairoaks' in *Pendennis*, was Thackeray's first real home since leaving India. The simple country life there must have been idyllic for a young boy, but increasingly boring for an adolescent who already knew something of the more sophisticated pleasures of London. The Carmichael-Smyths lived unpretentiously by choice, even before the loss of their money made strict economy necessary. The Major, on whom the character of Colonel Newcome was based in part, was a gentle, kindly man, very much under the thumb of his commanding wife. Thackeray, who called him 'father', was fond of him, and respected his integrity and unworldliness. But he had a certain amount of impatience with his stepfather's inability to stand up for himself, and the relationship of the husband and wife was not the model he chose when he himself came to look for a wife. Richard Bedingfield remembered that, 'He was convinced that a man ought to be superior in intellect to his wife. I mentioned some persons related to us, where the lady had most brains, and who had lived happily together. "I don't know how that was," he replied, "but, depend upon it, at one time the old gentleman ran some rigs." '[34]

His mother's undoubted intelligence, denied a creative outlet (later in life she tried, unsuccessfully, to write fiction herself), expressed itself in over-concern for her adored only son's success. Thackeray's performance at school was a disappointment to her, and her evangelical Christianity, which became more rigid as the years went by, led her to fear for his moral as well as his intellectual welfare. An atmosphere of loving disapproval clouded his adolescence, and contrasted sharply with the relaxed atmosphere of the Ritchie household where he so often spent half-holidays from school. As an adult, Thackeray sometimes had daydreams about becoming a country gentleman, but he was essentially a city dweller. Much as he respected the Carmichael-Smyths' austere and quiet way of life, he was also Richmond Thackeray's son, generous, free-spending, and self-indulgent, with a modest fortune of his own to

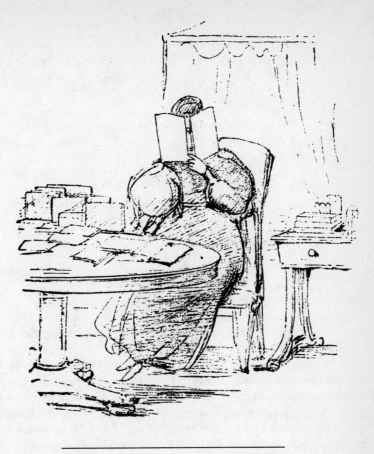

Mrs Carmichael-Smyth at Larkbeare

look forward to at twenty-one. His portrait of Pendennis, home from school after his father's death, lording it over the household as the young squire, reflects, with witty accuracy, his own situation when he left the Charterhouse in the summer of 1828.

Chapter 2

'The Education of a Gentleman' and the Education of a Writer

> Perhaps I misspent my time as an undergraduate.
> Perhaps I read too many novels, occupied myself too much with
> 'elegant literature' (that used to be our phrase),
> and spoke too often at the Union, where
> I had a considerable reputation.
>
> *Lovel the Widower*, Chapter 1.

Cambridge

For Thackeray the passage from boy to man was marked not only by his emancipation from the bullying of Dr Russell: 'On every possible occasion he shouts out reproaches against me for leaving his precious school forsooth!'[1] but by a sudden spurt of growth which turned him, almost overnight, from a boy to a young man. At the end of his time at the Charterhouse he had a severe fever lasting for several months, the first of the serious illnesses that were to punctuate his life. His head was shaved, a standard procedure then in prolonged fever, and he had to wear a wig through a hot summer.[2] While in bed he grew from being fairly small for his age – at fifteen he was five foot six – to his full height of six foot three. A contemporary at Cambridge remembered him as 'a tall thin large-eyed, full and ruddy-faced man with an eye-glass fixed *en permanance*'.[3] The short sight which had been ignored while he was at school was at last being remedied, if in a dandyish fashion in keeping with the 'buckish coat of blue-black with a velwet collar'[4] which he ordered in London on his way to Cambridge.

His illness had another effect on his Cambridge career: it was necessary to postpone his entry to Trinity from the beginning of the academic year, at Michaelmas 1828, to the following term. Before he left Charterhouse there had been some suggestion that he should be prepared for the university by the clergyman father of one of his schoolfriends. In the event he convalesced at home in Devon, and did some preliminary reading with his stepfather. It seems likely that the account in *Pendennis* of Pen's unsystematic but enjoyable gallop through the classics with Mr Smirke is based on Thackeray's reading with Major Carmichael-Smyth. The experience does not seem to have been of much practical use to him when he finally arrived at Trinity in February 1829, after the Lent term had begun. It was at this time, too, that he first burst into print in a local paper; not, as Pendennis does, with a sentimental verse effusion, but, characteristically, with a parody.

Trinity was, as it still is, the largest and one of the most prestigious Cambridge colleges, both socially and academically, and Thackeray revelled in having rooms on the same staircase as those once occupied by Newton, and boasted that one day their names would be remembered together. His late entry to Trinity does not seem to have been any handicap to him socially, whatever the effect may have been on his academic career. His rooms, on the ground floor just to the right of Trinity Great Gate, were not well placed for study: his letters home often refer to the difficulty of getting rid of unwanted callers.

Cambridge in the 1820s and 1830s was still dominated by the mediaeval syllabus which had kept it, like Oxford, behind the continental and Scottish universities in the development of new ideas in education. The mathematical tripos was the essential key to success, and though a classical tripos had been established in 1824, it was still necessary to have won honours in mathematics before being allowed to compete for it. The only qualifying test for entry to the university was membership of the Church of England, attested to by subscription to the Thirty-nine Articles. Consequently undergraduates were sharply divided into the 'hard-reading men' who were reading for honours, and those reading for a pass degree, who could occupy their time more or less as they chose. The punishing work schedules necessary to obtain high honours, which would lead to a coveted fellowship of a College; the narrowness of the course; and the often inadequate instruction, meant that many of the cleverest men of Thackeray's generation, Macaulay and Edward FitzGerald among them, opted out of the struggle and read only for a pass degree, spending their time in private reading which they felt would be of more use to them in later life. Thackeray, however, chose to read for honours, perhaps at the instigation of his ambitious mother, in whom he seems to have aroused that mixture of pride and irritation commonly felt by the parents of intelligent but lazy children. Dr Russell would hardly have advised such a course.

At first Thackeray's friends were mostly men who had been at school with him, but he soon made other acquaintances, such as John and Henry Kemble, the sons of the actor and nephews of Mrs Siddons. Though Tennyson and Thackeray were Cambridge contemporaries and later became good friends, they did not meet at the university. The two who became his closest friends, Edward FitzGerald and John Allen, he did not meet until Michaelmas term 1829. Cambridge was full of distinguished Thackeray relations: the Provost and Vice-Provost of King's were his cousins, two more Thackerays were Fellows of King's, and another cousin, Mrs Pryme, was married to the Professor of Political Economy. They asked their young kinsman to 'very, very stupid' parties, gave him good advice (which he ignored) on the management of his university career, and good, but insufficient wine: 'O such hock! never did I drink such hock! However there was only half a bottle of it between three – .'[5] His contemporaries provided livelier company. At first he went around with a Charterhouse friend, Carne, whose influence was not quite as sobering as Mrs Carmichael-Smyth would have wished. Together they serenaded an unknown girl, rode out to Wimpole and galloped in the park, spoke at the Union (where Thackeray, according to his own account, made an ass of himself), and kissed a pretty washerwomen. All harmless high spirits, but Thackeray found it necessary to reassure his mother that Carne's idleness was of benefit to him, since he was always rebuking him, and then found it necessary to live up to his own principles.

Such principles were unrealistic for Thackeray, though some reading men do seem to have carried them out. His early letters are full of plans to get up at four-thirty, go to his private tutor at six in the morning, and keep clear of wine parties. 'Tomorrow I intend to commence a steady, and systematic course of reading' is a typical promise.[6] For a while he paid the porter sixpence a week to wake him at six. But the struggle, particularly with mathematics, was too great. The tea parties of the serious reading men and the evangelical Simeonities gave way to wine parties: 'Reading men always have the largest wine parties,' he assured his mother, when on the point of giving one himself.[7] Like Pen he decided that 'private reading . . . was the only study which was really profitable to a man'; and he resumed his Charterhouse habit of omnivorous reading of novels and poetry, to which he now added history and biography. He bought 'a Gibbon for £2.10.0 it is not yet paid for',[8] Hume and Smollett's *History of England*, a life of Napoleon, and many other books, most of which he kept for the rest of his life.

He continued to make efforts to keep up his prescribed studies throughout 1829. 'I am just beginning to find out the beauties of the Greek Play . . . I pursue a plan of reading only the Greek without uttering a word of English.'[9] His private tutor was patient with him, and for a while he read Greek every day with a serious-minded undergraduate called Badger, a mature student, as he would be called

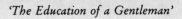

'The First Term'

'The Second Term'

25

nowadays, who was planning to become a clergyman. But the dry comment of his future son-in-law Leslie Stephen in his *Sketches from Cambridge*: 'The great difficulty of those whom destiny has marked for plucking is that they can neither keep their minds on one subject nor their bodies in one place'[10] was all too true of Thackeray.

Cambridge was full of delightful distractions, and though rowing was the only organized sport in those days, men rode, as Thackeray did occasionally, or swam in Byron's pool above Grantchester, or went for long walks. Other diversions were less innocent. The 'varmints' or 'sporting men' went to the races at Newmarket, as Thackeray and Carne did on one occasion at least, and many slipped up to London on illicit outings. Nearer at hand there were billiards at Chesterton, and the prostitutes of Barnwell and Castle End, unofficially tolerated by the University authorities, and kept in order by an occasional visit from the Proctor and his Bulldogs (the University police). Proctorial supervision did not prevent venereal infection from becoming known as 'Barnwell ague'. Drunkenness was considered a lesser offence than failing to attend chapel (not to pray, simply to register one's attendance), and the frequent town and gown rows, which often began after a wine party, when a gang of drunken undergraduates would issue forth to beat up the town 'snobs', were taken as a matter of course. On Guy Fawkes night such disturbances were an institution. Opportunities for running into debt were limitless. 'Put on a cap and gown and you can have tick for a thousand,' wrote a 'Trinity man' in 1827.[11] The Regency world of 'Corinthians' and 'Cyprians' which Thackeray had first come across in the pages of *Life in London* was still in existence, and he met the reality at Cambridge. He soon became known as a clever, non-reading man, and acquired friends among many different types of undergraduate, from the earnest John Allen, destined to become an archdeacon, who laboured to relieve Thackeray and FitzGerald of their religious doubts, to the shady Henry Matthew, who introduced him to the gambling set.

Thackeray made friends easily, if not always wisely, and began to make his mark in Cambridge not by intellectual brilliance – he was never one of the 'Apostles' – or by success in public speaking, but by his first foray into undergraduate journalism. A magazine called *The Snob* had been started by William Williams, a friend of Thackeray's, and Thackeray won acclaim by the publication in it of a neat parody of a typical prize poem, complete with explanatory notes, on the subject set for the Chancellor's Prize Poem for 1829, 'Timbuctoo'.[12] (The prize was actually won by Tennyson, with a hastily rewritten version of a poem originally called 'Armageddon'.) Writing was beginning to serve the same function as drawing in Thackeray's social life: 'Timbuctoo

Cambridge Habits

Cambridge Habits

recieved much Laud . . . The men Knew not the Author, but praised
the Poem, how eagerly did I suck it in!'[13] *The Snob* died a natural death
at the end of the summer term, though *The Gownsman* – no more
respectable than its predecessor – later took its place. Thackeray had a
lot of fun with them both, on one occasion making himself literally ill
with laughing while writing *The Snob* with Williams. His contributions
consisted almost entirely of parodies, burlesques and straightforward
copying of the style and subject matter of Theodore Hook's *Ramsbottom Papers* – the reminiscences of an illiterate vulgarian. Thackeray
gave his continuation of Mrs Ramsbottom's adventures a Cambridge
setting, and became adept at creating the mixture of malapropisms and
misspellings which Hook had borrowed from Smollett, and which
Thackeray was later to appropriate for his first real literary success, *The
Yellowplush Papers*. *The Snob* took up time that should have been spent
working for the May examinations: 'if I get a fifth class in the
examination I shall be lucky', he confessed.[14] He got a fourth; and went
off to Paris for the long vacation in a cheerful frame of mind with
William Williams, just graduated and engaged to tutor him.

Thackeray's first visit to the Continent does not seem, from the tone of his letters home, to have done much to dent his schoolboy insularity, though he was later to become far more appreciative of continental culture than most Englishmen of his generation. It was only fifteen years since Waterloo, and the average Englishman still regarded the French, the traditional enemy, with hostility and suspicion. Thackeray pronounced Notre-Dame 'not as fine as Exeter Cathedral', Tivoli 'nothing like our Vauxhall'. 'The Frenchmans cooking', wrote the future gourmet, 'I do not like as well as the Englishmans.'[15]

Between the lines of the letters designed for parental consumption, however, there are signs that what he later privately called 'the Incontinent' was affording the young man considerable pleasure. 'I wonder at your objecting to the Theatre-going', he tells his mother, 'for it gives me the best French Lesson possible';[16] and for a while the French actress Léontine Fay – 'the most delightful little creature I ever set eyes on'[17] – took the place in his heart occupied when he was a schoolboy by the English actress Mrs Yates. He saw Taglioni dance: 'who hath the most superb pair of pins & maketh the most superb use of them that ever I saw dancer do before.'[18] It may have been on this first visit to Paris that he had a somewhat closer association with the dancer Marie-Louise Duvernay, whom he referred to in 1833 as 'my ancient flame'.[19] She was a relation of the famous dancing-master Coulon, from whom Thackeray took the lessons he later used for a comic episode in *The FitzBoodle Papers*, where the lessons are abruptly ended when FitzBoodle bursts into a yell of laughter at catching sight in the mirror of the little master and his lanky pupil dancing together, 'which so offended the old man that he walked away abruptly and begged me not to repeat my visits.'[20]

Lessons at écarté were added to the mathematics with Williams, the French lessons with a M. Ori, 'a pleasant fellow enough, but dresses à la Snob',[21] and the dancing. Thackeray and Williams lived for a while in an 'idle, dissipated écarté playing boarding house' *chez* Mme la Baronne de Vaude. 'The situation is noisy but cheerful', he wrote.[22] A few days later he made the surprising discovery that 'I do not get on with my French so much as I expected for the people here are almost all English'.[23] The inhabitants included a Mrs Twigg, separated from her husband, whose dubious status alarmed Mrs Carmichael-Smyth, though her son assured her 'I never heard her speak a word which was not perfectly ladylike'.[24] Reproved by his mother for going to Frascati's, the smart gambling house, he responded with injured innocence:

it was a curious chapter in the book of life, the perusal of wh. has done me the greatest good – it has taught me not to trust so much in myself as before my pride or my ignorance would have led me to do; it has shewn me that I could not, (as few could) resist the temptation of gambling, & it therefore has taught me – to keep away from it ... I have discovered my temperament & inclination with regard to it, and the necessity wh. I did not then know of avoiding it.

The events of the next couple of years were to show that the lesson was not so simple nor so final as Thackeray wished his mother to believe, but the letter ends on a note which was to become characteristic of his view of life. However disingenuous it may be in this context, it expresses an opinion which was to become of fundamental importance to his writing:

may God grant that you never again call me avaricious and mean when I am but curious, that you never again think because I before was ignorant that therefore I was good; or that because I am now aware of my own weakness I must be wicked.[25]

Thackeray's second year at Cambridge was in several ways different from his first. The visit to Paris had made him restless, and the idea of academic honours seemed not only difficult of achievement, but increasingly irrelevant to his real interests. His introduction to gambling had fascinated him more seriously than he had admitted to his mother, and Cambridge had its share of dubious characters on the look-out for innocent young 'pigeons' ready for plucking. Chapters 18 and 19 of *Pendennis* give an authentic account (supported from other sources) of how a well-intentioned young man could be led astray by his desire to make a figure in the world, with 'little' dinners – the cookship at Trinity was said to be worth quite as much as the Mastership – a taste for fine bindings, rare prints, and good wines. This was the stage in Pen's, and Thackeray's, career, when the card-sharpers stepped in. In the brilliant sketch 'Captain Rook and Mr Pigeon', written ten years after he left Cambridge, Thackeray analysed the career of the card-sharper from the initial stage where he was himself a pigeon, to his seedy life as a plucker of innocent youth. The character of Deuceace in *The Yellowplush Papers* is an expanded version, and one end to such a story is told in 'A Gambler's Death' in *The Paris Sketch Book*.

On their return to Cambridge from the trip to Paris, Williams introduced Thackeray to Edward FitzGerald, whom he was tutoring for his final exams. They became friends at once. FitzGerald, neither a plodding 'reading man', nor a free-spending, coarse, irresponsible 'varmint', nor mindless 'sporting man', was just the companion Thackeray needed. FitzGerald encouraged him to think in intellectual terms that transcended the narrow limits of the University, and together they developed a crazy, almost surrealist kind of humour that marked an advance on the undergraduate parodies of *The Snob* and *The Gownsman*. The warmth and intimacy of their friendship continued to have an effect on both of them for the rest of their lives, even when they no longer saw very much of each other.

FitzGerald was in many ways quite unlike Thackeray. He had sufficient independent means not to need to think of taking up a profession. He was, too, abstemious and frugal by nature – he later became virtually vegetarian, and lived for most of his life in the country in increasingly reclusive simplicity. There is an amusing contrast between FitzGerald's charming but rarefied and unrealistic picture of Cambridge undergraduate life in *Euphranor*, written in the 1840s but not published until 1851, with Thackeray's more down-to-earth (and considerably livelier) accounts in *Pendennis* and *Lovel the Widower*. One of the characters in *Euphranor*, Lycion, could be meant for Thackeray: 'all the while he is pretending to be careless, indolent, and worldly, he is really bursting with suppressed Energy, Generosity and Devotion'.[26] FitzGerald was not without a streak of shrewd common sense, and it was he who warned Thackeray against Henry Matthew, who was later to appear as Bloundell, the gambling man who leads Pendennis into trouble. 'My dear old FitzGerald is always right about men: and said from the first that this was a bad one and a sham,' Thackeray told Jane Brookfield years later.[27]

By the end of his second summer at Cambridge Thackeray was deep in debts of 'honour', amounting to £1,500, which he paid off when he came into his inheritance two years later. Whether Matthew was the 'Captain Rook' who plucked the dandified young pigeon, or merely the means of introducing Thackeray to professional crooks, is not certain. But Matthew, like Deuceace, came to a satisfactorily miserable end. Thackeray went to see him in 1849:

I found an old man in a room smelling of brandy & water at 5 o'clock at Islington, quite the same man that I remember only grown coarser and stale somehow, like a piece of goods that has been hanging up in a shop window. He has had 15 years of a vulgar wife, much solitude, very much brandy & water I should think, and a depressing profession [Matthew had become a clergyman]: for what can be more depressing than a long course of hypocrisy to a man of no small sense of humour? . . . He can't walk, having paralysis in his legs, but he preaches every Sunday he says, being

Écarté

hoisted into his pulpit before service, and waiting there whilst his curate reads down below . . . He showed me his daughter of 15, a prettyish girl with a shrewish face, and bad manners – the wife did not show.[28]

Thackeray's growing awareness that Cambridge was bringing out the worst in him and suppressing his positive qualities led to an increasing impatience with his way of life. FitzGerald took his pass degree and left Cambridge in April 1830, and as a result of friction at home – he had an impossible mother – went to live in Paris for a while. This act of rebellion encouraged Thackeray to strike out on his own also, as he recalled in a Roundabout Paper, remembering a 'certain little Paris excursion (about which my benighted parents never knew anything) . . . Guilt, sir, guilt remains stamped on the memory, and I feel easier in my mind now that it is liberated of this old peccadillo.'[29]

He turned up quite unexpectedly on FitzGerald's doorstep in Paris, and was delightedly welcomed. He was, Fitz wrote to their friend John Allen, 'a little gayer than when I saw him last; but as kind as ever'.[30] The visit was brief, but by the time Thackeray got back to Cambridge for the summer term he seems to have decided that it would be his last: FitzGerald mentions a commission in the Registrar's office that Thackeray had applied for, in a letter to Allen of 16 May. Significantly, perhaps, no letters from Thackeray to his mother have survived for the period from November 1829 to July 1830, though she kept carefully almost all he ever wrote her. It is clear from a later letter that she was distressed by his decision to leave Cambridge without taking a degree, and that he was determined to have his own way.[31]

What was he to do in life? He had already dissipated part of his inheritance; the remaining £18,000 or so was not enough to keep him in idleness, nor would his mother's puritan conscience or his own ambition have allowed him to remain unemployed. The law seemed the only profession he could contemplate, though without much enthusiasm: 'a clergyman I cannot be, nor a physician, so I must drudge up poor & Miserable the first part of my life & just reach the pinnacle (or somewhere near it I trust, when my eyes will hardly be able to see the prospect I have been striving all my life to arrive at – These are the pleasures of the law.'[32] Meanwhile he set off for Germany, on a rather truncated and subdued version of the Grand Tour, armed with letters of introduction to important personages in Dresden which he was never to use. Making ready for the trip in London he had a few hasty German lessons, and characteristically took the opportunity to go to Kean's farewell performance.

Weimar

It was very agreeable for the English.
There were shooting-parties and battues; there was a plenty of balls and
entertainments at the hospitable Court; the society
was generally good; the theatre excellent,
and the living cheap.

Vanity Fair, Chapter 62.

France being still regarded with suspicion by the English middle-classes, young men in search of continental culture tended to be sent to Germany, the intellectual centre of Europe, and in particular to Weimar, home of Schiller and Goethe, 'the Athens of Germany'. Thackeray set out with no particular place or purpose in view: his relationship with his mother and stepfather was at a low ebb, and both sides probably felt a few months' absence would help to clear the air. He journeyed down the Rhine from Rotterdam to Cologne, sketching as he went, alert to picturesque scenes and figures, though the half-parodic chauvinism of his letters from Paris persisted: 'Yesterday the beauties of the journey began, & I really think the Rhine is almost equal to the Thames.'[33] He fell in with a German acquaintance from Cambridge, one Schulte, who took him to the University of Bonn and introduced him to members of the famous duelling clubs. He found them 'a wondrous stupid set of fellows'.[34]

As always when travelling he suffered from the fleas and bedbugs to which he seems to have been particularly sensitive, and wrote a comic poem for his mother on the subject. These verses, and a poem on the Dragon of the Drachenfels, show a distinct polishing of his talent for comic verse, and are an advance on any of his Cambridge squibs. His letters home are also full of plans for work and travel: he is writing an essay (at his mother's instigation) on Miracles; he is going to translate A. W. Schlegel's *Kunstlehre* (but later decides that this collection of lectures, by the translator of Shakespeare and one of the foremost literary critics of the German Romantic movement, is 'a spurious one');[35] he is on his way to 'Dresden pictures & Dresden Society';[36] he will settle in Cologne with 'some comfortable family'.[37] And then suddenly the news came to Larkbeare that he had arrived at Weimar, where an old schoolfellow assures him the place is exactly suited for him.

Weimar in 1830 was a principality living in the shadow of its former intellectual greatness. The Grand Duke Karl August, Goethe's intimate friend, patron and employer, had died in 1828, and his successor was less liberal minded and intellectually alert than his father, 'as silly a piece of royalty as a man may meet' was Thackeray's verdict on him.[38] The titans of the turn of the century, Goethe and Schiller, the philosopher Herder, and the lesser luminaries such as Wieland and the playwright Kotzebue (whose play *Lovers' Vows* precipitates the crisis in *Mansfield Park*), were all, except for the veteran survivor Goethe, long dead. It was symptomatic of the change that the little theatre founded by Karl August, of which Goethe and Schiller had both been managers, had become subject to Grand Ducal censorship. The great actor Ludwig Devrient, 'the Kean of Germany', still acted there, and had played in *Faust* in honour of Goethe's eightieth birthday, but in order to see him in *Die Räuber* Thackeray had to go to Erfurt, for the egalitarian sentiments of Schiller's youthful masterpiece were now 'a little too patriotic and free for our court theatre'.[39] But Thackeray was able to see performances of *Fidelio*, *The Barber of Seville* and *The Magic Flute*, with Hummel conducting the orchestra; and there was a performance in translation of Hugo's *Hernani*, which had caused a riot at the Comédie-Française only months before.

There were theatrical performances of some kind three times a week, a feast for a theatre-mad young man. Thackeray could go with a clear conscience, for the theatre in Germany had achieved a respectable status quite different from the *demi-monde* atmosphere of Covent Garden and Drury Lane, or the Paris theatres. One rather equivocal delight was a performance of Beethoven's *Vittoria*, a battle piece which incorporates the tunes of 'Rule Britannia' and 'God Save the King'. When Thackeray used this incident in *Vanity Fair* the narrator takes a straightforwardly patriotic line: the Englishmen 'stood bolt upright in their places, and proclaimed themselves to be members of the dear old British nation'.[40] The nineteen-year-old Thackeray observed it with a cooler eye: 'I never saw half a dozen men so excited as the English were, when Rule Britannia was played – I was amused with this celebrated piece of music.'[41]

The young Thackeray was more interested in the 'charming petite société' of Weimar than in the ideas of the German philosophers. The parental mixture of liberalism and piety he had grown up with still dominated his thinking, though he was beginning to be aware that it was not an adequate response to every situation in life. He dutifully set himself to learn the language under the tutelage of a noted eccentric, Dr Weissenborn, seeing a knowledge of German as a tangible, money-getting advantage which might help him to procure an attachéship and so avoid the dreadful prospect of going into the law. But his estimate of the merits of Goethe and Schiller was still firmly tied to ideas of morality, rather than purely literary judgements. Schiller, whose private life had been beyond reproach, was 'after Shakespeare *the* Poet';[42] perhaps because the grandeur of his tragic heroes raised fewer uncomfortable questions than the complex ambiguities of *Faust, Wilhelm Meister* and *Die Wahlverwandtschaften (Elective Affinities)*. Thackeray, like most Victorians, continued to consider the last a most immoral book. English sensibilities were outraged by Goethe's personal morality, his many liaisons, and his habit, as an old man, of falling in love with young girls. German society, on the other hand, had been shocked when Goethe abandoned his aristocratic and gifted mistress, Frau von Stein, for the humbly born and uneducated Christiane Vulpius in 1788. It made matters no better that he married her in 1806, in gratitude for her protection of him from Napoleon's soldiers.

Thackeray articulated the prejudice of his generation and his country in considering Goethe primarily as a libertine and 'little better than an old rogue'.[43] He paid lip-service to the writing; but dutifully, rather than with enthusiasm. 'I have read *Faust* with wh. I was of course delighted, but not to that degree I expected.'[44] He held the common opinion of his generation of Englishmen that *The Sorrows of Werther*, the runaway bestseller of Europe for fifty years, was sentimental rubbish, the habitual reading of housemaids. The current English translations were travesties of the original, and the comic sketches and stories of the 1820s and 1830s abound in Werther jokes, most of them very feeble. Thackeray himself wrote the last word on this distorted view of Werther in a ballad published in 1853 which gave the novel its final death-blow, as far as the English public was concerned.

> Werther had a love for Charlotte
>   Such as words could never utter;
> Would you know how first he met her?
>   She was cutting bread and butter.
>
> Charlotte was a married lady,
>   And a moral man was Werther,
> And for all the wealth of Indies,
>   Would do nothing for to hurt her.
>
> So he sighed and pined and ogled,
>   And his passion boiled and bubbled,
> Till he blew his silly brains out,
>   And no more was by it troubled.
>
> Charlotte, having seen his body
>   Borne before her on a shutter,
> Like a well-conducted person,
>   Went on cutting bread and butter.[45]

At the time this poem was published Thackeray himself was in Werther's situation – hopelessly in love with a married woman whose husband had finally lost patience with the situation, and ordered her to break off, or at least moderate the relationship. It was typical of Thackeray's divided nature that he could make this secret joke against himself, and publish it, while suffering as deeply as Werther.

Writing an account of his one meeting with Goethe for G. H. Lewes's biography of 1855, Thackeray modified his views to conform to the later English acceptance of Goethe's genius. The tone is softer, and the ranking is altered to 'the good Schiller and the great Goethe'; but an aura of wickedness, somewhat romanticized, still surrounds his memories.

His eyes extraordinarily dark, piercing and brilliant. I felt quite afraid before them, and recollect comparing them to the eyes of the hero of a certain romance called *Melmoth the Wanderer*, which used to alarm us boys thirty years ago; the eyes of an individual who had made a bargain with a Certain Person.[46]

Goethe does not seem to have found the tall young Englishman in any way remarkable. The old man had become a national monument, easily accessible to visitors, but very few of them elicited the affection and admiration which he expressed for the young Mendelssohn, also in Weimar in 1830. Thackeray visited him only once, but he did become accepted into the circle of Goethe's daughter-in-law, Ottilie. 'Very kind but withal a great bore' was Thackeray's verdict on the middle-aged Anglophile, a passionate admirer of Scott and Byron, whose salon was thronged with a succession of the young Englishmen passing through Weimar, from among whom she chose her lovers.[47]

English writers were all the rage in Weimar; to be English, and as Byronic as possible, was a passport to popularity with the girls. Flirting was made easier because the younger generation spoke English, and the mamas did not. The Grand Duke's little court was a curious mixture of old-fashioned formality and freedom; absurdly ceremonious, and yet welcoming any Englishman, even without letters of introduction, provided he wore the right clothes. Thackeray, whose fascination with dandyism persisted all his life, entered with enthusiasm into the question of court dress. Uniforms were much affected, and Thackeray, who described himself looking in court dress 'something like a cross between a footman and a Methodist parson'[48] prevailed on his mother to obtain a cornetcy in the Yeomanry of her landlord Sir John Kennaway and send him the uniform. He must have looked even odder in this than in the methodistical black-and-white of court dress, for though he expressed himself 'delighted', he did admit, 'I don't think the pink rosettes look well on the leather breeches, why the bawty [baldric] should be picked out sky blue I cannot concieve.'[49] He made fun of his own youthful pretensions when he came to describe the adventures of Jeames de la Pluche, the *arriviste* hero of one of his series in *Punch*, who goes to court in a uniform only slightly more absurd, topped by an 'Albert' hat 'with a plume like a shaving brush'.[50]

The winter at Weimar seems to have been a series of delightful parties in which Thackeray took part with enthusiasm, without ever losing a characteristic ironic detachment. There were balls, tea parties, evening parties, sledging parties, attendances at court, visits to the theatre; always something amusing going on. By English standards morals and religious observances were lax. Divorce, in the Protestant parts of

Germany, was acceptable and frequent, as were open liaisons. Behaviour was not perhaps quite as free as in the previous generation, when August Schlegel married the brilliant, witty widow Caroline Böhmer, who had just had an illegitimate child by a French officer, only to lose her to the philosopher Schelling. Biedermeier *Gemütlichkeit* was settling over Weimar by 1830. However, the girls still tended to be better read and freer in their behaviour than their English counterparts, and there are hints of puzzlement in Thackeray's letters as to exactly what game they were playing. He paid court first to the acknowledged beauty of the place, Melanie von Spiegel, 'the prettiest woman I ever saw in my life',[51] but between the letter of 20 October which announced this, and his next of 17 November, he had switched his affections to the rather more interesting Jenny von Pappenheim.

> The last time I wrote, I was, if you remember violently in love; I am still violently in love but it is with another person; Tho' as there are only two young ladies at the Court of Weimar with whom one can fall in love, I don't know what I shall do at the end of another fortnight, about which time I expect again to be free.[52]

The tone of this letter makes it sound as though neither involvement was very serious. Thackeray's biographers have assumed, on the basis of two anecdotes in Anne Thackeray Ritchie's *Chapters from some Memoirs* and the way in which the two girls are fictionalized in *FitzBoodle's Confessions*, that Thackeray was more genuinely affected by Melanie than by Jenny. The letters to his mother deliberately play down his feelings for both; but it is clear that whereas he gave up his courtship of Melanie, afraid that he was being encouraged to propose marriage: 'The old ladies here seem to be bent on marrying their daughters, two have told me that they did not wish *much* money for their Melanies or their Eugenies, but merely a competency – but I did not speak on the hint',[53] he was more than a little hurt by being thrown over by Jenny. He claims that 'my eternity only lasted 3 weeks, & was dissipated by a handsome young man, with moustachios who cut me out & cured me'[54] but a month later he is still protesting rather too energetically and with more than a touch of pique, that the flame has gone out. 'Flirting is a word much in vogue – but I think jilting is the proper term in this my (unfortunate or fortunate as you please) desertion.'[55]

Thackeray described Melanie as 'a very pretty girl' and Jenny as 'a very clever and amiable one'.[56] Jenny was the same age as he, the illegitimate daughter of Diana von Pappenheim and Prince Jerome

Napoleon. She had returned to Weimar with her mother in 1826, when von Pappenheim, tired of husbandly complaisance, insisted on a separation. The tolerant society of Weimar accepted them without question; Jenny was, like Melanie, a maid of honour at court. A portrait of her as a girl shows her as pretty and rather intense, with dark hair and eyes, a long nose and thin mouth. She belonged to Ottilie von Goethe's circle, and contributed poems in French, German and English to Ottilie's multi-lingual literary magazine *Chaos*, which appeared between 1829 and 1831. Later in life she wrote her memoirs, and remembered Thackeray as 'lovable' and well-liked, a gifted caricaturist; there is no hint that she ever felt more than friendship for him.[57] She read and enjoyed *Vanity Fair*, but presumably never came across *FitzBoodle's Confessions*, with its malicious parody of her as 'Ottilia'.

The experience of being jilted in favour of a moustachioed swell who was 'Heir to ten thousand a year – has several waistcoats of the most magnificent pattern, & makes love speeches to admiration'[58] was a passing humiliation; but there was another slight which Thackeray may have taken more seriously. He, like Jenny, submitted poems to *Chaos*: his were rejected. (After he had returned to England one mediocre set of his verses was published in the magazine: he had modified his natural bent for the comic to conform to the sentimentality of *Chaos*.)

The two girls, the pretty, Junoesque Melanie, with no intellectual pretensions, concerned only to please others and be happy herself, and the clever, competitive Jenny, formed a contrasting pair; and similar pairs appear, with variations, in almost all Thackeray's major fiction. Amelia and Becky, Laura and Blanche Amory, Rachel and Beatrix Castlewood, Ethel Newcome and Rosey Mackenzie; only in the last of these pairings is the simpler woman not preferred. They appear with least disguise in the last two episodes – really two parts of the same episode – of *FitzBoodle's Confessions*, published in *Fraser's Magazine* in 1843.[59] Thackeray subsequently tried to suppress the 'Dorothea' and 'Ottilia' episodes because of their autobiographical content.[60] He did suppress the 'Miss Löwe' episode, in which FitzBoodle falls in love with the daughter of a swindling Jewish merchant, which suggests that there may have been some basis of fact for this story too, though none has been uncovered.

FitzBoodle's Confessions, each episode of which recounts a youthful amatory misadventure of a bachelor clubman, now middle-aged, are comic satires at the expense of the narrator, who is humiliated in each episode except the last. FitzBoodle is not Thackeray: he is a crusty literature-hating philistine a good fifteen years older than his creator. Nevertheless he reflects, and is meant to reflect, certain prejudices which Thackeray was well aware of holding himself, and he does have some of his author's own adventures.

FitzBoodle, arriving in the little principality of Kalbsbraten-Pumpernickel, is first smitten with love for the solid charms of Dorothea von Speck. 'She was of the earth earthy, and must have weighed ten stone four or five, if she weighed an ounce.' Dorothea has the usual 'little stock of accomplishments'; is good-natured, healthy and happy. FitzBoodle's downfall in his pursuit of her is a literal one; he learns to waltz in order to cut out her other admirers, but when he tries out his new accomplishment he brings them both crashing heavily to the floor. Readers of *Pendennis* will recall that Pen suffers the same humiliation when dancing with Blanche Amory. FitzBoodle abandons his pursuit of Dorothea after this set-back, and, in revenge, falls in love with the intellectual Ottilia von Schlippenschlop. Her name is compounded from that of Frau von Goethe, and a Germanic version of Fielding's Mrs Slipslop, the elderly and unattractive chambermaid, much given to malapropisms, who takes a libidinous fancy to Joseph Andrews. Ottilia is a pretentious blue-stocking, who starts a literary magazine with her friends. FitzBoodle quotes a couple of examples of Ottilia's verses: a sentimental ballad on a maiden's suicide (with a Thackerayan parody of it) and a fairly straightforward poem on fairy-tales, which may be one of the poems by minor German authors Thackeray translated while he was at Weimar.

Ottilia is ethereal in appearance. 'You could not see her face, as it were, for her eyes, which were so wild, and so tender, and shone so that they would have dazzled an eagle, much more a poor goose of a FitzBoodle.' But she has an unforgivable vice: she is greedy. Worse, she is undiscriminating about food. 'She was always eating, and always eating too much. If I went there in the morning, there was the horrid familiar odour of those oniony sandwiches; if in the afternoon . . . I was choked by reeking reminiscences of roast-meat . . . She gobbled up more cakes than any six people present . . .' Unbelievably, this regime has no effect on Ottilia's appearance, except to give her a red nose. When FitzBoodle discovers her habits, he tries to tear himself from her: 'Marry a sarcophagus, a cannibal, a butcher's shop?' – but it is only when Ottilia devours a large quantity of bad oysters with relish that he leaves Kalbsbraten, never to return.

FitzBoodle makes it clear he is not against women eating: Dorothea has a healthy appetite in keeping with her size and general amiability. But there is something sinister about Ottilia's ravening greed. She is 'a ghoul, a monster, an ogress, a horrid gormandiseress'. A sketch-book in which Thackeray drew and wrote for the entertainment of a young

English girl, Caroline Vavasour, during his winter in Weimar throws a curious sidelight on FitzBoodle's memories of Ottilia.[61] The book contains two stories told in caricature sketches with captions, and a number of drawings depicting various kinds of torture. The first story concerns the marriage of Count Otto von Blumenbach to 'Ottilia, Amelie, Melanie, Jenny von Rosenthal'. The new Countess refuses to allow her husband beefsteaks for breakfast, but while he gets thinner, she grows fatter. Finally the Count discovers that his wife is a necrophagous cannibal who steals out to the churchyard at night to devour corpses. The pen-and-ink illustrations are full of lively and horrific detail.

The second story concerns a mother who kills and eats her own son, persuading her reluctant husband to join her at the feast. Among the torture drawings is one of a small boy threatened by a grim woman with a birch. It seems a strange collection to present to a young girl, and suggests a preoccupation, even an obsession, with devouring women that Thackeray was dealing with through exaggeration and humour. The preoccupation persisted, in modified and transmuted forms, into Thackeray's adult life and writings. FitzBoodle is clearly in danger of being eaten himself by the all-devouring Ottilia, and his escape brings the series of his 'Confessions' to an end on a note of relief, rather than

From the Weimar Sketch Book: The Count and his bride

From the Weimar Sketch Book: 'Now every day
the Count got thinner'

triumph. All Thackeray's bad women, and some of his heroines, have this devouring quality, though in the novels it is expressed in less direct and farcical terms. They tend to swallow up their men, and to demand more and more from them. Ottilia's literal greed is so absurd that it effectively destroys her attempt to be taken seriously as an intellectual. It may be, too, that gustatory appetite is here functioning as a submerged metaphor for sexual appetite: natural and healthy in Dorothea, perverted and indiscriminate in Ottilia. Thackeray wrote of Jenny that, 'The fond & free wanderings of her eyes ... had been tolerated on my part, because I thought that they were directed oftener towards my unprepossessing physiognomy than any other'; and he predicts that the man who has cut him out will one day be cut out in his turn.[62]

Thackeray was already suffering from the possessive element in his mother's love, and her unrealistic ambitions for him. He may also have resented his adopted sister's intellectual ambitions. Mrs Carmichael-Smyth had taken charge of her orphaned niece, Mary Graham, in 1826,

From the Weimar Sketch Book: The cannibal mother

From the Weimar Sketch Book: Necrophagy

and she became a member of the household until her marriage in 1841. She was four years younger than Thackeray, and they seem to have got on well enough as children. But Thackeray found her increasingly impossible in later life and wrote, at the time of her marriage, that he hoped 'she will sufftly. respect and admire her husband. Her Devonshire friends flattered Polly & did her no good.'[63]

While his unease with clever women was being confirmed by his experience with Jenny von Pappenheim, his mother was still bombarding him from a distance with sorrowful hints that he was a continual disappointment to her. He finally burst out with a long letter which is virtually a declaration of independence. It is a passionate indictment of his education at the Charterhouse and Cambridge, and of her lack of consideration of his feelings and wishes.[64] It is a remarkably well-argued and telling statement for a boy of nineteen, and makes clear how much Thackeray had grown up since leaving Cambridge. A later letter retracts and apologizes for the outburst, but the sense of a stubborn core within him, which semi-consciously pursued a path to self-realization, remained, though he was aware how absurd he must look to others, 'lying on my sofa, reading novels and dreaming of [fame]'.[65]

The real value of his nine months in Germany was not the acquisition of the language, or an education in German literature and ideas, but an increasing confidence in his ability to make use of experience in his own terms. He sketched a good deal while he was in Weimar: portraits, caricatures, landscapes. He used to entertain the children by doing rapid drawings of himself, emphasizing his broken nose, without taking the pen from the paper. He also stored up in his memory sights and sounds, details of appearance and conversation, which are used to great effect in the Pumpernickel chapters of *Vanity Fair*, where the little town, with its air of slightly *passé* grandeur and tolerant attitudes to sexual morality, provides the perfect setting for Becky at a precariously respectable stage of her career.

The golden interlude had to come to an end. Germany had already inspired Thackeray with his first scheme for a book: 'with a sketch-book a note-book & I fear still a Dictionary I could manage to concoct a book wh. would pay me for my trouble.'[66] But a long period of trial and apprenticeship was to intervene before he was able to attempt anything even at that modest level.

Chapter 3

The Idle Apprentice

'I know his haunts, but I don't know his friends, Pendennis'
the older man said. 'I don't think they are vicious, so much as low.
I do not charge him with vice, mind you; but with idleness,
and a fatal love of low company, and a frantic suicidal
determination to fling his chances in life away.
Ah, think where he might be, and where he is!'

The Adventures of Philip, Chapter 5.

It is not surprising that Thackeray once confessed an 'unaffected pity' for Hogarth's Idle Apprentice:[1] the story of his downfall might so easily have been his own. The next three years of his life were marked by a compulsive pursuit of activities which were at best a waste of time and money, at worst bordered on the disreputable. These were his prodigal years, in which he appeared to be spending his substance and getting very little in return. As it turned out, these disgraceful days and nights, which mounted, in spite of his intermittent attempts at reform, into months and years, became a rich source on which he continued to draw all his life. One can already sense in the letters and diaries of this period that the future writer is beginning to look over his own shoulder, to observe his own behaviour and motivations, not merely in an attempt at moral improvement (though there is an element of that too), but detaching himself from himself, in order to observe and store up his experiences for future use.

As a very young man he also began his lifelong habit of 'treating' schoolboys to a meal and the theatre, getting as much pleasure from observing their reactions of spontaneous delight as from the food and drink and the spectacle. He was not yet aware himself what this watchfulness was for: but his sense of separation from the diverse company in which he moved was not a straightforward matter of class snobbery. To the anxiety of status which he did undoubtedly feel – the whole complex matter of how to be a gentleman – there was being added the cool eye of the observer. He had already learned in the school of parody, if only at a crude and boyish level, to question the assumptions of any world, high or low, in which he chose to move. The structure of much of his writing, where the narrator often doubles as a character within, and a commentator on, the action, is implicit in this growing habit of self-observation.

When Thackeray came to write *Pendennis* in 1849, he allowed his hero, whose career in broad outline followed his own, to redeem himself fairly rapidly after his Cambridge excesses. Though Pen's brief attempt to read for the Bar is no more productive than his creator's, his advancement in the world of journalism is considerably more rapid, his aim more certain, and his renunciation of gambling and other expensive Cambridge habits complete, as Thackeray's most certainly was not. Pen at this stage of his way through the world is given a mentor, George Warrington, experienced, unpretentious, and at ease in all kinds of society. The simple underlying structure of the novel, based on Bunyan's *Pilgrim's Progress*, makes use of counterbalancing forces and their influence on the hero, shown pictorially in the design of the frontispiece. Thackeray discovered no such simple arrangement in the respectable and Bohemian worlds of London and Paris where he tried out his independence and abilities in the period between his return from Weimar and his marriage in 1836.

He arrived home from Germany in March 1831. He was ill on his return and went to Larkbeare where he found both the Carmichael-Smyths ill too. By the time he was able to go to London the Law term was almost over. It was a repetition of his late start at Cambridge. But he enrolled in the chambers of Mr Taprell, a special pleader, in the Middle Temple, and took rooms for himself at 5 Essex Court. 'Nasty black staircase as ever I see. Wonder how a gentleman can live in such a place,' comments Major Pendennis's servant Morgan on Pen's room at 'Lamb Court, Upper Temple'. After a while the initial euphoria of having a place of his own wore off, and his Essex Court chambers after two years seemed to him damp and horrible. But to begin with he was glad to establish himself in London on his own account, and plunged with enthusiasm into the pleasures of the town.

The study of the law was always *faute de mieux*: he said, in sharp contrast to his later anti-militarism, that he would have gone into the army if only there had been a war on, and some prospect of advancement. At first the Church and medicine were repugnant; after a year anything seemed better than law: 'I am thinking of turning Parson and being a useful member of society & not a cringing blustering sneaking bullying lawyer,' he wrote to his mother, half-joking and half-despairing.[2] Studying case law in Mr Taprell's chambers, where the sun never penetrated, was even worse than mathematics and classics had been at Cambridge. There must have been a depressing sense of *déjà lu* at Larkbeare when his letters arrived. 'It is very difficult to read dry law books & attend to them – I sit at t[hem] a good deal but proceed very slowly.'[3] He was more candid to Fitz. 'Of one thing I am determined that I never will practise the law, or at least will retire from it, before my business should occupy me too much.'[4] His diary, after months nominally spent in study, sounds a note of despair. 'I find I cannot read I have tried it at all hours & it fails – I don't know so much now as when I came to town & that God knows was little enough.'[5] In his drawings of himself at his high desk in chambers he is comically perched up so high that the tiny clerk bringing him a pile of law books has to climb a ladder to reach him. Law might be a socially elevated occupation, but it seemed to him for the most part out of touch with real life, and the preliminary training 'one of the most cold blooded prejudiced pieces of invention that ever a man was slave to'.[6]

The reluctant law student

He compensated by taking full advantage of the possibilities of life in London for a young man. He could, without compromising his position in good society, move from the world of dinner parties and balls to that of taverns, drinking clubs and saloons, gambling hells and brothels. Reminiscences of London life in the 1830s confirm the impression given in Thackeray's writings of the tawdriness of such haunts and their inhabitants, but until the charm of novelty wore off there was an excitement in places where, though the women were all, to some degree or other, 'fallen', the men came from differing backgrounds and brought very different experiences of life with them.

'The Interior of Hades'

Thackeray kept a diary from April to November 1832, and though this was censored by his daughter after his death, a fuller picture of his activities and thoughts is given by it, together with the letters and fragments of letters to FitzGerald that have survived, than is available for other periods of his life. The record is less blandly innocent than that of the young Pendennis. The hints in *The Newcomes* are closer to the reality, and in *Philip* he is even more outspoken, perhaps because Thackeray was, by the time he came to write it, further distanced from his own misdeeds. Pendennis, the by now middle-aged and respectable narrator, can stand for the author in the novel, and Philip is given the excuse of a wicked father, against whose hypocrisy the young man rightly rebels. The hot-headed, radical, impulsive Philip is not a self-portrait, but he shares some of Thackeray's characteristics, and his attitude to Bohemia accords with the way Thackeray's contemporary companions remembered him: that he was *in* that world, but not *of* it:

> Perhaps he liked to play the prince in the midst of these associates, and was not averse to the flattery which a full purse brought him among men most of whose pockets had a meagre lining. He had not emigrated to Bohemia, and settled there altogether. (*The Adventures of Philip*, Chapter 5, *Works*, 16, pp. 60–1)

However, the idea of the 'gentleman' who could occupy his time entirely by moving between respectable society and low life, at least until he married, was being overtaken by social changes which required a new definition of the term; one which was eventually to be crystallized to a great extent by Thackeray's own writings. It was never, in any case, an appropriate way of life for someone whose private income was as modest as Thackeray's.

Two events dramatized the changes which were taking place. The death of George IV in 1830 ended the Georgian era, and the passage of the first Reform Bill in 1832 symbolized the opening of a new one. When it looked for a while as though the Duke of Wellington's intransigent stand against reform might block the passage of the Bill, the country was in a state of near-revolution, and Thackeray thought it possible that William IV might be the last king of England, and the House of Commons be transformed into a House of Delegates. The French revolution of 1830 which had ousted Charles X, the last of the Bourbons, who had said he would rather chop wood than be a constitutional monarch like the king of the English, might have been repeated on the other side of the Channel, and Thackeray, who hero-worshipped Wellington, bought himself a big stick to defend himself 'against all parties' in the streets of London.[7] The Bill went through, and the agitation died down; but the sense that the old order had gone for ever was a true one, and though there were few immediate changes, the new flexibility in society was to turn out to Thackeray's advantage, both in his personal life, and in the material he was able to draw on for his fiction. The range of possible occupations for a man of his background was widening rapidly, and the attitude to journalists, like the attitude to actors and painters, was beginning to change. J. A. Roebuck, writing in 1835, still thought that a newspaper editor was not deemed to be a gentleman. But Melbourne in 1836 considered that no one could think it disgraceful or derogatory to be connected with the Press.[8]

Thackeray himself was ambivalent at this time. Too indolent and too unsure of his powers to settle to the respectable but daunting business of writing a novel, though he often thought about it, he frequented the society of journalists and painters, but tended to think and speak of them as his inferiors. Nevertheless, he was by the spring of 1832 seriously investigating the possibility of buying a newspaper, as an investment for his capital, which would come into his own control in July of that year, and to provide himself, as editor, with an occupation and a platform for his own writing.

While he was still uncertain about his future, much of his time was spent pursuing his two major obsessions, the theatre and gambling. Both in London, and in Paris, where he spent almost four months in 1832, he went to the theatre several times a week. Apart from the classics, Shakespeare in London, Molière in Paris, much of what he saw was ephemeral. Several of the French plays he saw were hissed off the stage. Thackeray's view of the theatre, and opera and ballet, was becoming more sophisticated and critical, but he still succumbed easily and happily to the atmosphere, and the actresses. He was charmed by Jenny Colon, and the famous Mlle Mars, now elderly, but still playing 'deliciously' in 'a pretty piece called Valerie'.[9] He was beginning to be initiated into life behind the scenes, too, but unlike Dr Johnson in a similar situation found amusement as well as temptation backstage, in the contrast of glamorous illusion and the hard vulgarity of 'two dancers abusing each other for scandal'.[10] Any fantasy of becoming an 'angel' was rapidly cured by a meeting with an actor 'who gave a melancholy account of his theatrical speculations'.[11] These experiences were to be turned to more profitable account in the early chapters of *Pendennis*.

The theatre was to become a paradigm in Thackeray's writing for the theme of youthful illusion. Just as young men in his novels are often taken in by the deceptive charms of an older woman, which cannot stand too close a moral or physical scrutiny, so the delights of the stage

Pantomime clowns

are seen by the eye of age and experience to be tawdry things; but with a regret that is like the regret of an old man for the illusions of first love. It is surprising to find this appreciation of a double vision of the world being expressed in a letter written when he was only twenty.

> I am sure that a young man's ideas however absurd & rhapsodical they are though they mayn't smack so much of experience as those of these old cold calculating codgers contain a great deal more nature & virtue.[12]

An understanding of this idea of the truth to be found in illusion is fundamental to an appreciation of Thackeray's kind of realism, which involves strategies a good deal more subtle than simply stripping illusions and self-deception from his characters. A passage in the *Roundabout Paper* 'De Juventute' charmingly elaborates the *ubi sunt* theme: but the unselfconscious youth he presents as his remembered self is a partly fictional character. The real Thackeray was already highly critical and self-aware.

> Ah, I remember a different state of things! . . . To see those nymphs – gracious powers how beautiful they were! That leering, painted, shrivelled, thin-armed, thick-ankled old thing cutting dreary capers, coming thumping down on her board out of time – *that* an opera-dancer? Pooh! . . . now, the dancing women and singing women are ludicrously old, out of time, and out of tune; the paint is so visible, and the dinge and wrinkles of their wretched old cotton stockings, that I am surprised how anybody can like to look at them . . . In the reign of George IV, I give you my honour, all the dancers at the opera were as beautiful as Houris. Even in William IV's time, when I think of Duvernay prancing in the Bayadère, – I say it was a vision of loveliness such as mortal eyes can't see nowadays. (*Works*, 17, p. 427)

Opera dancer

Young men are, in Thackeray's fiction, impulsive, subject to illusions, easily misled by bad company, but fundamentally innocent – original sin was never a concept that appealed to him. Life is shown to be a process of gradual disillusionment; layers of protective fantasy are removed from them by contact with the world, which gives little back in compensation. Thackeray, far less starry-eyed than many Victorians about the innocence of children – one thinks of the chilling self-absorption of George Osborne Junior, or the tantrums of the spoiled Clavering heir – reserves the theme of illusion betrayed for his young men, and, though less often, young women.

'Really London is to me only the place where the Theatres are,' he wrote to FitzGerald from temporary exile at Larkbeare.[13] But it was also the place where the gambling houses were. The theatrical obsession he saw later as a charming folly, but gambling, in everything he wrote, has its attractiveness ruthlessly stripped from it, though the element of addiction is strongly conveyed. Some of the best and harshest early writing is based on his own experiences of being taken in by experienced card-sharps; and he has little sympathy for the victim in such pieces as 'The Amours of Mr Deuceace' in *The Yellowplush Papers*, or the hard, brilliant sketch, 'Captain Rook and Mr Pigeon',[14] which lays bare the common progression by which the victim himself turns into the predator. As soon as he came of age, Thackeray was driven down to the city by his 'Mr Deuceace' to cash enough of his inheritance to redeem the 'debt of honour' of £1,500 he had contracted at Cambridge, but this lesson was not enough to cure him. The 1832 diary reveals – and was in part kept to remind himself – how much time and money was spent either in the public gaming houses in the Regent Street area, or at the kind of private gambling parties which he picks out as being the most dangerous for the novice in 'Captain Rook and Mr Pigeon'. He also sought out the equivalent places in Paris. The diary entries are full of shame. There are frequent promises to himself: '*the last time, so help me God*' – followed by immediate relapses. He lost more often than he won; and these losses added to the Cambridge debt must have eaten into his inheritance quite considerably. Before he reached his majority he had to ask his trustees for a hundred guineas to pay a debt of honour, and his account book for 1833 notes on 1 February, 'Lost at play £668'.[15]

Other accounts of the sporting world of the 1830s confirm the impression given by Thackeray's fictional portraits of gamblers. The dividing line between the professional gambler, however respectable and 'gentlemanly' his origins, and the common criminal was thin, often non-existent. Gambling mania swept England and the Continent in the 1820s and 1830s, and gamblers whose reputation in London became too unsavoury would move to Boulogne, as Deuceace does, then on to Paris, and perhaps make the circuit of the Belgian watering places, or the German principalities. Byron's friend Scrope Davies carried on a precarious existence of this kind at Ostend, surviving until 1852. For someone of Thackeray's temperament, gambling was all too easily available. He needed to take risks, to push himself to his limits; and he continued all his life to need the stimulus of constantly varied activity and change of scene. But he despised the gambling men, and himself for associating with them, while being bored with the lawyers and respectable relations and family friends who asked him to dinner more often than he wished. Paris and its environs, where he lived from August to November 1832, and again from September 1834 to the spring of 1837, was a relief. He spent his time there in much the same way as in London, reading French novels and seeing French plays instead of English ones, but without the ever-present guilt that the Middle Temple and the piles of unread law-books in his chambers represented. It was at this time that he learnt the fluent, if incorrect, French that became his second language. German, in spite of some continued attempts to translate from it on his return from Weimar, became merely the language in which he cloaked the record of his sins in his diary; later it was a source for comic names in his fiction. It was never a living language for him, as French was.

In Paris he idled away his time with expatriate friends and relatives – his favourite relations, the Ritchies, were now settled in the Place Vendôme. Sometimes he occupied himself less innocently: 'don't feel inclined to mention the expences or the occurrences of these days', one diary entry reads.[16] He read Balzac, Hugo, Paul de Kock, George Sand. He was critical of French romanticism, as he had been of German, accusing the French of labouring at 'a kind of eccentricity ... The gentlemen of the École Romantique have thrown away all these [classical] prejudices, but still seem no wise better or more poetical than their rigid predecessors.'[17] He read the French periodicals too, laying the foundations of a better understanding of French culture and politics than most English writers of his generation possessed. He spent time sketching in the country, and studying the paintings in the Louvre. It seemed a desultory existence. When in later years an aspiring writer asked the great author for advice, Thackeray replied that when he was young he read everything he could lay his hands on. Certainly the amount and breadth of his reading in his prodigal years is impressive.

Friendships with young men of his own class and background were an antidote to dullness and to low life. He spent several weeks in the West Country in the summer of 1832, campaigning for his friend Charles Buller, who had previously been Member of Parliament for a rotten borough swept away by the Reform Act and was now standing for West Looe. Thackeray and Buller were much alike in appearance; both six foot three, with broken noses. Harriet Martineau in her memoirs described a dinner party at the Bullers, at which the two young men made a ludicrous pair, seated one on each side of Mrs Buller.[18] But Buller, five years Thackeray's senior, had already begun to make his mark in the world, and was considered exceptionally promising. 'I wish to God, I could take advantage of my time and opportunities as C Buller has done,' Thackeray wrote in his diary.[19] Buller was more a man of the world in other ways, too. He kept a mistress, Theresa Reviss, variously described as an actress and 'a girl from the Baker Street Bazaar'. 'A very pretty disagreeable girl' Thackeray thought her.[20] She may have provided, in part, the inspiration for Becky Sharp. Other clever, entertaining friends lived in closer contact with the underworld than Thackeray did. He still saw something of Henry Matthew, though he found 'his recklessness & quiet with things hanging over him, wh. if discovered might leave him a beggar & an outcast' incomprehensible.[21] Savile Morton, one of the most amusing of his Cambridge friends, lived permanently in debt, and behaved 'shockingly' to women. FitzGerald and Thackeray helped to support a girl whom he had seduced and abandoned, but though they disapproved of his behaviour, neither of them ever completely broke with him. FitzGerald at one time attempted to raise money for him by finding a publisher for a selection of Morton's letters, without success. He had a fitting end, murdered by an outraged husband whose wife claimed that Morton was the father of her child.

Other friends retained from Cambridge days were the Kembles. Thackeray got to know the sisters, the actress Fanny and singer Adelaide, as well as renewing his intimacy with John and Henry. But by far the closest relationship of these years was the friendship with Edward FitzGerald. During the summer of 1831, much of which Thackeray spent at Larkbeare, with little to entertain him in the quiet, old-fashioned society of Ottery St Mary, they wrote to each other constantly, and at length: 'the immortal summer of foolscap' FitzGerald called it.[22] When Thackeray was in London, FitzGerald went to stay with him, or Thackeray would visit FitzGerald and other friends at Cambridge. They were closer in these years than they had been as undergraduates, and closer than they were ever to be again, though they continued to be friends for the rest of Thackeray's life. There were practical reasons for the waning of the intimacy in later years, for FitzGerald lived more and more in the Suffolk countryside, and became increasingly reclusive. Also, perhaps because of his childhood experience of a cold, unloving mother – he once overheard his grandmother tell her daughter, 'My dear, you are a very fine woman, *but a bad Mother*'[23] – he had little confidence in his ability to attract and hold affection. He told Thackeray early in their relationship that he was not to expect the same warmth when they met as there was in their letters, and in later years he tended to grumble that his old friends, Thackeray and Tennyson in particular, had become too grand to want to know him. In 1850 he wrote sadly to Frederick Tennyson, that he had little inclination to hunt up his friends, and that 'Thackeray is in such a great world that I am afraid of him; he gets tired of me; and we are content to regard each other at a distance.'[24] Yet it was to FitzGerald's care that Thackeray commended his daughters, when he was going to the United States for the first time in 1852:

> I should like my daughters to remember that you are the best and oldest friend their Father ever had; and that you would act as such: . . . the great comfort I have in thinking about my dear old boy is that recollection of our youth when we loved each other as I do now while I write Farewell.[25]

The few letters and fragments of letters of their youth that survived are a mixture of fooling and fantasy, and an outspoken emotionalism that seems almost lover-like to modern eyes. Young men today would hardly dare to write to each other in such terms, unless they were having a homosexual relationship, which Thackeray and FitzGerald certainly were not. They called each other by pet names, and wept at parting. Life without the other seemed to each dreary and blank; their friendship the only thing which gave it savour, as 'Old Fitz' expressed at length in a poem to 'my Willy'.[26] They openly referred to their feeling for each other as love. Nineteenth-century lack of explicitness about sexuality perhaps made it easier to be expressive of emotion in friendship; but there is a hint in FitzGerald's depressed but affectionate response to Thackeray's letter of 1852 quoted above that on his side there was possibly something more:

> your note . . . affects me partly as those old foolscap letters did, of which I told you I burned so many this spring; & why: – I was really ashamed of their kindness! If ever we get to another world, you will perhaps know why all this is so – I must not talk anymore of what I have so often tried to explain to you – Meanwhile, I truly believe there is no Man alive loves you (in his own way of love) more than I do.[27]

Sentimental friendships between people of the same sex in Thackeray's fiction are usually those of unmarried girls. The only exception to this is J. J. Ridley's hero worship of Clive, in *The Newcomes*, which is complicated by a class factor: J. J. is the son of a butler; Clive is a public-school boy. However, Thackeray does use the relationship to make a generalization which relates to his own relationship with FitzGerald:

> before the female enslaver makes her appearance, every lad has a friend of friends, a crony of cronies, to whom he writes immense letters in vacation, whom he cherishes in his heart of hearts; whose sister he proposes to marry in after life; . . . who is his hero. (*The Newcomes*, Chapter 12, *Works*, 14, p. 163)

Where women are concerned, however, the friendship is attacked, or condescended to as being a second-class, temporary kind of emotion which will disappear with marriage. This is, of course, part of Thackeray's attack on the sentimentality of debased romanticism; such exaggerated responses are not warranted by the circumstances. There is, too, a more sinister side to them: a trusting and innocent girl is being manipulated by a more sophisticated and unscrupulous one. Becky makes use of Amelia; Blanche Amory tries to breach Laura Bell's defences in the same way. The novels contain, of course, plenty of examples of the exploitation of one man by another, but not through sentiment, which is seen as a typically feminine mode of expression. Pendennis and Warrington drink and smoke together, visit theatres and taverns, talk and argue far into the night, as Thackeray and FitzGerald did; but they would never write to each other in the terms Thackeray and FitzGerald used. The relationship of two men in the novels is typically that of Mentor and Telemachus, rather than that of Orestes and Pylades suggested by Thackeray in a letter to FitzGerald. FitzGerald, always generous to his less fortunate friends, did give Thackeray money from time to time when he was in financial trouble, but he did not act Warrington to Thackeray's Pen. Warrington guides Pen through the snares of adult male society, and Pen in his turn performs the same function for Clive Newcome and Philip Firmin. These relationships are as much exemplary as realistic, part of the patterning of novels in which parents tend to be uncertain guides for their children.

FitzGerald's friendship was important to Thackeray as a writer, as well as in simple human terms of trust and intimacy. It is clear from what survives of the correspondence that Thackeray was using the long letters written to someone whom he could trust as a candid critic, who was also admiring of his talents, to experiment with the kind of intimate, conversational, easy style he perfected later. The two men egged each other on to perform, and criticized, or apologized for, 'dullness'. Thackeray would take off into elaborated fantasy. One letter imagines a trip to Spain that the two of them will take, and how the two heroes will fight off an attack by brigands. A gloomy reference to death by Fitz inspires a caricature and commentary which is criticized by FitzGerald in his next letter for exaggeration, 'excessive caricature will spoil it'.[28] Thackeray wrote pastiche letters to FitzGerald in the style of other writers; one 'as from Herrick . . . might have been made pretty but was poor enough', he confessed.[29] But the letters are works of art. The tiny drawings are done with the greatest care, often in watercolour, and his handwriting, though he is still using a sloping hand rather than the beautiful upright script he prided himself on in later years, is clear and attractive. Even after he had developed the upright hand, he continued to use the 'slantingdicular', when he wanted to write more rapidly, or, in his manuscripts, when he wanted to make a passage more prominent, for the printer. He must have been one of the few people to retain two quite different styles of handwriting throughout life.

FitzGerald, by nature more timid and secretive, did not expose himself to his friend in the same way: Thackeray heard only by accident from John Kemble that FitzGerald had written a play during the time

'Excessive caricature will spoil it'

when they were writing to each other so often. He was hurt: 'this is not open of him. Kemble says it possesses very great beauties. I should like to judge for myself,' he wrote in his diary;[30] but he said nothing to FitzGerald. There is nothing in Thackeray's correspondence to suggest that he ever knew about FitzGerald's Persian studies with Edward Cowell, and his translation of Omar Khayyám, published anonymously in 1859, on which his subsequent fame rested.

FitzGerald was perhaps such a satisfactory friend partly because of his apparent lack of ambition. Thackeray was full of anxiety about how best to use the powers he felt he had, and was wasting in 'seediness, repentance & novel-reading'.[31] Why did he feel himself superior to others – his mother for example – who he knew, if he were honest, 'could write much better letters & quite as good verses as I'? 'I see people do things far better than I can, & yet somehow my extreme good opinion of myself is by no means lowered,' he confessed.[32] He was contemptuous of Bulwer's novels, but envious of their success. *Eugene*

Aram might be 'humbug' and his own projected novel would be something better, but the novel remained unwritten; he was hardly ever at Taprell's chambers, and the realization that he must reform or 'be poor idle & wicked in a couple more years'[33] pressed on him.

It was then that Thackeray met a man who was to influence his professional life for the next ten years. William Maginn was one of the many Irish writers who dominated English journalism in the early nineteenth century. He came from Cork, where he had been seen as something of an intellectual prodigy; moved to Edinburgh, where he worked for *Blackwood's*, and then to London. His lively, scurrilous contributions eventually got him sacked from the habitually iconoclastic *Blackwood's*, and he became one of the founders of *Fraser's Magazine* in 1830. For several years he was its virtual editor. *Fraser's*, satirical, reactionary, constantly in trouble with libel suits, was one of the liveliest magazines of the 1830s. For convenience, an imaginary editor, 'Oliver Yorke', was invented for contributors to hide behind, though this fiction did not prevent the proprietor from being horsewhipped by an outraged author after Maginn wrote a scurrilous review of his novel. Thackeray subscribed to *Fraser's* from its beginnings, and introduced it to the Goethe circle at Weimar, perhaps with a certain mischievous intent, for *Fraser's* was in the forefront of the anti-romantic movement, and parodies of Byron and jokes about *Werther* appeared regularly in its pages. *Fraser's* high Tory politics were not in line with Thackeray's views, but Tories and Radicals were on some issues closer to each other than either to the traditional Whigs, and he does not seem to have found them offensive. Its no-nonsense attitude to literature certainly appealed to him. He submitted a translation of a German poem to the magazine in 1831, but it was rejected, and his first known contribution was a 'version' of Béranger's 'Le Roi d'Yvetot', published in 1834.

According to a circumstantial but probably unreliable account by Francis Mahoney, 'Father Prout', another of the Irish literary mafia who wrote for *Fraser's*, it was he who introduced Thackeray to Maginn in 1832.

Thackeray was a young buck in those days: wanted to make a figure in literature – la belle affaire! So he thought he must help himself to a magazine. It is an expensive toy. A magazine wanted ... an editor. I recommended Billy Maginn ... Before Maginn could go into the matter he must have 500L for deck-clearing ... This was a startling beginning; but Maginn was not to be had on any other terms. He was the only available man at the time ... Thackeray was obliged to come to Maginn's terms.[34]

Maginn never edited the *National Standard*, the paper Thackeray bought in 1833, but it does seem to have been through him that Thackeray made his way at last into the world of London journalism and began to get some of his pieces accepted for publication. And he did lend Maginn money, at once realizing how foolish he had been to do so; he got little of it back. After Maginn's death he replied wryly to a request to contribute to a memorial to him that he had done enough by way of giving him bread, 'let other philanthropists give him a stone'.[35] However, though their professional association may have been less close than Mahoney suggests, Maginn certainly influenced Thackeray as a writer. Many of Maginn's pieces for *Blackwood's* and *Fraser's* might have been written by the young Thackeray. Maginn was an early popularizer of anti-romantic attitudes, who thought that Byron's poetry was over-rated, but that his letters should be published 'entire . . . unmutilated and unasterisked':[36] he was furious at the burning of Byron's autobiography. He was consistently opposed to bombast and sentimentality, everything, in fact, that Thackeray came to characterize as 'humbug', and saw as the besetting sin of his age. He loved parody, and early in his career wrote a burlesque novel, *Whitehall, or the Days of George IV*, which attacks all the targets Thackeray later lampooned in *Mr Punch's Prize Novelists*.

Maginn reinforced some of Thackeray's prejudices, and encouraged him to take up *Fraser's* attitudes. The celebrated vendetta against Bulwer, which Thackeray pursued vindictively, and beyond reason, began in *Fraser's*. But Maginn was the first congenial and lively companion Thackeray had found who took learning seriously. He was erudite; and as well as showing Thackeray 'the mysteries of printing and writing leading articles'[37] he read Homer with him. His attempt at another kind of education shocked his young pupil. Maginn took him to a common brothel, where Thackeray felt 'very disgusted & sickened to see a clever & good man disgrace himself in that way'.[38] Maginn was constantly in debt, and by 1837, when Thackeray began to write regularly for *Fraser's*, he was a chronic alcoholic, and was finished as a writer. But his personality was immensely attractive:

> Barring drink and the girls, I ne'er heard of a sin –
> Many worse, better few, than bright, broken Maginn.[39]

Thackeray saw other sins ignored by Lockhart's memorial verses, notably the poverty into which his wife and family were plunged by Maginn's irresponsibility. In 1849, after Maginn's death, he portrayed him as 'Captain Shandon' in *Pendennis*, unconcernedly in and out of prison for debt, and spending whatever money he acquired on drink. Thackeray omits Maginn's ways with the girls. 'Captain Shandon' (whose name may also contain a dig at 'Father Prout', who wrote the enormously popular song 'The Bells of Shandon') is seen as a less significant figure for Pen's literary career than Maginn was for Thackeray's. It is the reliable Warrington who effects Pen's introduction to the literary world; which guarantees at least an element of respectability in literary Bohemia.

By May 1833 the law studies had been tacitly dropped, and Thackeray was hard at work on the *National Standard*, which he had acquired from F. W. N. ('Alphabet') Bayley. 'We have got free of the Old Bailey and changed the Governor,' Thackeray announced in his first editorial. His literary manners had not yet much to distinguish them from those of the 'low literary men' whose company he despised. The paper, a weekly, gave him, for the first time in his life, more work to do than he had time for. He seems to have written most of it himself, with the help of one assistant, and illustrated it too. Much of it was ephemeral, done under pressure, and certainly not in the class of Dickens's early journalism. He was well aware of this, knowing even at the time that it was poor stuff. Near the end of his life he drew a comic picture of the narrator as youthful editor in *Lovel the Widower*.

> I daresay I gave myself airs as editor of that confounded *Museum*, and proposed to educate the public taste, to diffuse morality and sound literature throughout the nation, and to pocket a liberal salary in return for my services. I daresay I printed my own sonnets, my own tragedy, my own verses . . . I daresay I wrote satirical articles, in which I piqued myself upon the fineness of my wit, and criticisms, got up for the nonce out of encylopaedias and biographical dictionaries; so that I would be actually astounded at my own knowledge. (*Lovel the Widower*, Chapter 1, *Works*, 17, p. 74)

The specious excuse that 'it looks well to have a Parisian correspondent'[40] gave him the chance to spend time away from London, where he felt increasingly depressed and found it difficult to make friends. 'I shall go back to Paris I think, & marry somebody,' he threatened in a letter to his mother, complaining that after three years in London he did not have a single female acquaintance.[41] The only compensation for the dreariness of London was the recently founded Garrick Club, of which Thackeray became a member in 1833. The Garrick had strong connections with the theatre and journalism, and was considerably more free and easy than other London clubs. It remained Thackeray's favourite among the many to which he later belonged. It was, he said, a place where gentlemen 'drop their absurd English aristocratical notions'.[42]

The *National Standard* was becoming an increasing burden. When he bought the paper he still had a certain amount of his inheritance intact, but by October 1833 almost all of it had been lost in the collapse of the Indian banking houses in which his money, and much of his stepfather's, was invested. He kept the paper going until the beginning of 1834, hoping that sales might pick up. Then the question had to be faced again, and with more urgency than before; how was he to earn a living? His income was now no more than a hundred pounds a year.

His thoughts had already begun to turn back to art, his first enthusiasm, while he was still involved with the *National Standard*. To become a student in one of the Paris ateliers was cheap, no more than a pound a month, and the *vie de bohème* relaxed and agreeable. By October he was established in the Paris atelier of a landscape painter, and later he attended life classes, as well as spending much time copying paintings in the Louvre. Gambling seems to have ceased abruptly with the realization that he was now dependent on the charity of his relations until he could earn his own living. He claimed to feel much happier without the money he had lost. At first he was satisfied with his progress in painting, and with the freedom from English class snobbery. In *The Paris Sketch Book* he writes of the artist in France 'being caressed by hosts and hostesses in places where titles are laughed at, and a baron is thought of no more account than a Banker's clerk . . . This country is surely the paradise of painters and penny-a-liners.' The life of the young artist was 'the easiest, merriest, dirtiest existence possible . . . how he passes his evenings, at what theatres, at what *guinguettes*, in company with what seducing little milliner, there is no need to say'.[43] He returned with reluctance to London to attend to the *National Standard* and other business matters, and may have attended an art school in London for a few months. The description of 'Gandish's' in *The Newcomes* is probably based on the school run by the Academician Henry Sass. Through Maginn he made the acquaintance of painters such as Daniel Maclise, who sketched him as a young buck with sketch pad and pencil in 1832, and included him in the second version of the Fraserian group portrait in 1835. George Cruickshank later gave him lessons in engraving; other painter friends were George Cattermole and Frank Stone.

He went back to Paris in the autumn of 1834, this time in the company of his grandmother, Mrs Butler, and at her expense. The dashing Mrs Butler does not seem to have mellowed with the years, and

Thackeray, who until then had hardly known her, found her sarcastic tongue hard to bear. 'I am at the moment writhing under the stripes of her satire & the public expression of her wrath,' he wrote to his mother.[44] She picked quarrels with him constantly over trivial matters: a lost letter, a pair of boots. Finally Thackeray could put up with it no longer and moved out to a room of his own in the Rue des Beaux Arts, where he lived until his marriage. He said they were better friends when they were living apart, and in a way he admired the fierce old lady for her independent mind and freedom of expression. She became the inspiration for the capricious, card-playing old women who tyrannize over, and spoil, young men in his novels.

His first enthusiasm for art as a profession began to wane, as he came to the depressing realization that he would never make a painter. 'I have got enough torn-up pictures to roast an ox by ... I have become latterly so disgusted with myself and art and everything belonging to it, that for a month past I have been lying on sofas reading novels, and never touching a pencil,' he wrote to Frank Stone in April 1835.[45] In the same month he applied unsuccessfully for a job as Constantinople correspondent to the *Morning Chronicle*. Though he never entirely gave up the fantasy of becoming a painter – late in his life he was still hoping to have the time to take up art seriously – he became convinced that illustration and caricature were what he was best fitted for.

The months as an art student were not wasted. The trained eye and the facility in drawing which daily practice had given him were of use to the writer, as well as the caricaturist. 'I have no head above my eyes,' he said once,[46] and 'seeing is certainly better than book-reading ... it would be a good plan I think for a man in my trade to give up reading altogether for, say, a year: and see with nobody else's eyes but his own.'[47] The eye for detail which the short-sighted boy had early acquired was sharpened and focused by the habit of looking for significant detail in a landscape or portrait, and carried over into his observation of the absurdities and foibles of nineteenth-century society. In *Mrs Perkins's Ball*, his Christmas Book for 1847, he not only notes that the back-drawingroom door has been taken off its hinges for the occasion, but adds that it has been 'placed upstairs under Mr Perkins's bed'.[48] The contrivance and anxiety of giving a party in a modest house not designed for such ostentation are conveyed without comment or elaboration.

Thackeray's first published 'book' was in fact a little pamphlet consisting of eighty lithographed cartoons of ballet dancers. *Flore et Zephyr*, by 'Theophile Wagstaff', published in 1836.[49] His love of the ballet, and his recognition of its absurdities and incongruities, are

FLORE ET ZEPHYR
Ballet Mythologique
DEDIÉ
À
par
Théophile Wagstaff
LONDON, PUBLISHED MARCH 1st 1836 BY J. MITCHELL, LIBRARY, 33, OLD BOND St
à Paris chez Rittner & Goupil, Boulevard Montmartre.

Flore

Taglioni as Flore, by A. E. Chalon

exposed in these caricatures. The debt to other caricaturists, Daumier and Chalon in particular, is obvious, but the drawings are among the best Thackeray ever made, their comic exaggeration restrained and melancholy. The frontispiece is an unmistakable caricature of Chalon's lithograph of Taglioni in the role of Flore, in the old ballet which was revived for her in 1831. Thackeray probably saw it in London in 1833, when Taglioni danced with the veteran Albert as Zephyr; his Zephyr is an elderly, *passé* dancer having difficulty with his leaps and his simulation of despair and adoration. Six of the cartoons depict the ballet; the last two show the very different scenes backstage; Flore wrapped in a shawl receiving the adoration of a vulgar young swell and a stout middle-aged man; Zephyr consoling himself with a pint of porter and a pinch of snuff. Each lithograph is signed with a modified form of the WMT monogram Thackeray had already designed for himself, with the M omitted, so that it can stand, to the uninitiated, for 'Theophile Wagstaff'. The letterpress consists of a bare caption, in French, to each cartoon. In its bald, bleak way, *Flore et Zephyr* presents, in microcosm, the fascination with illusion and reality, and the unwincing social realism that were to persist in Thackeray's writing.

Zephyr

Backstage

Backstage

Both found literary expression in *The Paris Sketch Book*, not published until 1840, under Thackeray's by then well-established pseudonym 'Michael Angelo Titmarsh', but made up of material gathered, and pieces published, in the 1830s. It is a curate's egg of a book, which would never have found a publisher in a less expansive literary age. The 'sketch' as a literary form was an early-nineteenth-century phenomenon, though only Dickens immortalized the form with *Sketches by Boz* and *Pickwick Papers*. A less considered and literary form than the essay, the sketch trades the latter's shapeliness and conscious elegance for immediacy. It developed naturally with the enormous expansion of periodicals, and was directed at a new readership, whose attention had to be captured rapidly. The visual style of caricature was its natural complement, and the new method of publishing fiction in numbers, with illustrations which often made their effect by grotesque exaggeration, grew out of it. For Thackeray the sketch was a natural form, an extension into words of the miscellaneous drawings which had always decorated his letters, and much of his early writing has this sketchlike quality.

The sketch was often a travel-piece, aimed at the new middle-class tourist, for whom the Continent was opened up by the years of peace

Attwood

and the increasing ease and speed of travel. *The Paris Sketch Book* opens
with a vivid account of the horrors of crossing the Channel. The second
piece is a comic cautionary tale of a travelling salesman who fancies
himself as a Byronic hero and lady-killer, who is thoroughly fleeced by
an unscrupulous French couple. It combines several of Thackeray's
hobby-horses: the baneful effect of ill-digested romanticism; the
dangers of gambling; the troubles that will befall the 'little man'
attempting to jump class barriers. It is not enough to be one of 'Nature's
gentlemen'; the wickedness and the good manners of the aristocrat are
both out of reach of the tradesman. It is a sour little tale; but even more
bleak is 'A Gambler's Death', based on a real incident which Thackeray
witnessed. It is one of his first wholly successful transformations of
reality into art.

The story is simple enough. A young man who had been at school
with 'Titmarsh' turns up again in Paris as a professional gambler, and,
claiming acquaintance, borrows his last five pounds. 'Attwood' has a
run of luck, repays Titmarsh, and lives like a lord for a while. Then,
inevitably, he loses everything, and shoots himself with a pair of
borrowed pistols. Titmarsh hears the news from another of Attwood's
acquaintances.

> 'Here's a pretty row!' said Gortz, quoting from his letter: – 'Attwood's
> off – have a bit of beefsteak?'
> 'What do you mean?' exclaimed I, adopting the familiar phraseology of
> my acquaintances: – 'Attwood off? – has he cut his stick?'
> 'Not bad,' said the feeling and elegant Fips – 'not such a bad guess, my
> boy; but he has not exactly *cut his stick*.'
> 'What then?'
> '*Why, his throat*.' The man's mouth was full of bleeding beef as he uttered
> this gentlemanly witticism.

A Gambler's Death

The poverty of the emotional response is matched by the slang expressions; the mutual rapacity amounting to cannibalism is conveyed by the mouthful of bleeding beef; the destructiveness of such a way of life is epitomized in the gambler's death. The final twist comes when, instead of the moral which contemporary readers would have expected, Thackeray breaks off the last fragment of the tale, and gives that as the moral. Attwood's friends go to his early-morning funeral, still half drunk.

MORAL

'When we turned out in our greatcoats,' said one of them afterwards, 'reeking of cigars and brandy-and-water, d—e sir, we quite frightened the old buck of a parson; he did not much like our company.' After the ceremony was concluded, these gentlemen were very happy to get home to a warm and comfortable breakfast, and finished the day royally at Frascati's. (*The Paris Sketch Book, Works*, 2, pp. 122, 124)

Not all of *The Paris Sketch Book* is as original as this. However, it contains Thackeray's most famous caricature, probably inspired by Philipon's even more famous 'Poire': 'Rex. Ludovicus. Ludovicus Rex', another variation on the theme of illusion and reality, which illustrates

REX.   LUDOVICUS.   LUDOVICUS REX.

'Rex. Ludovicus. Ludovicus Rex'

'Meditations at Versailles', one of Thackeray's most outspoken attacks on heredity and privilege. The phallic sword-hilt of the final figure of the weak little man metamorphosed into king is a startling emblem of the brutal force that underlies the power of the figurehead. Other pieces of interest are those on French painting, plays and novels; 'Caricatures and Lithography in Paris' is particularly relevant to his growing interest in book illustration.

Thackeray lived a hand-to-mouth existence for a couple of years, picking up whatever journalism came his way. 'The deuce is in it if I can't make my own livelihood in a couple of years,' he wrote to his mother on his twenty-fourth birthday.[50] FitzGerald, always generous, offered to subsidize him, and devised a scheme, which came to nothing, to publish the Sir Roger de Coverley pieces from the *Spectator* with illustrations by Thackeray. But this desultory way of life could not go on for ever. He was already beginning to feel older than his years, and he needed something to provide a focus and meaning for his existence. By September 1835 he had found it.

Chapter 4

Marriage

Philip's old college and school cronies laughed
at hearing that, now his ruin was complete, he was thinking about marriage.
Such a plan was of a piece with Mr Firmin's known
prudence and foresight.

The Adventures of Philip, Chapter 21.

Few young men can ever have shown more eagerness to get married. From the age of twenty it was a constant theme in Thackeray's letters, often accompanied by a drawing of Mr and Mrs Thack. with a numerous train of children. He fell easily in and out of love with suitable and unsuitable girls, 'suitability' being judged at this stage by the standards of the time; a young man with only a modest amount of money, and later, none at all, had better look out for a girl who would bring a portion with her. If pretty Theodosia Pattle (one of the seven beautiful Pattle sisters, one of whom was to become Virginia Woolf's grandmother) had '£11,325 in the 3 per cents' he'd have popped the question.[1] He was severely practical on the advisability of *not* being in love with one's wife:

> I saw my ancient flame Duvernay at the French Opera the other day, & wondered how I could have ever been smitten – Now this would be an awkward circumstance in marrying a wife, it will be better I think not to be in love with her at all – only to have a kind of respect, & esteem for the sharer of one's couch, & the payer of the baker's bills.[2]

This was all very sensible and must have been reassuring, if a little chilling, to an anxious parent; but when Thackeray really fell in love, he did it with a wholeheartedness and lack of concern for practicalities which must have reminded his mother of her own romantic history. It is amusing to compare letters written within a few months of each other by FitzGerald and Thackeray on the subject of love and marriage. FitzGerald writes:

'Mr and Mrs Thack'

And now, my dear Boy, do you be very sensible, and tell me one thing . . . – shall I marry? – I vow to the Lord that I am upon the brink of saying 'Miss—do you think you could marry me?' to a plain, sensible girl, without a farthing! There now you have it – The pro's and con's are innumerable, and not to be consulted: for I have at last come to a conclusion in morals, which is this: that to certain persons of a doubting temper, and who search after much perfection, it is better to do a thing slap dash at once, and then conform themselves to it.[3]

FitzGerald did not marry the lady. Thackeray's letter is to his cousin William Ritchie, but he evidently wrote in a similarly rapturous strain to FitzGerald.

I am arrived at such a pitch of sentimentality (for a girl without a penny in the world) that my whole seyn, être, or being, is bouleversé or capsized – I sleep not neither do I eat, only smoke a little and build castles in the clouds; thinking all day of the propriety of a sixième, boiled beef and soup for dinner, and the possession of the gal of my art.[4]

Under the linguistic fooling, the depth of feeling and commitment is unmistakable, and it was typical of the young Thackeray that the 'gal of my art' should be as nearly penniless as he was. Marriage, like gambling, was a neck or nothing enterprise. For the rest of his life he continued to admire those who married on 'nothing a year', and to help them financially when he was in a position to do so. This socially acceptable way of living on the edge and, in due course, providing hostages to fortune, always appealed to him. He had taken several steps on the path which led Captain Rook to perdition. Now he would learn his lesson and become one of Pigeon's resourceful children who are 'born in poverty and may bear it, or surmount it and die rich'.[5]

Marriage was also the generally approved answer to the problem of finding an acceptable sexual outlet. In his diary for 1832 Thackeray records having 'just come from talking of debauchery and its consequences – wh. have made me long for a good wife & a happy home' and two days later found himself 'growing loving on every pleasant married woman I see'.[6] He already had personal experience of the consequences of debauchery; an early gonorrhoeal infection left him with a stricture of the urethra which caused him much suffering for the rest of his life, and perhaps contributed to his premature death. He was not, like Charles Buller, in the social or financial class of young men about town who kept a mistress in a separate establishment, as his own father had done, nor would this have satisfied the eager idealism instilled by his mother.

Isabella Shawe

Isabella Shawe was only seventeen when they met in a Paris boarding-house; one of those establishments against which he was to warn the naïve traveller in *The Paris Sketch Book*: 'In the first place, you have bad dinners; and secondly, bad company. If you play cards, you are very likely playing with a swindler; if you dance, you dance with a—person with whom you had better have nothing to do.'[7] Isabella was red-haired, tiny, 'the diminutive part of me', he called her.[8] All his friends seem to have been charmed by this 'nice, simple, girlish girl'.[9] She had a good, well-trained singing voice, and according to one account drew well, but she was not otherwise remarkable for 'accomplishments', and she was not clever, which was all to the good as far as Thackeray was concerned. She was unaffected and natural, qualities he always admired in women. He fell immediately and entirely in love with this artless, timid girl, still very much under the thumb of her formidable widowed mother, who 'talked as big as St Paul's',[10] though she had neither money nor the social position she felt was owed to her. Mrs Shawe was the impoverished relict of an Indian Army officer, and she and her five children lived among the English expatriates in Paris, at that time cheaper than England. It was an isolated society, '*Cranford En Voyage*' as Anny Thackeray later described her paternal grandmother's Paris circle,[11] which mixed very little with the French.

A tone of loving disappointment, even decided disapproval, in Thackeray's early letters to Isabella reveals that his total commitment was not at first reciprocated. He was ready for marriage, as soon as possible; she was not. Thackeray blamed Mrs Shawe, who was certainly against the match, either because, like Mrs Baynes in *Philip*, she had some more apparently suitable husband in mind for her daughter, or simply because she felt that Isabella had plenty of time in which to find a husband with money or a steady profession. But Isabella's apparent coldness and disinclination to express her feelings in her letters, or in person, her indolence – she habitually stayed in bed all morning – even perhaps her chronic constipation, which was evidently so much a matter of family concern that Thackeray referred to it both facetiously and seriously in his letters during their engagement, suggest some complicity in her mother's dominance. All seem pathetically negative forms of self-assertion, designed to keep her in the nursery. Mrs Shawe's younger daughter, Jane, never escaped from her mother's arbitrary and capricious rule, and, like her sister, suffered a mental breakdown in later life. Isabella, pulled from her mother by the strength of Thackeray's loving determination, eventually found the role he cast her in too difficult to sustain. She relapsed again into a retreat from reality, and this time nothing and no one could rouse her.

For the time being, however, Thackeray's love throve on opposition. Major Carmichael-Smyth, anxious to do what he could to make up to his stepson for his responsibility for the financial muddles in which most of Thackeray's money had disappeared, became the prime mover in setting up a new radical journal, mainly in order to give Thackeray a job. Undismayed by the failure of the *National Standard*, Thackeray felt sure that the new paper, *The Constitutional and Public Register*, would flourish. He was appointed Paris correspondent, at a salary of £400 a year, and wrote exultantly to Isabella:

> My father says I could not do better than to marry, my mother says the same. I need not say that I agree with the opinion of my parents – so, dearest, make the little shifts ready, and the pretty night caps; and we will in a few months, go & hear Bishop Luscombe read, and be married, and have children, & be happy ever after, as they are in the Story books – Does this news please you as it does me? are you ready and willing to give up your home, & your bedfellow, and your kind mother, to share the fate of a sulky grey headed old fellow with a small income, & a broken nose?[12]

Isabella was not ready and willing. Thackeray's impetuosity and his open, though perfectly proper, expression of desire upset her; and Mrs Shawe seems to have persuaded her that to marry Thackeray would not only be imprudent, but would cut her off from her family. Things mounted to a crisis in July 1836, when Mrs Shawe attempted to part them altogether. Thackeray steadfastly refused to believe that Isabella did not love him. 'I am sure,' he wrote to her, 'though you may not perhaps be yourself aware of it, that your own heart has never as yet had fair play, and that where your words are questioned rudely, and your feelings scarcely permitted to shew themselves, there is no wonder that a certain habit of coldness & indecision should have sprung up.'[13] The picture of Isabella before their marriage which emerges from this and other letters is a good deal less steadfast than the romanticized portrait of her as Charlotte Baynes in *Philip*. She seems closer to the pathetic, superficial little Rosey Mackenzie of *The Newcomes*, attached to her mother by fear and dependency, clinging and kissing in public, but having her ears boxed in private.

Guided by her mother, Isabella objected to Thackeray's ardour, and his 'improper' expression of it. He replied in terms that Dobbin might have used to Amelia: 'take me or leave me – I never can love you as I have; although you fancy that my love for you was not "pure" enough.'[14] He won the battle, probably more through his steady persistence than in some dramatic scene such as that in *Philip*, where the inhabitants of the boarding-house range themselves with the persecuted

Charlotte and force her mother to give in. They were married on 20 August 1836, at the British Embassy in Paris, and Mrs Shawe, whose consent was necessary, since Isabella was still a minor, was a witness.

The marriage began blissfully. Away from her mother, Isabella was warm and loving, and Thackeray, who had an assured income from *The Constitutional* for articles on French politics, mostly hack work which could be done without much creative effort, happily succumbed to his wife's indolence. 'Fancy that out of the 24 hours we spend at least eleven in bed,' he wrote, half-ashamed, half-boasting, to his high-minded mother. 'My little Puss bating the laziness is the best little wife in the world; I never knew a purer mind or a better temper, or a warmer heart.'[15] The reiterated 'little' which Thackeray always used to describe his wife (later it became 'the poor little wife'), is perhaps ominous; but she was both very young and very small compared with her tall

Mr and Mrs Thackeray

husband, who had already, at twenty-five, begun to think and write of himself as older than he really was. He delighted in and responded to her immaturity and irresponsibility, and their marriage recalls that of David and Dora Copperfield; though Thackeray made fewer attempts at instilling ideas of domestic economy into his charming child-wife. The pathetically short years of married happiness confirmed the pattern for Thackeray's view of women; and it is the portraits of 'good' women in his novels which have done as much as anything to reinforce the critical estimate of him as a typically Victorian writer whose doll-like women are simple to the point of being feeble-minded.

In a letter to Isabella before their marriage, Thackeray gave an eccentrically all-embracing definition of frivolous women:

> a woman who occupies herself all day with her house and servants is frivolous, ditto she who does nothing but poonah-painting and piano forte, also the woman, who piddles about prayer-meetings, and teaches Sunday schools; into wh. 3 classes, I think, the race of women are divided.[16]

He is joking, of course; but it is difficult to see what an unfrivolous woman was supposed to be doing. Thackeray certainly didn't want or expect her to go out to work, qualify for a profession, or compete in any other way with men. His sharp attack on women's 'accomplishments' in his story *The Ravenswing*, where he calls them 'prison work, done because there was no other exercising-ground for their poor little thoughts and fingers',[17] echoes much of the serious contemporary criticism of female education; and girls' schools were among the earliest of his satiric targets. Yet his dislike of his own education was such that he would have deplored any attempt to model girls' schools on the great public schools. In *The Irish Sketch Book* he compares the practical education of the Templemoyle Agricultural Seminary favourably with that of the public schools: 'all the world is improving except the gentlemen',[18] but he does not anywhere in his writings have any positive suggestions to make about improving the education of women. His clever daughter Anny was to suffer from his lack of interest in women's intellectual training, and his devaluation of female intelligence. He exhorted her to be 'humble-minded' as her mother had been, good rather than clever. Loving her more than her quiet younger sister, he often seemed, when they were young, to approve of her less; though his delight in her quickness and self-assertive personality, so like his own, undermined his declared preferences as she grew up.

Thackeray seems to have wanted his women to embody one form of the ideal feminine, the child's view of a perfect mother, which had been permanently embalmed by his childhood experiences. A child in constant contact with his mother soon learns to adapt to her reality, and gradually to see her as a person like himself. Thackeray's early separation from his mother, and his unhappiness at school, were not extreme or unknown experiences for a boy of his background, but they left a mark as profound as Dickens's more obviously traumatic background, repeatedly referred to in his writing. As an adult Thackeray learned to accept the reality of his mother, and to identify her failings, as well as appreciating her goodness. But he, like Poe, never lost the longing for an infantile paradise, which he embodied in a female Peter Pan from whom nothing is expected but love. No real, fully adult woman could play such a role for long in marriage. Thackeray's unerring choice of Isabella, a girl from whom every possibility of self-realization had been removed by her mother's combination of indulgence and destructive overbearingness, gave him, for a while, the loving 'humble-minded' companion he needed. He preserved the image of her at that time entire and unblemished by her subsequent madness. 'What a whirl of life I've seen since then, but never her better I think,' he wrote to her sister Jane in 1848; 'don't you recollect her singing and her sweet sweet voice? She goes to Epsom tomorrow when you sail for India. Go, stay, die, prosper, she doesn't care. Amen. Her anxious little soul would have been alarmed at my prosperities such as they are.'[19]

Though Thackeray's early experiences may have led him towards his personal expression of this concept of woman as all heart and no mind, it was an idealization which suited his age. It is difficult to make the imaginative leap backwards into the state of mind of a society which saw women's primary need as protection, rather than emancipation. The sexual and economic exploitation of women was perceived as wrong; but the only alternative suggested was that men should set women apart, as a higher order of moral beings not expected to struggle with the everyday business of life. What now seems obvious – that women should be given more control of their own lives through political and educational reform – was seen as dangerous to women themselves. The anti-romantic backlash saw that woman was, in realistic terms, the victim of the Byronic hero. Thackeray, in common with other anti-romantic writers, suggested that romantic fiction itself contributed to the exploitation of women. The down-trodden Caroline in *A Shabby Genteel Story* retreats into 'these tender, kind-hearted, silly books: the only happiness which Fate had allowed her was in this little silent world of fancy', and is all the more ready to see a cynical seducer as the hero of a novel.[20] But instead of envisaging a state of affairs in which a woman might take on the role of hero herself, Thackeray agreed with Victorian society in its attempt to tighten the protective net cast around women, and to extend to the poorer women the sexual protection the better-off enjoyed. Young men were not supposed to have any sexual experience before marriage; children were kept 'innocent' as long as possible; the public schools were cleaned up and the obsessive campaign against masturbation was started.

All this repression naturally led to hypocrisy. Thackeray saw the hypocrisy – it was one of his major targets – without seeing that he was, in his acceptance and endorsement of this attitude to women, contributing to it. He assumes, for example, that women do not want to work outside the home. If they do so, it is another example of their exploitation by men. Yet he knew women who worked: Fanny Kemble (whom he came to dislike heartily), her sister Adelaide, a good friend of his, and, later, Charlotte Brontë and Harriet Martineau. He employed women as servants, and as governesses for his daughters, and was a kind and considerate employer to them. Yet he seems to have shut his mind to the possibility that any of them might actually have enjoyed their employment, and taken a pride in earning a living. The hypocrisy of women themselves is one of the attributes he repeatedly praises. Their concealment of domestic unhappiness, in particular, is seen as heroic, their pretences to, and about, their husbands admirable.

During the happy honeymoon months of late 1836, none of this would have seemed relevant to the young couple. They stayed in bed in Paris, and *The Constitutional*, unsuccessful from the first, slid ever deeper into financial trouble. It was a bad moment for even an efficiently run Radical newspaper. Radical views were unpopular because of nervousness over the Chartist movement, and Radical representation in Parliament had almost disappeared. By January 1837 Thackeray was talking with comic despair of the 'two people who read' *The Constitutional*,[21] and turning his hand to other things. He had not entirely given up the attempt to make money as an illustrator, and there was a proposal that he should provide the illustrations for Ainsworth's forthcoming novel, *Crighton*. Nothing came of it, though Thackeray promised 'I work better than I did four months ago, and as quick as a house on fire.'[22] He also proposed himself as illustrator for *Pickwick Papers* – again without success – when the original illustrator, Seymour, committed suicide. He offered the (largely unwritten) *Paris Sketch Book* to Macrone for £50, explaining that he wanted to be made to write, and to bind himself to do so. By April *The Constitutional* was in a state of collapse, the Directors refused to put up any more money to save it, and it ceased publication on 1 July.

The Thackerays came to London in April, and lived with the Carmichael-Smyths at Albion Street, near Hyde Park, where their first child, Anne Isabella, was born on 9 June. The birth was 'a bad business'; the homoeopathic doctor favoured by Mrs Carmichael-Smyth bungled the delivery, and Thackeray had to bring in another. Mrs Shawe was also in attendance, and her presence was not conducive to a calm atmosphere. Isabella was feverish and unwell after the birth. As always when things seemed as bad as they could be, Thackeray began to produce work which, though uneven in quality, more and more often showed his characteristic gifts emerging.

There were plenty of openings for an ambitious young writer needing to make money in a hurry. Even after he had established his family in England, Thackeray often travelled to France to collect material for articles, writing affectionately to Isabella that he felt as though he had left one of his legs behind when he was parted from her. Magazine pay was mostly low, and Thackeray was not at first in a position to hold out for good terms, but there were many periodicals competing with each other for a rapidly expanding middle-class readership. Now that Thackeray was 'writing for life' as Carlyle put it,[23] not just playing at authorship, he made full use of his literary contacts. Journalism was aggressive and exploratory in the 1830s and 1840s. Competition encouraged an attacking, entertaining style of writing, which suited Thackeray's feeling for the absurd, hatred of hypocrisy and pretentiousness, and taste for burlesque.

Thackeray's first published piece of fiction, the short story 'The Professor', which appeared in *Bentley's Miscellany*, then edited by Dickens, in July 1837, is a reductive burlesque of romantic fiction. It takes the standard plot of the innocent young girl deceived by a mysterious stranger, and shows up its threadbare falsity by translating it to a seedy world of oyster bars and petty swindling, using a popular folk hero, or villain, Dando the oyster-eater, as the central character. The story includes comic attacks on various forms of pretension: the social ambitions of tradesmen, the genteel sharp-practice of girls' schools which provide 'accomplishments' instead of education, the false ideals instilled by romantic writers. The story is Thackerayan in its delight in visual detail, reductive simile and deliberate anachronism, but it is not significantly different from many comic stories of the time. With the creation of the footman Charles Jeames Yellowplush, whose reminiscences began to appear in *Fraser's Magazine* at the end of 1837, Thackeray established himself as a writer of fiction who had a unique and instantly recognizable narrative method: one which works by stripping off layers of pretence. The observer is himself observed, and the assumptions the narrative has first encouraged the reader to make are undercut, forcing him to look again.

The establishment of Yellowplush, who was followed by such personae as 'Major Gahagan', 'Ikey Solomons', and his longest-lasting alter-ego, Michael Angelo Titmarsh, was a vital step for Thackeray as a writer. With them he devised a form of narrational presence which is not authorial, as in Fielding's novels, nor quite the same as a narrative told by a character in the story, but something between the two. It was a flexible technique which enabled him to add layers of commentary, mediating his own ambiguous view of the world through his mouth-piece, in ironic and satirical terms. By using a servant as the narrator in *The Yellowplush Papers* he also made an invisible man suddenly apparent, and created a plausible near-omniscient narrator, one who was likely to make the reader uneasy, even as he laughed at Yellowplush's familiarity with the contents of his master's pockets. No middle-class household of the period, however impoverished, consisted solely of the family. When the Thackerays moved from Albion Street early in 1838 to a rented house, 13 Great Coram Street, they often didn't know where the next five pounds was coming from, yet they had a couple of maids, a cook, and an old manservant, John Goldsworthy, who had been with the family at Larkbeare, and who seems to have been taken on as an obligation. His wages were paid (with considerable irregularity) by Mrs Butler, and the yellow plush of his old livery breeches gave Thackeray his title.

Thackeray was unusual in his consciousness of servants as people; one of the *Roundabout Papers* he wrote in the last years of his life shows a vivid awareness of the dishonesties and hypocrisies forced on them by their anomalous position:

> Do you suppose you can expect absolute candour from a man whom you may order to powder his hair? . . . Why, respectful civility is itself a lie, which poor Jeames often has to utter or perform to many a swaggering vulgarian, who should black Jeames' boots, did Jeames wear them and not shoes. (*Works*, 17, p. 487)

This awareness made Thackeray a good employer, and he had a close relationship with several of his servants. But he was always aware of the power that knowledge of family affairs inevitably gave them. Yellow-plush is only the first in a series of menservants in his fiction who know infinitely more about their masters than the masters know about them, and who turn that knowledge to account.

Yellowplush, Gahagan and Titmarsh

Yellowplush was brought into existence as a suitable reviewer of a ridiculous book of etiquette, written for those with no knowledge of polite society by one who clearly had no knowledge of it himself. It was to be expected that a review in *Fraser's* should attack any attempt by those who aspired to social status to join the company of gentlemen. But Thackeray, while satirizing the book, mounts an attack on society too, by making the expert authority who reviews the book a footman. 'I expect you will pay handsomely for it; for it is good fun,' he wrote to James Fraser.[24] His readers clearly agreed, for Thackeray was at once commissioned to write more Yellowplush pieces.

One aspect of the Yellowplush 'fun' that can seem heavy-handed to modern readers, though it was popular at the time, is the comic substandard language in which the pieces are written. Making fun of the speech of the uneducated may seem a cheap way of reaffirming class boundaries, but it was a standard form of humour for nineteenth-century writers, and no one seems to have found it offensive. One highly intelligent and much valued servant of Thackeray's in later years used to write to the papers signing his letters 'Jeames de la Pluche'. The Yellowplush way of writing became for Thackeray a sign of affection, an intimate 'little language', which he used in his letters to his wife, and he wrote proudly of his daughter Anny, 'she's a real daughter of Yellowplush, isn't she?' when she wrote to him: 'Papa I'm very unhappy and I don't know Y.'[25] As used by Yellowplush, however, it became more subtle, serving the satiric purpose of supplying a kind of subtext of which the narrator himself is unaware. The misspellings and distortions of language reveal emotions and relationships only hinted at in the text. When Yellowplush refers to the 'bennyviolent' gentleman who sent him to school; or says that Mrs Shum made her stepdaughter 'retchider and retchider'; or explains of the downtrodden Miss Kicksey: 'abommanating dogs, she never drove out without her ladyship's puddle in her lap',[26] he is enriching and renewing language, not debasing it. His creative way with words and fresh, unsentimental view of the world correlates with his sharp view of society: 'These fashnable gents have ways of getten money, witch common pipple doant understand . . . If he had been a common man, you'd have said he was no better than a swindler.'[27]

Thackeray saw the correspondences between the position of the servant and that of the writer. Each is an observer, ignored, sometimes despised, by the society through which he moves. He is in it, but not of it, until he reveals the power which his silent observation has given him. In the Yellowplush stories which made use for the first time of Thackeray's experiences in the gambling world of Paris and London,

Yellowplush triumphant

Yellowplush serves the gambler Deuceace by acting as his spy as long as it suits him, but he transfers his allegiance without compunction, using what he knows about his master for his own ends. The writer is the servant and entertainer of his public – or so it thinks – until he holds the mirror up to show who is really being satirized. The similarity is made explicit in the final Yellowplush Paper, 'Mr Yellowplush's Ajew', where the two professions are comically compared, and Yellowplush turns down the chance of becoming a writer, to remain a footman: 'The work's not so hard – the pay is better: the vittels incompyrably supearor.'[28] He changes his mind, however, on learning that 'Bullwig' (Bulwer) has just been made a baronet, deciding that he'd much rather have a coat of arms than a coat of livery. He will learn to spell, and write a novel just like Bullwig's – which means, in Thackeray's eyes, ceasing to be a writer of any interest or significance.

The popularity of Yellowplush encouraged Thackeray to 'strike for wages' as he put it. Finding that other *Fraser's* contributors were being paid more, he demanded twelve guineas a sheet (sixteen magazine pages) for Yellowplush's adventures, with an extra two guineas for an illustration. He was beginning to gain confidence in his writing abilities, and his next contribution to *Fraser's*, the story *Catherine*, was his longest piece so far, and his first attempt at handling an extended plot.

Catherine began as a parody of the Newgate novels of Bulwer and Ainsworth which romanticized murderers and highwaymen; and it appeared, month by month, through 1838, as Ainsworth's *Jack Sheppard* appeared in *Bentley's*. *Catherine*, like the Newgate novels, was based on a true murder case taken from the Newgate Calendar; one deliberately chosen for its sordid and mercenary character, and unpleasant details. Thackeray himself came to feel that it was 'a mistake all through'. The reason for this, he felt, was that he hadn't handled the story harshly enough: 'the author had a sneaking kindness for his heroine, and did not like to make her utterly worthless.'[29] The heroine, corrupted in early youth, self-seeking, financially grasping, an unnatural mother and finally the murderer of her husband, is certainly the opposite of everything Thackeray admired in women. As a forerunner of Becky Sharp, Catherine is crude enough, yet the portrait is of interest in pointing the way to Thackeray's most brilliant successes. He was not yet fully aware that his great strength as a writer lay precisely in his ambiguity of response, that 'sneaking kindness' for the sheer energy and inventiveness of the less admirable characters.

At the level of parody the story is a failure, for the targets are too wide and the attack loses focus. Nevertheless it is an interesting failure. Carlyle praised it, perhaps because it contains passages of vividly realized and atmospheric historical writing: the story relies as much on Thackeray's reading of eighteenth-century authors as it does on burlesque of his contemporaries. The crowded scene-setting of the opening paragraphs echoes Carlyle's technique in *The French Revolution*, which Thackeray had reviewed enthusiastically, and reveals the extent of Carlyle's influence on Thackeray's early writing.

As a literary exercise, *Catherine* has considerable interest as Thackeray's first exploration of the underside of the eighteenth century, the world of Fielding's *Jonathan Wild*. He was also trying out, tentatively, the narrative technique which he finally perfected in *Vanity Fair*: using passages of commentary to connect past to present, particular to universal; creating an 'open' rather than a 'closed' self-contained story. The original parodic purpose is catered for rather unsatisfactorily by passages of burlesque modelled on the styles of Ainsworth and Bulwer, which are not integrated with the rest of the story, and distract from it. Apart from the narrative experiments, the story is chiefly interesting for the creation of characters who seem like sketches for those in later novels. Galgenstein, who reappears in *Barry Lyndon* as a minor character, is a first attempt at Barry himself; and

Isabella and Anny

Brock, the most interesting character in *Catherine*, has some of the chameleon-like characteristics of Father Holt in *Esmond*. The story is also significant for the explicit reiteration of the belief, tacitly assumed in the later novels, that evil is as natural and inescapable a part of the human psyche as good, and that impulses for both are to be found in the best and the worst of men.

Thackeray's domestic life continued to give him great happiness. 'Here have we been nearly 2 years married & not a single unhappy day,' he wrote to Isabella in March 1838.[30] But it made him, prophetically, 'almost tremble for the future'; and the first sorrow came a year later, with the death of their second daughter, Jane. She had been born in July 1838, so easily and quickly that Thackeray was out fetching the doctor when she arrived. Isabella, unencumbered this time by mother or mother-in-law, recovered rapidly from the birth. 'She produces children with a remarkable facility,' Thackeray told her mother.[31] Jessie Brodie, a devoted and indispensable nurse, joined the family to look after the two little girls. But Anny, aged sixteen months, became gravely ill in September, and after her recovery Jane contracted a respiratory illness and died the following March.

Both parents were deeply saddened by her death, but Thackeray found it possible to throw himself into his work. He was writing articles and reviews for a number of periodicals, including *The British and Foreign Review*, edited by his friend John Kemble, and *The Times*. He was also doing illustrations, not only for his own stories, and these sometimes gave him trouble and took up more time than he could afford. Three etchings done by a new patent process failed and had to be done again on wood-block. It was an exhausting way of life, but, as Isabella wrote to Mrs Carmichael-Smyth, 'I doubt if William would like any regular work half so much as what he is doing now.'[32] It was not so easy for her. She described herself as (characteristically) 'rather sluggish' and as spending time 'quietly reading, or *sleeping* or musing'.[33] It was a natural reaction to bereavement, but it may have marked the beginning of her renewed retreat from reality. Her own picture of her passivity is countered, however, by charming glimpses from Thackeray's letters of her playing with Anny, entering with child-like enthusiasm into the little girl's games of make-believe. 'Miss Thackeray and her mother are at this moment dragging carts round the room, and yelling Taytoes in a way that precludes all possibility of grammar: Miss T remarks that the taytoes are very dear at a penny a bushel, and that she will only give five francs – I believe that on this matter the daughter knows very nearly as much as the mother, who has a noble want of the organ of number. The Child is the same, for though she knows all her letters, we can not get her to count two.'[34] Both parents delighted in the child left to them. 'There is a grand power of imagination about these little creatures, and a creative fancy and belief that is very curious to watch,' Thackeray wrote to his mother, vowing that Anny should have plenty of fairy stories, rather than the moral tales of Miss Edgeworth.[35]

The household became increasingly disorganized, however, and the noise and continual interruptions made working at home more and more difficult.

> There is no lack of work; but the deuce is the wear & tear of it: and the wear & tear of London – there has not been five minutes cessation of knocks & bell-ringing this blessed day: and between times my wife comes in with the prettiest excuses in the world.[36]

He formed the habit, which remained with him all his life, of writing elsewhere, in clubs, or public houses, on journeys to the country, or abroad. When his writing was going badly he became 'dreadfully cross to my poor little wife in consequence. She had much better let me go away on these occasions, but she won't.'[37] There were perpetual money worries, and various schemes were proposed for economy: that Brodie should be replaced by a cheaper country girl (fortunately Thackeray vetoed that) or that part of the house should be let. Mrs Butler, 'GM', joined the household to help with expenses, and managed to upset the gentle Isabella with her authoritarian ways.

Isabella made constant efforts to please her mother-in-law and husband. 'We continue *good children* in getting up of mornings,' she wrote when she was seven months pregnant with her third child.[38] But she was being asked to turn herself into a different kind of wife from the 'Little Trot' Thackeray had delighted in. She was still only twenty-one, and she did her best to be practical and economical, and not to be possessive. 'W. gets up early works hard all day and then I let him gad of an eveng.'[39] But after the birth of a third daughter, Harriet Marian, in May 1840, she became increasingly low-spirited. Thackeray became gloomy and irritable too, but so preoccupied with the pressures of work and poverty that he failed to see how serious Isabella's depression was. Going to see the public hanging of Courvoisier, a valet who had murdered his master, gave him 'the blue devils', and was the occasion for one of his sharpest and most attacking pieces of journalism.[40] Already overburdened with work, writing and drawing for *Fraser's*, preparing *The Paris Sketch Book* for publication, writing articles for *The Times*, he seized on the idea of going to Belgium to collect material for another sketch-book. It was clearly a way of getting clear of the noisy misery of home, and though Isabella begged him not to go he insisted. She began to laugh as he left her.

The fortnight's trip was a brief respite, but when Thackeray returned he was alarmed at Isabella's state. On medical advice he took her, with Brodie and the children, to Margate. At first Isabella seemed better. Thackeray did not know until years later that while he was attempting to keep up with his writing commitments – an article for *The Times* on Fielding, and *A Shabby Genteel Story* for *Fraser's* – Isabella, walking on the beach with Anny, threw the little girl in the sea. She instantly pulled her out again, but it was a traumatic moment that the child never forgot.[41]

A Shabby Genteel Story reflects the sadness and guilt that Thackeray felt about Isabella, though the story, of a down-trodden little Cinderella taken in by a plausible rogue and tricked into a false marriage, had no literal connection with her life. The heroine, Caroline Gann, is given some of Isabella's characteristics, however: she is pale, freckled and thin, and has a ranting, would-be genteel Irish mother. The story is set in Margate, in the back streets Thackeray walked through thinking of his story, and his present situation. George Brandon, the villain of the story, is more careful than his author to avoid entanglements, but his background is the familiar one Thackeray so often castigates in his early work, to which he himself belonged. Brandon too went to public school and university.

> I should like to know how many such scoundrels our universities have turned out; and how much ruin has been caused by that accursed system which is called in England 'the education of a gentleman.' Go, my son, for ten years to a public school, that 'world in miniature;' learn 'to fight for yourself' against the time when your real struggles shall begin . . . You have learned to forget (as how should you remember, being separated from them for three-fourths of your time?) the ties and natural affections of home . . . My friend Brandon had gone through this process of education, and had been irretrievably ruined by it. (*A Shabby Genteel Story*, Chapter 2, p. 299)

Though Thackeray felt that his marriage had saved him from becoming a Brandon, an inveterate womanizer like his friend Savile Morton, his doubts about himself surface more than once in Brandon's character. 'Give me joy; for in a week's time it is my intention to be violently in love, – and love is no small amusement in a watering-place in winter,' Brandon writes to his friend Lord Cinqbars, echoing a letter of Thackeray's from Weimar. Like Thackeray, Brandon is an accomplished parodist and caricaturist, accomplishments seen as typical of his cynical and opportunistic attitude. Like Caroline, Isabella also suffered from neglect – his neglect – and her mother's bullying vulgarity. He blamed his mother too, and 'GM' for misinterpreting Isabella's depression as sulkiness. Thackeray wrote to his mother warning her that she and Polly Graham (who had been in attendance at Harriet's birth), must not reprove Isabella any more about her 'faults':

> in the course of her depression the poor thing has worked up these charges so as to fancy herself a perfect demon of wickedness – God abandoned & the juice knows what: so that all the good of your reproof was that she became perfectly miserable and did her duty less than ever.[42]

Years later he wrote to his mother that she had never properly appreciated Isabella's unaffected goodness and simplicity. Mrs Carmichael-Smyth's gloomy evangelical piety, increased during her life in Paris by her attachment to the ideas of the French Protestant preacher Monod, was eventually to convince her son that his children should live with him, rather than their grandmother. Already, during the first phase of Isabella's illness, he was arguing with her over religion, objecting to her fanatical anti-Catholicism and narrow-mindedness with a typically open-minded argument in favour of toleration. 'Indeed it is something noble I think to think even of this difference: that God has a responding face for every one of these myriad intelligences, and a sympathy with all.'[43]

The return from Margate was a depressing one. 'There is something in the air of this dismal Coram Street that seems to give us all the blue-devils,' Thackeray wrote to his aunt Ritchie.[44] They soon set off again, this time to join Isabella's mother and sister in Cork, so that Isabella might be looked after by her relations, while Thackeray gathered the materials for a travel book on Ireland, for which he had arranged a contract – much better than any he had managed hitherto – which included an advance of £120 to finance the expedition. Thackeray was at last becoming a recognized author, even though most of his work had appeared over pseudonyms, in periodicals. He did have to deposit his plate-chest with Chapman and Hall, as a 'kind of genteel pawn'.[45]

The Irish trip was doomed to failure, and Thackeray can only have undertaken it in a spirit of desperation. Only ten days earlier he had considered that they had escaped from 'a pretty kettle of fish' in the form of a threatened visit to London by Mrs Shawe.[46] He had always found his mother-in-law quite impossible, and was convinced she was bad for both her daughters. Nevertheless, the family set sail for Cork on 13 September. He had written Mrs Shawe a conciliatory letter: 'you & Jane must look to the little woman and get her back to spirits again.'[47]

The journey from London to Cork took three days and four nights. On the second day Isabella tried to kill herself by jumping out of the water-closet window into the sea. It was twenty minutes before the ship's boat even saw her; but by a miracle she was found, floating on her back and paddling with her hands. She continued 'quite demented' throughout the voyage, making further attempts at suicide, and Thackeray had to watch her day and night. He slept with a ribbon round his wrist and attached to her waist, so that any attempt to get out of bed woke him at once. Brodie took entire charge of the children. 'I never saw anything more beautiful than that woman's attention to the children on board the steamer. She was sick almost every ¼ of an hour, but up again immediately staggering after the little ones feeding one & fondling another. Indeed a woman's heart is the most beautiful thing that God has created and I feel I can't tell you what respect for her.'[48]

When they reached Cork Mrs Shawe's behaviour ran true to form. Though she had a spare bedroom she refused to have Isabella in the house 'on account of her nerves'.[49] The Thackerays took lodgings next door, where Anny made friends with the entire household, and acquired a decided brogue. Thackeray recorded his gratitude to the inhabitants of this 'kind, poor, generous, barebacked house' when he came to write *The Irish Sketch Book*. Mrs Shawe was, in contrast, so violent and abusive that Thackeray concluded that she must be mad. This appalling Irish episode, added to Mrs Shawe's behaviour in trying to prevent the marriage in the first place, created an *idée fixe* about mothers-in-law which pervades his fiction. It is at its fiercest in *The Newcomes*, where Clive's mother-in-law Mrs Mackenzie, 'the Campaigner', with her violent accusations against Clive and his father, and her treatment of her daughter, which alternates indulgence with insensitivity and cruelty, is based on Thackeray's experiences of Mrs Shawe. Like Colonel Newcome, he could 'scarcely get a meal at her home but I am obliged to swallow an insult with it'. 'In the midst of all this trouble she can't keep her monstrous tongue quiet.'[50] Isabella's condition fluctuated, and at first Thackeray felt it did her good to be with her sister; at other times she was depressed and suicidal, not noticing or caring for her children. Brodie, deeply scornful of Mrs Shawe, kept them all going: 'without her I don't know what would have become of us all'.[51]

On 9 October Thackeray made the sudden decision, with the doctor's approval, to bring them all home. Nothing was said to Mrs Shawe until all the arrangements had been made, and they set off by the shorter sea route to Bristol. Thackeray wrote desperately to his mother from Clifton, asking her to come to them, and to raise money for them

Caricature of Mrs Shawe

somehow. The publisher's advance had all been used up, and no work on a book had been possible. Mrs Carmichael-Smyth was unable to come, and the pathetic cortège set off again, this time to Paris via London, with the loyal Brodie as Thackeray's only support. The last part of the journey, in a French *diligence*, remained imprinted on Anny's memory.

> I wanted to get out and walk, and they wouldn't let me, and I cried on and on . . . My father . . . struck a match, and lit up a little lantern, which he held up to amuse me. But I only cried the louder. Then he said gravely, 'If you go on crying you will wake the baby, and I shall put out the candle;' so I went on crying, and I woke the baby, who began to cry too; then the man in the corner scolded again, and my father blew out the lantern, and suddenly all was dark. I could not believe it, never before had I been so severely punished . . . I suppose I went to sleep on my father's knee at last . . . The next thing I remember is arriving quite cheerful at Paris, and my grandmother and my grandfather coming down the curling stairs to meet us in the early morning and opening their arms to us all.[52]

Those open arms, the contrast of his mother's behaviour with that of Mrs Shawe, began a new phase in Thackeray's relationship with her. He had never really been alienated from his mother, but there had been times when he felt that she was rigid and narrow-minded and overbearing, not only in her attitude to religion, but in her attempt to push him into a conventional way of life which did not suit him. He was to feel these things again. But her uncompromising acceptance of the burdens he was now to lay on her, at a time when the Carmichael-Smyths' finances were still extremely precarious, won his lasting respect and admiration.

Chapter 5

Days of Trouble

His days of trouble had now begun in earnest, and, indeed,
he met them like a man. He wrote incessantly for the periodical works of the
day, issued pamphlets, made translations, published journals
and criticisms, turned his hand, in a word, to
any work that offered, and
lived as best he might.

'Fielding's Works', *The Times*, 2 September 1840.

The parallel between Thackeray's own days of trouble and Fielding's was poignant and inescapable. Like Fielding, he had lost his inherited wealth, and was finding that the only way in which he could make money was as a literary hack. The grand if diffuse ambitions of earlier days seemed as far from realization as ever, and he clung to Fielding's example. Fielding, too, had been born a gentleman, lost everything, and by unrelenting effort made himself into a major novelist. The two novelists have always been compared – first by Thackeray himself – as stylists, satirists and moralists. The identification, at this stage of his life, was as much emotional as literary.

His brief marriage was over, though it was a long time before he accepted that his wife's condition was irreversible, and the doctors too were hopeful at first. A post-partum depression, unusual in its severity, probably tipped Isabella over into permanent psychosis. The Shawes were not an emotionally stable family. Thackeray seems to have had considerable justification for thinking Mrs Shawe unbalanced; Jane Shawe had a later breakdown, and one of the sons was an alcoholic. Isabella's granddaughter, Leslie Stephen's eldest child Laura, was mentally retarded, or psychotic. Later in life, like her grandmother, she lived in contented seclusion, happy as long as she was spared the problems of the everyday world. Isabella seems to have been able to cope with life as long as too many demands were not made on her, but the stress of marriage, motherhood, bereavement and constant financial anxiety eventually proved too much for her fragile mental balance.

There was no effective treatment, though everything that could have been done at that date was tried out. The arrangements that Thackeray,

with loving concern, eventually worked out for her care, could hardly
have been bettered. He first tried placing her in the highly regarded
Maison de Santé at Ivry. She was also, for a while, at Chaillot, under the
care of Dr Puzin. Thackeray's experiences of these relatively enlightened places convinced him that institutional care was not right for
Isabella. The English madhouses were far, far worse. Thackeray's friend
Bryan Procter, poet and Commissioner in Lunacy, took him to see his
favourite place in London 'which makes me quite sick to think of even
now. He shook his head about the other places.'[1]

In the early days of her madness Thackeray from time to time made
efforts to look after Isabella himself. He took her for a day's outing
from the Maison de Santé, and under the influence of his affection and a
couple of glasses of champagne (the magic potion of *L'Elisir d'Amore*,
as he recalled), Isabella became her old, charming self:

> actually for the first time these six months the poor little woman flung
> herself into my arms with all her heart and gave me a kiss, at which
> moment of course the waiter burst in. This only served to mend matters
> for the lady went off in a peal of laughter, the first these six months again,
> and since then I have had her at home not well, nor nearly well, but a
> hundred times better than she was this day week.[2]

He took her home; but, as he was to discover, fluctuations of this sort
are in the nature of the illness.

If they were all to survive, he had to write almost continuously, and
he found that it was impossible for him to act as his wife's nurse and get
any work done. For a while he engaged a woman to look after her at
home, and noted how much easier the task was for a paid nurse, who
was not emotionally involved. Then, at the Carmichael-Smyths'
insistence – for they had added hydropathy to homoeopathy in their
fascination with unorthodox medical procedures – he took Isabella for a
'water-cure' at Boppard, on the Rhine. His account of the treatment in a
letter to FitzGerald reveals his habitual scepticism, and his way of
coping with suffering by comic distancing, as he describes how he
shared the 'immense sluicing of the water-pipe' with Isabella:

> It would have made a fine picture – Mrs Thack in the condition of our
> first parins, before they took to eating apples, and the great Titmarsh with
> nothing on but a petticoat lent him by his mother, and far too scanty to
> cover that immense posterior protuberance with wh. nature has furnished
> him.[3]

The violence of the treatment, which alternated sweating with the 'immense sluicing', seemed to rouse Isabella from her apathy for a while, but eventually proved no more effective than anything else. She slipped back into her previous condition of 'perfect indifference, silence and sluggishness', with occasional fits of agitation, and rare times when she 'played the nastiest pranks' or rambled distressingly. She was not unhappy, Thackeray thought, but cared for nothing, 'except for me a little', not even her children. She seemed 'about sixteen years old'[4] and continued to look far younger than her real age for the rest of her long life, frozen in an eternal adolescence, in sharp contrast to Thackeray's premature greyness.

Thackeray eventually had to acknowledge that Isabella was better away from him and the children; being with him agitated and disturbed her. She stayed at Chaillot until 1845, when he was able to arrange for her to come to England to be looked after in a private family at Camberwell, where she had her own rooms and personal attendant, supervised by 'an excellent worthy woman', Mrs Bakewell. 'The difference in the poor little woman's appearance is remarkable now that she has some one to look after her and keep her clean,' Thackeray reported to his mother.[5] He still hoped that one day, perhaps when their daughters were grown up, she would be able to live with them again, but Isabella remained with Mrs Bakewell until her death in 1894, by which time she had long been a widow, though it is unlikely she was aware of it. Most of the time she was gentle, quiet and withdrawn, passively content with her secluded half-life. In the early days, when her recovery was still hoped for, Thackeray told his mother to let the children see her often; later he came to feel that her intermittently erratic behaviour would be disturbing for them. Though he continued to visit her, Anny and Minny (as Harriet was always called) were brought up with the ideal of their 'humble-minded' mother kept before them, but not the reality of her condition.

For about eighteen months from the time he arrived on his parents' doorstep with Isabella and the children, Thackeray lived mostly in Paris. But his mother's household depressed him, as he wrote frankly to FitzGerald, still one of his most intimate correspondents. He was always on the brink of quarrelling with 'the Governor'. He longed for FitzGerald to visit Paris and cheer him up, for he had 'another long weary winter' (of 1841–2) ahead of him. The children, too, 'are not half the children without their mother', and it made his heart sick to be parted from her.[6] It was difficult to work in these circumstances, and he really needed to be in London to pick up whatever journalism was available. There is a striking contrast between the almost arrogant confidence of the letters to Fraser at the time when Yellowplush was appearing, and one written in March 1841 begging for work to pay Isabella's board at the asylum, and apologizing for his high and mighty attitude following the agreement with Chapman and Hall for the Irish book: 'think of my little wife so wretched yonder, and I am sure you will lend a hand to save her,' he entreated.[7] Fraser responded, and Thackeray continued to write for *Fraser's* until his commitments to *Punch* (which paid better) eventually swallowed up most of the time he devoted to journalism.

It is not surprising that *The Great Hoggarty Diamond*, written soon after Isabella became insane, was not a success with the public, though Thackeray always thought it the best thing he had done before *Vanity Fair*. Stylistically it is an uneasy mixture of the earlier, Yellowplush exuberance and a sentimental melancholy clearly due to his private circumstances. The narrator, Sam Titmarsh (cousin of Michael Angelo) begins as a likeable vulgarian, laughing himself sick over the sketches of Theodore Hook, as Thackeray had done as a schoolboy. Then, with the account of the abject poverty of Sam and his young wife, and the death of their child, the tone alters drastically. The change is too extreme, perhaps because the events being described are so close to the writer's own experience. The inexplicable ups and downs of fortune, though they are given a fairy-tale explanation in the shape of the magical diamond, express the feeling of helplessness at the vagaries of fate which Thackeray must have been experiencing. The ostensibly happy ending is too hurried to be convincing, and the drawings lack much of Thackeray's customary energy. His later affection for the story was due in part to his feeling that his cynical, satirical side was always overemphasized by critics, at the expense of his emotional capacity. 'If it does not make you cry I shall have a mean opinion of you. It was written at a time of great affliction, when my heart was very soft and humble', he wrote to Mrs Brookfield in 1848.[8]

By May 1842 Thackeray was back in the gloomy Coram Street house, sharing it with his adoptive sister, now married to Major Carmichael-Smyth's younger brother, Charles. 'GM' was also there from time to time. It was not a good arrangement. The Carmichaels (they had dropped the 'Smyth') were hypochondriacal and domestically incompetent, 'worse than we were I think such dirt and cobwebs on the walls, suffered so calmly!' Thackeray complained.[9] He felt Mary was jealous of him and that she thought his mother would prefer his children to her little boy 'and I think you will to[o]' he added complacently.[10] He disliked her pretentiousness, and the continual disturbances in the house. It made matters worse that Mary had generously lent him £500; nevertheless, he could not pretend to feelings that he did not have: 'the fact is, somehow, that she doesn't *agree* with me.'[11]

Except in *A Shabby Genteel Story* and *The Great Hoggarty Diamond*, the depression that Thackeray frankly admitted to in his letters at this time (though almost always with a self-admonitory rider added, or a joke about Byronic melancholy) is seldom noticeable in his published writings, though its unacknowledged presence adds an edge of questioning scepticism. He continued to contribute fiction, art criticism and literary criticism to *Fraser's*. He also wrote for the *Foreign Quarterly Review*, the *Morning Chronicle*, and occasionally for *The Times*. He also wrote regularly, and at first secretly, for 'a low paper called *Punch*', and many other periodicals, including the American magazine *The Corsair*, and the Indian *Calcutta Star*. Asked by his cousin Richard Bedingfield for advice on becoming a journalist, Thackeray told him that it was 'a bad trade at the best'.[12] He felt himself becoming a hack, writing only for money. The question of journalism as a proper occupation for a gentleman, though it continued to put him on the defensive, had become as irrelevant as it was for Fielding. He could never quite make ends meet, however hard he worked. His parents took on the responsibility of the children; he borrowed from his grandmother and from Mary; and FitzGerald, ever generous, paid at least one month's fees for Isabella's maintenance. He was continually having to dun editors for fees due to him, and to ask for higher rates of pay. The big novel he had dreamed of so long, which was to make his name, was put off no longer from laziness and inadequacy, but because the pressures of work left no time for it.

Yet the writing he produced from 1840 to 1846, when he at last started work on *Vanity Fair*, is often impressive. The experience of writing for different periodicals, and creating different personae, all distinct characters with different styles and backgrounds, gave him the opportunity to experiment with the varied styles and levels of discourse that were to become a distinctive part of his major fiction. The most important of these personae was Michael Angelo Titmarsh, an impoverished artist and writer, who was by now a well-established *Fraser's* character.

Thackeray increasingly used Titmarsh as an *alter ego*, closely identified with himself. The Titmarsh of *The Second Funeral of Napoleon* is a narrator and commentator who, though characterized as an elderly cynic, speaks directly for the author, and is quite different in tone from the Titmarsh who is a character in, as well as author of, *The Paris Sketch Book* of only a year earlier. *The Second Funeral*, published with the accomplished anti-war ballad 'The Chronicle of the Drum', is an attack on what Carlyle, in his 1840 lectures on *Heroes and Hero-Worship*, described as sham hero-worship. Thackeray gives an eye-witness account of the pretentious ceremonial that was mounted for the return of Napoleon's body to France, and its reinterment at Les Invalides. He, like Carlyle, saw Napoleon as a charlatan and quack, wrapped in 'a paltry patchwork of theatrical paper-mantles, tinsel and mummery';[13] but, unlike Carlyle, draws the conclusion, from his dead-pan description of the funeral junketings, that all hero-worship is a sham. History camouflages the real character: it is 'written on fig-leaves'. The narrator, borrowing an image from Carlyle and improving on it, imagines how, at the Day of Judgement 'we shall see Pride with his Stultz clothes and padding pulled off, and dwindled down to a forked radish'.[14] No dignitaries are spared: a comic deflation of the pretensions of the church is added to Thackeray's habitual dislike of the army: 'The archbishop's mitre may be about a yard high; formed within probably of consecrated pasteboard . . . On the two peaks at the top of the mitre are two very little spangled tassels that frisk and twinkle about in a very agreeable manner.'[15]

The Second Funeral contrasts public sham with private reality; feigned grief with the good humour of the French crowd 'on the alert

'*How to astonish the French*'

for a festival';[16] the military concept of 'gloire' with the usefulness of the *garde municipal à cheval* 'armed for the special occupation of peace-keeping . . . not the most glorious, but the best part of the soldier's duty'.[17] In a little vignette of an English family (his own, in fact) nervously issuing forth to see the show, secretly convinced that the French were about to turn on all the English in Paris and murder them, he makes gentle fun of his mother's lack of common sense; but he also compares personal, familial love with the sham pomp and mourning of the official proceedings. Contrasts like these were to become one of the recurrent themes of the novels. The piece also contains the germ of *The Book of Snobs*, in an attack on the process by which Napoleon and his generals turned themselves into a mock-aristocracy: 'Give in a republic an aristocracy ever so little chance, and it works, and plots, and sneaks, and bullies, and sneers itself into place, and you find democracy out of doors.'[18] In one of the most outspoken passages on the idea of the gentleman, Thackeray, after conceding that 'there *is* a good in gentility; the man who questions it is envious, or a coarse dullard not able to perceive the difference between high breeding and low', goes on to postulate a highly practical basis for the difference:

> nature does make *some* gentlemen – a few here and there. But art makes most. Good birth, that is, good, handsome, well-formed fathers and mothers, nice cleanly nurserymaids, good meals, good physicians, good education, few cares, pleasant easy habits of life, and luxuries not too great or enervating, but only refining, – a course of these going on for a few generations are the best gentleman-makers in the world, and beat nature hollow. (*The Second Funeral of Napoleon, Works*, 3, p. 439)

Gentility, for a nineteenth-century writer, was separated by the narrowest of margins from the stark necessities of the poor, as Thackeray knew from personal experience. *The Second Funeral* 'hugely praised by the press has sold but 140 copies'.[19] In 1842 Thackeray visited Maginn, in prison and penniless, shortly before he died leaving his wife and children destitute. The lesson was not lost on him. His personal generosity to friends in trouble throughout his life, and his concern in later years to leave enough at his death to keep his wife and daughters in comfort, were legacies of these anxious years.

It may have been partly as a contrast to his real situation that he created a new writing persona for *Fraser's* in 1842. The Honourable George FitzBoodle, who presents himself to the editor as a potential contributor, is a middle-aged clubman, confirmed bachelor, and aristocratic philistine. He is also another version of the footman Yellowplush, from the other side of the green baize door. He too scorns literary men and claims a cosmopolitan sophistication which he is willing to pass on (at a price) to *Fraser's* readers:

> a man to be amusing and well informed, has no need of books at all, and had much better go to the world and to men for his knowledge. There was Ulysses, now, the Greek fellow engaged in the Trojan war, as I dare say you know; well, he was the cleverest man possible, and how? From having seen men and cities, their manners noted and their realms surveyed, to be sure. So have I. I have been in every capital, and can order a dinner in every language in Europe. (*Works*, 4, p. 202)

Like Yellowplush, FitzBoodle can't spell, but dismisses this as a minor consideration: 'Let one of your understrappers correct the spelling and the grammar of my papers: and you can give him a few shillings in my name for his trouble.' But where Yellowplush retained the cunning of a street arab, and invariably triumphed over his betters, FitzBoodle is as naïve and gullible as a schoolboy, and his bluff, no-nonsense stance is combined with an absurd romanticism. Thackeray made use of material from his own life for FitzBoodle; even FitzBoodle's passion for tobacco, which leads to the loss of his first love, was one he shared. 'What a splendid father has been thrown away upon you!' he told his friend Richard Monkton Milnes (who didn't smoke) when told he might smoke anywhere in the house but in Richard's room.[20] FitzBoodle also rather unexpectedly shares Thackeray's views on the propriety of marrying for love, even if it means marrying out of one's class.

However, though FitzBoodle suffers some of Thackeray's own reverses, in the 'Pumpernickel' episodes discussed in Chapter 2, the character that is built up by the careful use of a deliberately restricted register of language is as distinct from that of his creator as any of the people in the novels. This way of distancing autobiographical material, first used more tentatively in parts of *The Paris Sketch Book*, is developed with FitzBoodle, and finally used to full effect in the novels. It marks a move away from the pure fantasy of Yellowplush, and that of the Irish adventurer Major Goliah Gahagan. His 'Adventures', burlesquing military memoirs in Munchausen style, were republished with the *Yellowplush Papers* and some of the more outrageous Michael Angelo Titmarsh pieces as *Comic Tales and Sketches* in 1841. Though Thackeray's writing was now developing in other ways, republication in volume form of these magazine pieces marked another stage in his increasing acceptance by the public.

FitzBoodle's willingness to put his personal experiences on paper, and publish them for gain, is a very ungentlemanly thing to do for one who insists so much on being a gentleman. His suggestions, in 'FitzBoodle's Professions', for new occupations for gentlemen (auctioneer; 'dinner-master'; being a foreigner) parody and make ridiculous the contemporary anxiety about 'correct' and 'incorrect' occupations, and, by implication, the legitimacy of journalism. Thackeray, from habit and necessity, was gaining confidence in his chosen profession.

Men's Wives, a series of four stories on the theme of marital disharmony, which appeared in *Fraser's* in 1843, again has FitzBoodle as narrator, but here, as a commentator on, and narrator of other people's stories, he begins to change character. He still adopts the tone of a man of the world, but he comes closer to one of the narrative voices that is heard later in the novels. He might be defined as the public voice, the downright, average man who appears to be articulating the author's own beliefs and prejudices, only to be subtly undercut by another, conflicting point of view. The private Thackeray of the letters and reported conversations remains closer to Titmarsh, though he was quite capable of assuming the FitzBoodle mantle (or evening coat) when it suited him. The change is gradual; in the first of the stories, 'Frank Berry's Wife', FitzBoodle is still a character in the story. It is a slight piece about a henpecked husband, contrasting his valour in fighting when a schoolboy (described in a parody of Pierce Egan's *Boxiana*) with his subjection to a pretentious, cold-hearted woman. The interest lies less in the characters (though Mrs Berry is worthy of a place in *The Book of Snobs*) than in FitzBoodle's expanded literary powers. There is a description of the Berrys' dingy, gimcrack pavilion that characterizes the people who live in it in Thackeray's sharpest manner, and FitzBoodle, once so loftily non-literary, begins to reveal that he does read, if selectively. Describing Mrs Berry's collection of 'Annuals' he comments, 'I had rather that Mrs FitzBoodle should read "Humphry Clinker"!'

'The Ravenswing', the second of the stories, is far more substantial, one of the best of Thackeray's shorter works. It is a complex story, and the protagonist is one of the few Thackeray heroines to be actively engaged in the world. Morgiana Crump belongs more to the world of Titmarsh than of FitzBoodle; she is the daughter of a publican and a music-hall performer (though there is a hint that her real father is a lord, the publican's erstwhile employer). The cheerful, sleazy, easy-going life of the theatre, to which Thackeray returns in the early chapters of *Pendennis*, is evoked in the opening pages of the story. Morgiana and her mother are harmlessly addicted to this life, and the narrative makes use of the gossipy style and the kind of allusions which they themselves would have used.

The story is the only account of marriage in *Men's Wives* where the wife, and not the husband, is the exploited and suffering party, though the theme of wifely suffering is of course common elsewhere in Thackeray's fiction. Morgiana is not seen as wholly blameless for this; her social ambitions lead her to fall for a rotter whom she falsely supposes to be a gentleman. Otherwise she is sympathetically presented. She is cheerful, hard-working, utterly loyal to her awful husband and a good mother to her child. She even cuts off the splendid hair which gives her her nickname, to help pay her dissolute husband's debts. When she becomes a professional singer to support him she struggles to maintain her equilibrium in a position that Thackeray sees as an impossible one; that of a respectable woman in the *demi-monde* of the theatre. 'She was an honest woman, visited by that peculiar class of our aristocracy who chiefly associate with ladies who are *not* honest.' In respectable houses she is treated 'with that killing civility which our English aristocracy knows how to bestow on artists', while also despised by the tradesmen of her own class to whom her husband owes money. A person 'admirably disposed by nature to be happy', she is subjected to a seduction attempt by one singing teacher, whom she routs with the weapon of laughter; verbal and physical abuse from her husband; and the deadening atmosphere surrounding a second music teacher, based on the composer and teacher Sir George Smart, who did much to make the profession respectable. Thackeray's description of the funereal gloom of the 'Thrums' and their dank old house brilliantly suggests that when propriety invades the stage, all the glamour and fun fly off into the wings. The Victorian theatre was beginning to change its character, and Sir George Thrum is most astute in combining the old with the new: 'Respectability has been his great card throughout life', but 'he does not neglect the little arts of popularity, and can condescend to receive very queer company if need be.'

Thackeray's friend Adelaide Kemble had a brief career as a professional singer, from 1839 to 1842, when she married and retired from the stage. During that short time she established herself as one of the best singers of her generation, and the Ravenswing's experiences may have been based on what Mrs Sartoris, as she became, told Thackeray about it. His heroine, too, gives up her career as soon as she has the security of a happy second marriage. Thackeray saw work outside the home as exploitation for women, but *The Ravenswing* also contains a long tirade on the exploitation of women within the home.

Mrs Walker gave up her entire reason to her lord. Why was it? Before marriage she had been an independent little person; she had far more brains than her Howard. I think it must have been his moustachios that frightened her and caused in her this humility. (*Works*, 4, p. 388)

There is also an attack on the slavery of useless 'duties' and the production of hideous 'works of art' by the 'ladies' whom Morgiana aspires to join. As ever, Thackeray is not logical about this. He despises the amateurism of the ladies' needlework, but feels that the world of professional artists is too corrupt for women. Nevertheless the story is one of Thackeray's sharpest commentaries on the general condition of women in his time.

Stylistically, 'The Ravenswing' is one of Thackeray's most assured early works. The dialogue, the comic use of appropriate simile (after Captain Walker has compared Morgiana's eyes to billiard balls, they 'fell plump, as it were, into the pocket of his heart'), the sure balance and cadence of the sentences, all contribute to a sense of satisfaction and enjoyment in a story which might have been depressing, even tragic. But as the narrator comments, on a causeless burst of laughter from Morgiana and her mother: 'Why need there be a reason for laughing? Let us laugh when we are laughy, as we sleep when we are sleepy.'

'Denis Haggerty's Wife' is, by contrast, a story of unrelieved gloom, one of Thackeray's savage attacks on Irish mothers-in-law. Haggerty is a cheerful fool who is tricked into marrying a girl who had earlier rejected him, after she has been blinded and made hideous by smallpox. The wife and her mother make his life hell, and Thackeray's own bitterness about Mrs Shawe is evident: 'She's never paid her daughter's income since the first year, though she brags about her sacrifices as if she had ruined herself for Jemima.'[21] (Isabella's allowance was often not paid, and had to be wrung out of Mrs Shawe.)

The savagery of this story was probably prompted by the trip to Ireland which Thackeray made in 1842, to fulfil his obligation to write the book commissioned two years earlier, which reawakened memories of the way he had been treated then. *The Irish Sketch Book* (Thackeray would have preferred the more unassuming 'Cockney Travels in Ireland') was the first book he publicly acknowledged under his own name. It is nominally by 'Titmarsh', but in the dedication to the Irish novelist Charles Lever he laid aside this 'travelling title' and signed himself W. M. Thackeray. The pseudonym and the man behind it had finally joined hands; an important step in establishing his literary reputation, and one which showed that Thackeray thought more of *The Irish Sketch Book* than his off-hand comment on it might suggest. He told his mother it was 'a clever book . . . but beside the point. If it will amuse people, however, that is all I ask.'[22]

It was the first of his books to be widely reviewed, and apart from the Catholic *Tablet*, which took exception to his attacks on priests, the reviewers were mostly enthusiastic, commending his originality, his keen sense of the ridiculous and his hostility to humbug. But the Irish were furious. Charles Lever, not in the least mollified by the dedication to him, first wrote a temperate review in the *Dublin University Magazine*, but then drew a virulent portrait of Thackeray as 'Mr Elias Howle' in his novel *Roland Cashel* which appeared in 1850. His anger had probably been intensified in the intervening years by Thackeray's parody of his Irish novels in *Punch's Prize Novelists*, but his portrait of Thackeray as 'a publisher's man of all-work, ready for every thing, from statistics to satire, and equally prepared to expound prophecy, or write squibs for "Punch" ', a travel writer who has come to Ireland to laugh at its errors and misfortunes, was close enough to the truth to hurt. In order that there should be no mistake, Lever went on to describe Thackeray's physical appearance, unpleasantly caricatured but recognizable, and his habit of sketching the company and making notes about them, and to suggest, completely untruthfully, that Thackeray made a habit of not paying his share of a restaurant bill. 'It is a heavy infliction that we story-tellers are compelled to lay upon our readers and ourselves, thus to interrupt our narrative by a lengthened description of a character not essentially belonging to our story,' Lever concludes primly.[23] To the obvious retort, 'Why do it, then?' the only answer can be that it relieved Lever's sense of grievance and would be popular with his Irish readers.

Thackeray had hoped for FitzGerald's company, but Fitz, in a mood of depression, decided against the trip: 'Except for a journey of two days I get dull as dirt,' he explained.[24] Thackeray felt let down, but wrote cheerfully enough from the Shelbourne, then as now the grandest hotel in Dublin, praising the physical splendours of a chambermaid at Llangollen, and discussing the Irish mixture of grandiose pretension and squalor which he found everywhere. During the next four months he travelled all over Ireland, making voluminous diary notes, and sketching on the spot. He was often amused by what he saw, occasionally moved or delighted. But mostly he found Ireland and its inhabitants, already in a state of semi-starvation, even before the terrible famine which began in 1845, predictably depressing.

The book is full of prejudice, and Thackeray knew it. He knew that forty years would not suffice to make sense of Ireland, let alone three months: 'And where in the midst of all the lies that all tell, is a stranger

'A Car to Killarney'

to seek for truth?'[25] He was personally influenced by his knowledge of Mrs Shawe, and the London Irish he had known, and he accepted too easily the literary stereotype of Castle Rackrent slovenliness and decay. He deplored the hand-to-mouth poverty, without correctly diagnosing where the responsibility lay. The great virtue of the book is its immediacy. It unfolds Ireland to the reader as the writer saw it, recording his impressions and his changes of perspective as he travelled on, without attempting to sum up. Thackeray's ideas on the tragic tangle of Irish affairs have the merit of unpretentiousness, even where, as the *Tablet* complained, 'The writer doesn't falsify his impressions, but his impressions are false. He has a *crick* in his imagination.'[26] It is one of Thackeray's most personal books; both in the writing and the drawing he is constantly present in the happenings he presents, and his idiosyncratic eye brings a freshness to the least promising subjects. The moth-eaten exhibits in the Trinity College Museum, for example, set the tone of decay and neglect which is a main theme of the book:

a very *seedy* camelopard . . . the straw splitting through his tight old skin and the black cobbler's wax stuffing the dim orifices of his eyes. (*The Irish Sketch Book*, Chapter 1, *Works*, 5, p. 19)

His acquaintance with poverty had hitherto been limited to the shabby-genteel; nothing he had seen in Paris or London had prepared

him for the widespread destitution of Ireland. He was honest enough to
reveal that he found it disgusting. In Cork, and the whole of the west
and south of Ireland, beggars 'come crawling round you with lying
prayers and loathsome compliments, that make the stomach turn . . . In
this fairest and richest of countries, men are suffering and starving by
millions . . . The epicurean, and traveller for pleasure, had better travel
anywhere than here: where there are miseries that one does not dare to
think of; where one is always feeling how helpless pity is, and how
hopeless relief, and is perpetually made ashamed of being happy.'[27] This
passage is followed by a description of slum children in a public garden
at Grattan's Hill which delicately takes the reader, by a gradual and not
too shocking transition, back into a world of affection and hope in
which happiness is again possible. Yet the final image of the paragraph
inexorably re-establishes the realities of the poor in Ireland:

> What a strange air of forlorn gaiety there is about the place! – the sky itself
> seems as if it did not know whether to laugh or cry, so full is it of clouds
> and sunshine. Little, fat, ragged, smiling children are clambering about
> the rocks, and sitting on mossy doorsteps, tending other children yet
> smaller, fatter, and more dirty . . . 'Tell me who is it ye love, Jooly?'
> exclaims another, cuddling a red-faced infant with a very dirty nose.
> More of the same race are perched about the summer-house, and two
> wenches with large purple feet are flapping some carpets in the air. It is a
> wonder the carpets will bear this kind of treatment at all, and do not be
> off at once to mingle with the elements: I never saw things that hung
> to life by such a frail thread. (*The Irish Sketch Book*, Chapter 7,
> *Works*, 5, p. 87)

Rural Ireland

His visit to an Ursuline Convent shocked him in a different way. The isolation of the nuns from the world of family affections seemed horrible to him. He always found religious extremism distasteful – Quakers as well as Catholics are attacked in the book – and extremism in women seemed particularly unnatural. He thought that a woman giving up the world 'commits suicide upon her heart'. 'What call has she to give up all her duties and affections? And would she not be best serving God with a husband at her side, and a child on her knee?'[28] Was he perhaps thinking there was something equally wilful in Isabella's withdrawal from her husband and children?

Bright spots in Ireland were the graceful good manners, and the more free-and-easy relationship of children with their parents. He was impressed by the Agricultural School at Templemoyle, where the boys were given a good general education as well as a practical one, without being burdened with the classics. But the scenery, which impresses most visitors, he confessed himself unable to describe adequately, in words or pictures. The great sights, Killarney, Connemara, the Giant's Causeway, were not to his taste. The Causeway he found overpoweringly gloomy: 'When the world was moulded and fashioned out of formless chaos, this must have been the *bit over* – a remnant of chaos! Think of that! – it is a tailor's simile. Well, I am a Cockney: I wish I were in Pall Mall!'[29] Lever sees this kind of reference back to his London readers as a way of sneering at the Irish: 'How pleasantly could he flatter their town-bred self-sufficiency, how slily insinuate their vast superiority over all other citizens.'[30] But this refusal to be impressed by romantic scenery has its moral side, as well as being a comic ploy. It is escapist to admire landscape when the people who live in it are starving, and when the land might, with cultivation, be rendered less picturesque but more profitable. Travelling between Clifton and Westport he was explicit about this:

> we passed miles of ground that evidently wanted but little cultivation to make them profitable; . . . This spectacle of a country going to waste is enough to make the cheerfullest landscape look dismal; it gives this wild district a woful look indeed. (*The Irish Sketch Book*, Chapter 19, *Works*, 5, p. 224)

Chapman and Hall nervously censored some of his attacks on Catholics, and Thackeray was gloomy about the book's prospects. But the travel book was beginning to become a popular form, and though *The Irish Sketch Book* was not a best seller, it did help to establish his reputation, and the Irish experiences were a mine he continued to quarry for his fiction.

'*A Pleasure-boat at the Giant's Causeway*'

The infant school at Dundalk

On his return, Thackeray spent as much time as possible with his family in Paris. He missed his daughters more and more; staying with Charles Lever he at once became a favourite with the children, and when a Dublin child in its nurse's arms called 'Papa, Papa' after him it gave him 'such a turn of the stomach as never was'.[31] He wrote tender letters to Anny, perfectly judged to appeal to a small child, and kept in constant touch with their development through letters to his mother, worrying particularly over Minny, whose life had begun so inauspiciously. He was determined to bring them to live with him in London, and made serious, though unsuccessful, attempts to find a house more suitable than Coram Street for the children and his parents too, if he could persuade them to leave Paris.

Thackeray with Anny

He gave up Coram Street in May 1843 – he was spending so little time there that the expense was unjustifiable – and divided his time between Paris and lodgings in London, first in Jermyn Street and then in St James's. Henry Vizetelly the engraver, who got to know him at this time, described his simple bachelor life in 'an exceedingly plainly furnished bedroom, with common rush seated chairs and painted French bedstead, and with neither looking-glass nor prints on the bare, cold, cheerless-looking walls'.[32] It was a long way from the extravagance of his undergraduate lodgings at Cambridge, and it is no wonder that his 'clubbability' became more pronounced at this time. The Garrick in particular gave him a daytime base where he could work, and eat, and meet his friends.

It was in these years without a family that the pleasures of the table, always a temptation for him, became a partial substitute for home life. He was always eating and drinking too much, and always regretting it. He turned his weakness to good journalistic use, as he did all the large and small experiences of life. 'Memorials of Gormandizing', which considers eating as one of the fine arts, is one of the best known of the 'gustative' articles. Very much in the *Fraser's* tradition with its easy, anti-romantic air, it contains, as a bonus, a delightful 'version' of Horace's ode 'Persicos odi'.[33] A more savage later piece for *Punch* is 'A Dinner in the City', a remorseless account of dreary gluttony. More

'*A Dinner in the City*'

generally, Thackeray took up the *Fraser's* tradition of using food and drink as reductive imagery. Consider the description of Mrs Hoggarty's miniature of her dead husband:

> In the middle of the brooch was Hoggarty in the scarlet uniform of the corps of Fencibles to which he belonged; around it were thirteen locks of hair, belonging to a baker's dozen of sisters that the old gentleman had; and as all these little ringlets partook of the family hue of brilliant auburn, Hoggarty's portrait seemed to the fanciful view like a great fat red round of beef surrounded by thirteen carrots. These were dished up on a plate of blue enamel. (*The Great Hoggarty Diamond, Works*, 4, p. 5)

Thackeray was travelling a good deal in these years. A trip to Belgium and Holland produced 'Little Travels and Roadside Sketches' for *Fraser's*[34] and one of his cleverest ballads, 'Carmen Lilliense', written out of the unpleasant experience of being left penniless when his pocket-book was stolen, which manages to burlesque both Villon and Goethe.[35] In August 1844, when he was half-way through his first full-length novel, *The Luck of Barry Lyndon*, he accepted at short notice the offer of a free passage through the Mediterranean to the Near East, to write a travel book about the places where the steamer called in. Carlyle scornfully compared Thackeray's acceptance of the P. & O. Company's offer to 'the practice of a blind fiddler going to and fro on a penny ferry-boat in Scotland, and playing tunes to the passengers for halfpence'.[36] This puritanical reaction annoyed Thackeray considerably, and virtually put an end to their friendship. Carlyle's early influence on Thackeray had already changed, and the younger man now saw the views of the older as a challenge. Carlyle's gibe weakened the tie still further.

Self-portrait

Cornhill to Cairo is a sadder book than *The Irish Sketch Book*, marred by a sentimentality which looks forward to the tone of Thackeray's last journalism, *The Roundabout Papers*. It is permeated by a longing for his children, and is very much the book of a man who does not want to be in the exciting places he describes. But it was more widely reviewed than *The Irish Sketch Book*, and it sold better, going quickly into a second edition. Thackeray had written to Bedingfield in 1845, 'I can suit the magazines (but I can't hit the public, be hanged to them).'[37] Now he was beginning to hit the public; but not with the best of which he was capable.

Barry Lyndon, which was serialized in *Fraser's* from January to December 1844, made no concessions to sentiment. Its acerbity may be the reason why it was not published in volume form in England until twelve years later. It made so little impression on the literary world that it was not reviewed at all when it appeared in *Fraser's*. Thackeray found it a difficult book to write, partly because an historical novel required a good deal of research, and he was overloaded with journalistic commitments. There are few signs of strain visible in the story, though Thackeray is still experimenting with form. The footnotes by the 'editor' FitzBoodle are rather crudely used to direct the reader towards a correct reaction to Barry's first-person narration, as though the author could not yet trust the power of his own narrative to undercut or emphasize the boastfulness and brutality of the self-styled hero. But the story itself, his first extended exploration of the eighteenth century, conveys the mixture of squalor, makeshift and brutality, with a thin veneer of elegance, that had so struck him in Ireland, and it is entirely fitting that the autobiographical narrator is an Irishman.

Barry Lyndon is, as *Catherine* had been, an attack on the romantic view of history. Barry tells his story as a worn-out old man of sixty in 1800, looking back over the previous forty years. To let an impudent villain condemn himself out of his own mouth was an audacious technical feat; Fielding himself did not attempt it in *Jonathan Wild*. Thackeray brought it off brilliantly. The opening parodies the family chronicle novel which goes back over the centuries to establish the importance of the hero's forebears, but it also establishes Barry's inflated sense of his own importance, which easily turns into a fantasy about his origins, intelligence and looks. Barry's double standards are economically made clear: an attempt by the Barrys to murder the English would have been 'a just massacre'; when the opposite happens it is 'odious butchery'. But Barry as a young man is not without his attractions, for a totally unlikeable character would not have the hold that he must exert over the reader. The pattern of age looking back to youth with indulgence works as satisfactorily here as it does in Thackeray's more straightforward *ubi sunt* passages.

Barry conforms to the habits of more approved characters in other ways too: he falls in love, foolishly but forgivably, with his older cousin; loses such notional 'inheritance' as he has, and is forced to leave home and seek his fortune. But though the pattern is the same as in the later novels, Barry's solutions to his problems are always entirely in character. The hard-work ethic which Pendennis, Clive and Philip all subscribe to in the end is replaced by lies, blackmail and bullying. The fact that he is a very ineffective villain, who ends up having lost everything, is not empty moralizing, but entirely in character. His end can be foreseen from the beginning of the story: there is no Dickensian unmasking or reversal. Everyone, except for a time Barry's unfortunate wife, is well aware of his intrigues and the ruthlessness with which he carries them through. Thackeray adds to the credibility of his villain by making him capable of affection, for his first love; for his mother, who, in a kind of grotesque foreshadowing of the mother-love of Helen Pendennis, sticks to her son when everyone else has abandoned him; and for his son, who dies as a result of Barry's indulgence, which leads to the child's fatal disobedience. The ties of blood always mean more to Barry than those of friendship or marriage. He has no objection to being a spy, but when he finds that the man he has been set to watch is his own uncle, family loyalty once more takes precedence, and the two set up in an alliance of joint villainy. This too accords with the Irish background, and the kind of society depicted in *Castle Rackrent* and *Ormond*.

Barry Lyndon is a brutal book, and Thackeray didn't care for it himself, and told Anny not to bother to read it when it was at last reprinted. It may reveal aspects of the writer he preferred not to dwell on, for there is a certain relish in the way Barry mistreats his wife and stepson, and in the descriptions of the nastier aspects of war. Barry is a truthful narrator – he is too complacent to feel that he needs to lie about his behaviour – and sees clearly enough how war brutalizes all those who take part in it. His commentary is realistic:

> It is well for gentlemen to talk of the age of chivalry; but remember the starving brutes whom they lead – men nursed in poverty, entirely ignorant, made to take a pride in deeds of blood – men who can have no amusement but in drunkenness, debauch, and plunder. It is with these shocking instruments that your great warriors and kings have been doing

their murderous work in the world; and while, for instance, we are at the present moment admiring the 'Great Frederick,' as we call him, and his philosophy, and his liberality, and his military genius, I, who have served him, and been, as it were, behind the scenes of which that great spectacle is composed, can only look at it with horror. (*Barry Lyndon*, Chapter 4, *Works*, 6, p. 71)

Barry's attack on Frederick the Great is in marked contrast to the Carlylean view of heroes, and he is dismissive of the techniques of historical novelists: 'These persons (I mean the romance-writers), if they take a drummer or a dustman for a hero, somehow manage to bring him in contact with the greatest lords and most notorious personages of the empire.'[38] Barry himself comes in contact mostly with other rogues, and there is a satisfactory consistency to his lively, sordid, eighteenth-century world. It is a book that appeals more to our anti-heroic age than it did to Thackeray's own, with its passion for the past. When he came to write *Esmond* Thackeray himself fell into some of the traps he had correctly diagnosed in other writers. *Esmond* is a more elegant, in some ways a more enjoyable book than *Barry Lyndon*, but the earlier novel has a sharper eye for historical truth.

Thackeray's children came to London with their grandmother in the summer of 1845, for a glorious visit. Anny was eight, Minny five; old enough to enjoy thoroughly all the treats their indulgent father had arranged for them. He found parting with them again hard to bear, but was characteristically self-aware in making a distinction between true feeling and what he called 'abstract pathos': 'I never could bear to think of children parted from their parents somehow without a tendency to blubbering: and am as weak to this day upon the point, as I used to be at school.'[39] His own childhood experiences overwhelmed him whenever he thought of his daughters, and he felt the separation from him was unnatural, and must be ended. The affairs of the *Constitutional* were still not completely cleared up, and the threat of bankruptcy hanging over Major Carmichael-Smyth, which had caused their move to France, was still there. Thackeray, though he was nearer being able to make a satisfactory living, had lost £500 he could ill afford, by speculating in railway shares. His letters throughout 1845 and 1846 are full of longing for the children, and anxiety about them. Anny was giving her grandmother trouble. She was a clever, plain, self-willed little girl. 'I am afraid very much she is going to be a man of genius,' Thackeray wrote, proud, but slightly alarmed by her resemblance to himself.[40] His house-hunting became more determined, and at last he found a suitable house in the quiet suburb of Kensington, 13 Young Street, where, he thought, they could all live together. But the Carmichael-Smyths were still reluctant to return, and at last he decided that, in spite of his unwillingness to deprive his mother of them, the children should come to live with him, whether she came too or not.

Chapter 6

Punch

The world gives up a lamentable portion of its time to
fleeting literature: authors who might be occupied upon great works
fritter away their lives in producing endless hasty sketches . . .
Let us take a stand at once, and ask, 'Why should
not the day have its literature?'

'A Brother of the Press on the History of a Literary Man,
Laman Blanchard and the Chances of
the Literary Profession',
Works, 6, p. 550.

His connection with *Punch* at last gave Thackeray the financial security
that enabled him to set up a home for his children in London, in 1846.
Punch was something new among English periodicals, a lively, satirical
paper deliberately aimed at the respectable middle classes. Earlier
English satirical papers such as *The Age* and *The Satirist* had been
scurrilous rags, footman's reading in Thackeray's fiction, which often
made their money out of blackmailing public figures, threatening
exposure unless they paid up. *Punch* modelled itself instead on the
French paper, *Charivari*, with its brilliant political and social cartoons
by Daumier. At the outset, in 1842, *Punch*'s purposes were still unclear,
and FitzGerald sent Thackeray a message urging him not to go into it.
Thackeray was dubious too, and kept his association with it quiet. He
adopted a haughty tone when Bradbury and Evans, who soon took over
as proprietors as well as printers of the paper, abruptly terminated his
first series, 'Miss Tickletoby's Lectures on English History'. He had
done his best, he wrote, 'just as much as if I had been writing for any
more dignified periodical'.[1] But though he was hurt that his rather lame
efforts in the 'Comic History' genre, later made popular in the paper by
Gilbert à Beckett, had failed, he continued to write, and draw, for
Punch, and by December 1843 he was on the regular staff. *Punch* paid
more than double what he got anywhere else, and he increasingly had
'my own way with the worthy Mr Punch'.[2] By the summer of 1844 he
was exulting, 'Mr Punch is the great card: and I have made some great
hits there.'[3]

HALF AN HOUR BEFORE DINNER.

*Niminy and Piminy staring at the Ladies seated in a circle in the
drawing-room.*

Niminy. " That's a fain woman in yallah."
Piminy. " Hm !—pooty well."

Punch *cartoon*

Thackeray was valued in the *Punch* office as a useful all-round contributor who could fill up space with an article, a comic ballad, or a wood-cut which might often illustrate someone else's joke or article. He was not entirely happy about this. The work for *Punch* took up more of his time than he liked, and the messenger boy often had to be kept waiting while he finished an article or drawing. The 'dignity of literature' obsession returned with the greater financial security that writing the undignified provided, and bedevilled his relationships with some of the other writers on the paper.

Punch in its early years was a radical paper. It campaigned for causes such as the abolition of capital punishment and imprisonment for debt, and on behalf of better pay and conditions for working people, particularly the desperately poor women garment-workers: Thomas Hood's 'The Song of the Shirt' was featured in the Christmas number for 1844. Douglas Jerrold, also on the *Punch* staff, who wrote many of the most polemical pieces himself, was on uneasy terms with Thackeray from the beginning. It was a clash partly of personality, partly of politics, partly of origins, which cannot have been made easier when Jerrold's popular series, *Mrs Caudle's Curtain Lectures*, was surpassed by Thackeray's *The Snobs of England*. Thackeray felt more comfortable with the public school men on *Punch*, such as Leech, who had been at the Charterhouse with him, than he did with the self-made men, the editor Mark Lemon and Jerrold. Lemon thought Thackeray seemed too great for ordinary conversation; Jerrold said, 'I have known Thackeray for eighteen years, and I don't know him yet.'[4] When Thackeray finally resigned from the paper in 1851 he wrote to Evans, 'I am sure that it is best for my reputation and the comfort of some of that crew that I should be out of it . . . I fancied myself too big to pull in the boat; and it wasn't in the nature of things that Lemon and Jerrold should like me.'[5] He was not popular, either, with the engravers who turned his drawings into wood-blocks: Birket Foster recalled that he was the only one of the contributors who never spoke to them.[6] Yet many of the younger generation of *Punch* contributors remembered his kindness to them, and even his relationship with Jerrold was not always antagonistic. Thackeray claimed that Jerrold was a vulgarian who ate peas with his knife, wanted to abolish the aristocracy, and yet toadied to them. But when Jerrold was put up for membership of the Reform Club, and specifically rejected the idea of asking Thackeray to sponsor him, fearing his 'crotchets', Thackeray nevertheless did his best to get him elected. 'I think we have got the little man in' was his lordly way of putting it.[7]

'The Club Snob'

Thackeray enjoyed, too, the schoolboyish and decidedly bawdy intimacy of the all-male weekly dinners, frankly detailed in Henry Silver's unpublished *Punch* diary. Smut seems to have provided a lingua franca which temporarily erased differences of background and political viewpoint for these journalists, many of them highly sophisticated in other contexts, enabling them to relate to each other without nervousness or rivalry for the short period of the meal and the discussion about the forthcoming number of the paper. Thackeray's sentimental ballad 'The Mahogany Tree', portraying for public consumption a group of worldly middle-aged men as 'boys', now seems mawkish, but it appealed to mid-Victorian sentiment, and truthfully represented, however unconvincing it may now seem, one side of Thackeray's uneasy relationship with his brothers of the press. He continued to attend these dinners after he had resigned from the staff in

1854, and was present at one only a fortnight before his death. *Punch* became, in effect, another club for him for the rest of his life, and when he became editor of the *Cornhill Magazine* he instituted weekly dinners of the same kind for his contributors. His private sense of humour, as recorded by Silver, was not sophisticated. He revelled in puns – the worse the pun, the better he liked it – and joined in the teasing of the new young contributors who were sometimes shocked by the stories told by their elders. If this was the level of conversation he was used to when not in the company of women, it is no wonder that, in the preface to *Pendennis*, he explains that it cannot be reproduced in the book.

The more serious purpose of the dinners was to decide on the main political cartoon for the forthcoming number, and to discuss the general shape of the paper. Much of what *Punch* stood for in the 1840s was in line with Thackeray's own youthful enthusiasms, and it might have been expected that he would feel more in sympathy with its Liberal politics than with *Fraser's* Toryism. His conclusion to 'Going to see a man hanged' – which appeared in *Fraser's* – was firmly against capital punishment: 'I fully confess that I came away down Snow Hill that morning with a disgust for murder, but it was for *the murder I saw done*.'[8] But he felt that Jerrold's radicalism, and in particular his anti-clericalism, went too far: 'that savage little Robespierre' he called him.[9]

It cannot be denied that he felt that reform was safest when it came from above, filtered through the educated, gentlemanly classes. It was partly due to Thackeray's increasing influence that by the end of the decade *Punch* was abandoning its radical stance and concentrating on amusing its readers, not disturbing them. By the 1880s Ruskin was characterizing Mr Punch as 'a polite Whig, with a sentimental respect for the Crown, and a practical respect for property' who 'holds up for the general idea of perfection ... the British Hunting Squire, the British Colonel, and the British Sailor'.[10] This was very different from the early years, when *Punch* (and Thackeray) ridiculed the Royal Family for being philistine and pretentious, attacking the sentimental cult of the Royal children, and the expense to the nation of the couple's philoprogenitiveness. Albert's addiction to slaughtering birds and animals let out of bags in front of him, was another target. Military glory of all kinds, already satirized many times by Thackeray, was presented as ludicrous and outmoded. Social pretensions and 'shams' of all kinds were lambasted, most devastatingly by Thackeray in *The Snobs of England, By One of Themselves*. *Punch* even achieved the distinction of being banned in France on one occasion, on account of an article by Thackeray which made fun of Louis Philippe. Yet it was over *Punch's* attacks on Louis Napoleon that Thackeray finally broke with the paper.

'Military Snob' (The Duke of Wellington)

At first Thackeray participated in *Punch*'s attacks and lampoons (never on private aspects of their victims' lives) with apparent relish. He learned to adapt his writing to the taste of *Punch* readers, without abandoning his own tone of voice. His mastery of the conversational style was now complete, and the management of different levels of narrative, which was to become so important for *Vanity Fair*, was now much more assured. He added further writing personae during this time, and 'the Fat Contributor' invented for *Punch* is older and more staid than Titmarsh, yet less pretentious than FitzBoodle, managing to be, like *Punch* itself, comic for serious purposes. The F.C.'s despatches from the Near East are sharper and more personal than the accounts of the same places in *Cornhill to Cairo*. For *Punch* the Royal Palace in Athens is 'built in the style of High-Dutch-Greek, and resembles Newgate whitewashed and standing on a sort of mangy desert', and the Temple of Theseus is 'of the exact colour and mouldiness of a ripe Stilton cheese'.[11] *Cornhill to Cairo* also records Thackeray's disappointment with modern Athens, but he is more respectful, and more conventional, about the ancient monuments. 'I thought I could recognize the towering beauty of the prodigious columns of the Temple of Jupiter.'[12] *Punch* readers were told that the Fat Contributor never wished to set eyes on them again. Perhaps the dignity of literature had to be more carefully upheld in the official, book-length account of the journey than in the weekly column.

Punch also gave him a public platform for the exercise of his two earliest talents, drawing and the making of comic verses. Both were a continuing part of his private life, used to entertain adults and children of whom he was fond. A rhymed alphabet survives, which he created for a little boy who was having trouble learning his letters,[13] and part of another he drew for Anny. He illustrated his letters with comic drawings too, from his childhood to the end of his life. Many of his ballads and comic verses, published as a collection in 1855 and 1856, first appeared in *Punch*. Compared with some Victorian comic versifiers, Thackeray's ballads are mild, even genial. His nautical ballad, 'Little Billee', often recited by him at convivial male gatherings, avoids a cannibalistic denouement – little Billee is rescued in time. Gilbert's later rewriting of the same story, 'The Yarn of the "Nancy Bell" ', is much fiercer. His Irishman's view of the Great Exhibition of 1851 manages to send up the whole vulgar enterprise without being personally offensive to any of those responsible for the excesses:

> There's fountains there,
>   And crosses fair;
> There's water-gods with urrns:
>   There's organs three,
>   To play, d'ye see?
> 'God save the Queen,' by turrns.
>
> There's statues bright
>   Of marble white,
> Of silver, and of copper;
>   And some in zinc,
>   And some, I think,
> That isn't over proper.
>   ('The Crystal Palace', *Works*, 7, p. 160)

Thackeray's verses are often *pièces d'occasion* which haven't survived as well as the pure fantasy of Lear: even when the *Ballads* volume first appeared, Clough, who was fond of Thackeray, felt they were 'indifferent stuff'.[14] They served their purpose in *Punch*, and were well up to the magazine's standards.

Thackeray's illustrations, including many of those in *Punch* as well as in the novels, are grotesque distortions of his original intentions, for he never applied himself to learn the technique of drawing for the wood-block. However, he did learn much about the telling use of illustration for satirical purposes. The influence of Daumier is obvious everywhere in early numbers of *Punch*, and Thackeray also learned directly from the other *Punch* artists, Leech in particular. When a small cut is not identified by Leech's rebus (a leech in a bottle) or Thackeray's own signature for his *Punch* drawings of a pair of spectacles, it is often

'*Dining-out Snob*'

Punch *initial*

difficult to tell the two artists apart. By the spring of 1843 Thackeray was writing to his mother, 'I've been making a lot of drawings and the Punch people are beginning at last to find out that they are good.'[15] Practice in doing small vignettes rapidly, and the *Punch* habit of expanding or commenting visually on the verbal content of a joke or article, helped him when it came to creating the illustrations for *Vanity Fair*. The *Punch* initials, in particular, were exercises in ingenious visual humour of a kind which he continued to use for the rest of his life.

The greatest opportunity *Punch* gave him, however, was the space given to the series *The Snobs of England* (reprinted in 1848 as *The Book of Snobs*). It ran for a year, from February 1846 to February 1847, establishing him as the satirist of early Victorian society, and preparing the way for *Vanity Fair*. He was ultimately to regret the label of satirist, and try to shake it off; he disliked, too, that *Snobs* associated him irrevocably with *Punch* in the public mind. It was his last major journalistic exercise in his early style, before his energies were increasingly absorbed by novel writing. Though it was designed for a particular periodical, and with a defined aim, it was far from ephemeral, and has continued to be one of Thackeray's most popular books: it is one of the few of his works currently in print.

The title *The Snobs of England* and the 'Prefatory Remarks' are a parody. A series of books of moral advice and instruction for women had recently appeared: *The Women of England, The Daughters of England, The Mothers of England*, and so on. The author, Mrs Ellis, was one of *Punch*'s butts. Her conclusion, that it was the fate, and the duty, of the women of England to 'suffer and be still' was one Thackeray came perilously close to voicing himself on numerous occasions; but he was not above using her as a starting point. The 1848 version omitted several chapters, as well as altering the title; Thackeray claiming to feel that they were so stupid, personal, and snobbish, that they should not be reprinted. Yet these chapters contained some of his best writing on matters that recurrently preoccupied him, such as the dignity of literature, the army, and flunkeydom: the servant as a mark of conspicuous consumption.

The etymon of 'snob' is a journeyman shoemaker. Thackeray first met the word at Cambridge, where it was widened in meaning to include any tradesman, hence someone not a gentleman or 'nob'. This sense seems to have survived for a considerable time: there is a Bab Ballad by Gilbert, published in *Fun* (a rival to *Punch*) in 1867, called 'Seaside Snobs', about vulgar crowds in Margate, swearing and dropping *h*s.[16] There are snobs of this sort in Thackeray's gallery; the Raff Snob, the Englishman abroad, 'who is heard yelling "We won't go home till morning!'' and startling the midnight echoes of quiet continental towns with English slang'.[17] The word, however, gradually came to be associated with lower-class strivings for gentility, usually depicted as ludicrous and doomed to failure. In this sense Hook's Mrs Ramsbottom (who was revived as a character in *Punch*) is a snob, and so is Pogson, the duped commercial traveller in *The Paris Sketch Book*. Most of the snobs decribed in *The Snobs of England*, however, conform to Thackeray's much wider definition, 'He who meanly admires mean things, is a Snob.'

WIGGINS AT HOME.

WIGGINS AT BOULOGNE.

WIGGINS AT SEA.

'The Raff Snob'

'University Snobs'

Snobs does not attempt to be a complete microcosm of 'the condition of England', the most central of *Punch*'s concerns in the 1840s. Nor does it fully explore what is now thought of as the essence of snobbery, the rejection of others for not possessing money, class, honours, qualifications, or esoteric knowledge. There are no 'intellectual snobs' in Thackeray's gallery. There are two chapters on University snobs, but they are all, from professors to undergraduates, tuft-hunters and toadies who cultivate the empty-headed lordlings among them. 'A society that sets up to be polite, and ignores Arts and Letters, I hold to be a Snobbish society.'[18] Thackeray's central idea is of a positive snobbery, which rules, and often ruins, the lives of those who concentrate all their energies on admiration and imitation. However, the first chapter does show a different kind of snobbery at work, when the narrator is revealed, apparently accidentally, as a negative snob, one who will reject a friend who has saved his life, because he eats peas with a knife, or take advantage of a rival who cannot conform to the habits of an alien society. Here the narrator is 'one of themselves', while his supposed examples of snobbish behaviour are innocents abroad; the chapter might be an apology to Jerrold. Of course alienation from the narrator must only be temporary, or the balance of the piece would be upset, and throughout *Snobs* Thackeray cleverly keeps the balance between castigating his subjects, and revealing the narrator's own fallibility and prejudice.

Thackeray's main educational point, in the most didactic of his books, is that snobbery inevitably interferes with the simple enjoyment of life for the snobs themselves, often frantically trying to keep up appearances on an inadequate income. He repeatedly insists in his writing, not only in *Snobs*, that pretentious dinner-party giving can bring a family to the brink of ruin. This is the theme of 'A Little Dinner at Timmins' of 1848, which relentlessly details, step by step, how an easy-going husband allows himself to be coerced by his wife and mother-in-law into a useless display which is financially disastrous.[19] An objection to society's insistence on show was not confined to Thackeray, but it was a natural attitude for a man who felt himself to be a gentleman and objected to the idea that he should beggar himself to prove it. When he was making another attempt to persuade the Carmichael-Smyths to return to England permanently, in 1848, he wrote that it was possible to live perfectly simply without loss of dignity. The Carlyles did so, and entertained 'the best company in England'. But he went on to explain rather defensively that he couldn't live like that. 'I want a man to be going my own messages . . . there must be a cook and a woman about the children.'[20]

The apologetic tone is characteristic of his ambivalent attitude to servants. He tended to take refuge in a series of evasions: it was all right to employ a woman, but not a man. Or perhaps it was all right to employ a man, in certain circumstances, but not to dress him up in livery. There is a wittily appropriate description of a greengrocer's boy transmuted by snobbery into a page, in 'Hobson's Choice', a *Punch* piece of 1850.

> His name was changed from Peter to Philip, as being more genteel: and a hat with a gold cord and a knob on the top like a gilt Brussels sprout, and a dark green suit, with a white galoon stripe down the trouser-seams, and a bushel of buttons on the jacket, were purchased at an establishment in Holborn. (*Works*, 8, p. 494)

In *Snobs*, the Pontos employ a young chameleon:

> a boy called Thomas or Tummus. Tummus works in the garden, or about the pig-sty and stable; Thomas wears a page's costume of eruptive buttons. When anybody calls, and Stripes is out of the way, Tummus flings himself like mad into Thomas's clothes, and comes out metamorphosed like Harlequin in the pantomime. (*The Book of Snobs*, Chapter 26, *Works*, 9, p. 399)

Thackeray continued to find pages' uniforms irresistibly comic. On his 1853 visit to America he startled the young Henry James, incarcerated in a tight jacket with a row of brass buttons, by telling him he would be

'Thomas and Tummus'

known in England simply as 'Buttons'.[21] Snobbish display particularly offended him in children, and on another occasion he terrified the eight-year-old Alice James by examining her dress and exclaiming, in mock-horror: 'Crinoline? – I was suspecting it! So young and so depraved!'[22]

Thackeray was also fascinated by the details of the extraordinary dress of flunkeys, men-servants in livery, which was a survival from the eighteenth century, and by military uniforms, and he often equates the two. He felt that the livery was not only an anachronism, but a divisive one. The uniform was unfair to the man who had to dress up in gold lace and powder his hair, for it cut him off from ordinary human beings, conferring a false sense of importance on both employer and servant. The flunkeys are used throughout *Snobs* as 'types of their masters in this world',[23] and *The Peerage* is 'a sort of gold-laced and liveried lackey to History'.[24] The illustration used as the frontispiece to *The Book of Snobs* (where its meaning is not entirely clear) was originally more appropriately placed in one of the chapters suppressed in 1848. The anxious little man (Lord John Russell in court dress) is pleading with the magnificent flunkey who scornfully bars his way, appealing to the resemblance between their dress in the Abolitionist catch-phrase: 'Am I not a Man and Brother?' In this chapter the politicians who fawn and flatter and scheme for office, taking ridiculous ceremonial appointments, 'First Lord of the Dustpan, or the Head Groom of the Pantry', are equated with the footman who gets his livelihood by being turned into an object, a piece of ostentatious display.

Walter Bagehot, in his essay 'Sterne and Thackeray', described the English social system as being one of 'removable inequalities'.[25] Thackeray saw more clearly how difficult they were to remove. In his

'The persecution of British Footmen'

'Am I not a Man and a Brother?'

attacks on the outward and visible signs of difference, he suggested that uniforms and the like are not only a waste of money, but actually help to prevent the creation of a society where inequalities can be gradually phased out. But in a later article, 'Waiting at the Station', he despaired of inequalities of birth ever being overcome in England: only by emigration to the new countries of the colonies could former servants become self-respecting and independent. He attacked the complacent assumption that because one man in a million had surmounted the class barrier, all could do so.[26] By 1850, when 'Waiting at the Station' was written, he felt that the reform of society was too complex a matter to be influenced by ridicule or propaganda. The same disillusion prompts the ending of *Lovel the Widower*, where the most interesting character in the story, the butler, also has to find his happy ending in the colonies. But in 1846 society still seemed to be in flux, capable of being reformed by example and ridicule.

Snobs, which began as a rather formulaic series of examples of snobbery, starting at the top with 'The Snob Royal', who was, of course, Thackeray's old target, George IV, gradually developed over the months into little vignettes, by way of illustrative incidents and character studies. With 'Country Snobs' (Chapters 24 to 30), Thackeray created a self-contained cautionary tale with well-developed characters. The Pontos could live an agreeable, unassuming country life – something like that Becky imagines for herself as a gentleman's wife with five thousand a year – but are ruined by their anxiety about keeping up appearances, and by the extravagance of their officer son. Thackeray was by this point well launched on the writing of his 'Novel without a Hero', and the two enterprises nourished each other, the novel gaining structure and tautness from the experience of writing, over a period of a year, to a specific theme; the pieces for *Punch* showing, as the months went by, an increasing preoccupation with narrative.

Thackeray's long apprenticeship to parody also culminated in *Punch*, in the 1847 series, *Punch's Prize Novelists*.[27] He managed to cause a good deal of offence with these wickedly accurate and funny 'versions' of popular novelists of the day. He had intended to include Dickens, but Bradbury and Evans took fright, feeling that he was too much of a popular hero to be attacked, even in *Punch*. It would have been fascinating to see whether Thackeray could have caught Dickens's tone as perfectly as he did those of the novelists he subjected to his scalpel, those who are less known and seldom read today, though they were all popular best-sellers at the time. He could not resist his old enemy 'Sir E. L. B. L. Bart', and the high-flown abstract nonsense in which Bulwer Lytton dressed up his sordid Newgate subject matter in *Eugene Aram*

'Country Snobs'

and *Paul Clifford*. He is sharp, too, on the idiocies of historical novels
in which every other character turns out to be a famous personage.

Bulwer Lytton must by now have been hardened to Thackeray's
attacks, but Disraeli, his second victim, was deeply offended by
'Codlingsby', which accurately catches the manner of *Coningsby*, but
does not attempt to give any account of its underlying political and
social purpose. Thackeray had reviewed *Coningsby* when it first
appeared in 1844, in the *Pictorial Times*. His review was phrased in
offensively personal terms, comparing Disraeli's style to his dandyish
appearance: 'As the bodily Disraeli used to be seen some years ago about
town, arrayed in green inexpressibles with a gold stripe down the seams,
an ivory cane, and, for what we know, a peacock's feather in his hat –
Disraeli the writer in like manner assumes a magnificence never thought
of by our rigid northern dandies, and astonishes by a luxury of conceit
which is quite oriental.'[28] Disraeli eventually got his own back, after
Thackeray's death, in his last completed novel, *Endymion*, where
Thackeray is portrayed as St Barbe.

Codlingsby

Charles Lever, Thackeray's third victim, retaliated more promptly,
and with surprising venom: Thackeray's 'Tale of the Fighting Onety-
Oneth' was affectionate and lively, a pastiche rather than a parody of the
jovial Irish military novels which he thoroughly enjoyed himself. It has
none of the attack on literary pretentiousness that was Thackeray's
prime parodic target, and his version of G. P. R. James, the endlessly
prolific and popular historical novelist whose books inevitably began
with two horsemen slowly wending their way through a mountainous
landscape, was similarly genial. He was sharper in his attack on Mrs

Mrs Perkins's Ball

Gore, whose literary concerns were closer to his own: when her novel *Cecil* was thought to be by him he was by no means displeased. But he is unsparing of her fashionable mannerisms in 'Lords and Liveries, by the Authoress of "Dukes and Déjeuners", "Hearts and Diamonds", "Marchionesses and Milliners", etc. etc.'. Much of the impact of *Vanity Fair* can be traced to a careful dissection of the fashionable society novelists, of whom Mrs Gore was one of the most skilful and prolific.

Thackeray was now busier than ever, with the work for *Punch* and other periodicals, the big novel at last under way, and the first of his

Christmas Books, *Mrs Perkins's Ball*, to be written, and illustrated, in time for the Christmas market. But his determination to get his children back didn't weaken. He first moved his wife to England, and then insisted that his mother must either return to England and live with him and the children at Young Street, or give them up to him. He was, as he wrote to Jane Shawe, 'child-sick . . . and when I see . . . a pair of little girls at all resembling my own, become quite maudlin over them'.[29]

The emotional gaps in his life had been filled to some extent in a rather different way by his renewed friendship with William Brookfield, a friend from Cambridge days, and his wife Jane, who rapidly became far more important to him than her husband was. He met her first in 1842, soon after her marriage, and though they took to one another at once, Thackeray was cautious about his feelings at first. 'I don't think I have fallen in love with anybody of late, except pretty Mrs Brookfield,' he joked in a letter to Isabella in 1843,[30] and to his mother he wrote three years later than he had been in love with her 'these four years – not so as to endanger peace or appetite but she always seems to me to speak and do and think as a woman should'.[31] He managed to deceive himself about the extent of his emotional involvement, attempting, with partial success, to channel his longings into the conscious desire to have his children with him, his wife within visiting distance, and his household organized so that he could, at last, make a real start on his big novel.

The Brookfields' marriage had been a love-match. Brookfield was one of those men, brilliantly promising at university, who never fulfil expectations. Socially he was not much of a catch for Jane Elton, whose father, though he earned his living as a writer – he had been a contributor to the *London Magazine* – was heir to a baronetcy, and whose uncle was Henry Hallam the historian, father of Tennyson's friend Arthur Hallam. Brookfield, who entered the church as a means of advancement, rather than from any sense of vocation, achieved the preferment he hoped for only late in life, remaining for many years a penurious and obscure clergyman who became an Inspector of Schools to augment his income. Jane, eleven years younger than her husband, became progressively disenchanted by the man who had dazzled her when she first met him at the age of sixteen. In the early years of their marriage they were so poor that at one time Brookfield was reduced to living in the crypt of St James's, Piccadilly, where he was curate, while Jane went home to her family. She seems to have borne this penury patiently and cheerfully; her unpretentious courage in adversity was one of the things that Thackeray most admired about her, and incidents from the Brookfields' simple way of life – Jane mending her husband's trousers, and sending out for twopenny tarts for dessert – were woven into his writing. As early as 1844 he describes the neglected Arabella sewing 'white ducks – Wagstaff's white ducks – his wife was making them into white ducklings for little Fred'.[32]

In many ways Jane Brookfield was the opposite of Isabella. She was five foot nine inches tall – so tall for a woman in those days that her father nicknamed her 'Glumdalclitch'. Her letters are lively, gossipy and outspoken; she was clearly a woman with a good opinion of herself, and not in the least 'humble-minded'. She must also have been emotionally devious, in a way that Thackeray particularly abhorred in women, but failed to perceive in her. This was perhaps more forgivable in a woman of her generation than it would be today. When she wrote to her husband, in 1845, that she was 'foolishly, blindly fond' of being liked and admired, and that 'If I had not the restraint of very deep affection for you, and some restraint of conscience, I should be, I believe, still on the look-out for conquest'[33] she was deceiving either Brookfield or Thackeray, as well as herself, perhaps. During the years that Thackeray was falling ever more irretrievably in love with her, she and Brookfield were writing daily when they were separated, in terms of affectionate banter which show perfect confidence. Brookfield writes: 'Thackeray observed on Saturday night that you had the sweetest voice he ever heard. And now you wretch, have I told you enough? I don't know what mischief I haven't done by repeating men's praises of you.'[34] Another letter refers to 'Master Moxon and Alfred [Tennyson] . . . and as the latter (indeed both) are among your seven hundred and ninetynine lovers . . .'[35] The Brookfield letters were published by her son partly as an attempt to squash public speculation about her relationship with Thackeray; but it is clear at this time (1846) Thackeray was not seen as any particular threat to the marriage.

The transfer of the children from the care of his mother in Paris to the pretty bow-windowed house in Young Street was not altogether straightforward. Thackeray felt guilty at depriving her of them after she had cared for them so devotedly, taking the place of their mother for six years; yet he felt they should be with their natural parent, for his sake as much as theirs. 'Continual thoughts of them chase I don't know how many wickednesses out of my mind,' he explained,[36] and he continued to feel that his children constituted a moral shield for him – reversing the usual pattern of parental protection. Later, at his moment of greatest temptation over Jane Brookfield, it was the thought of the children – his and hers – that stopped him from attempting to seduce her.[37] He was also concerned at his mother's increasingly gloomy state of mind, which was later to intensify to the point where he wondered whether she were not becoming actually mad.[38] Her hypochondria made her fear continually for her family's physical welfare, and Thackeray had, more than once, to put his foot down about using orthodox doctors, rather than the homoeopathic practitioners she favoured. Her concern for their spiritual welfare, and her stern brand of evangelical Christianity, had already caused friction between them. Henriette Corkran, the daughter of *The Times* Paris correspondent who was an old friend of Thackeray's, remembered Mrs Carmichael-Smyth purveying a gloomy brand of Christianity very much at odds with her son's unfailing kindness to children: 'Her description of Hell was terrible.'[39]

Thackeray had still not given up all hope of Isabella's recovery, and he did not want his mother to play too large a maternal part in the children's lives. He was prepared, at this point, to have her to live with him, but this she would not do. There was, then, the problem of who was to look after them. A governess would be needed, to teach them, and to take charge of their physical welfare. He would not send them to school: after his own experiences at the Charterhouse he was determined they should escape 'rough words and brutal treatment'.[40]

The 'governess question' was much aired in *Punch* during the 1840s; someone on the staff (probably Jerrold) was indignant at the treatment of this exploited class; and their meagre salaries, poor conditions of work and equivocal status were the subject of several articles. The governess question was a problem for the Thackeray household too; but it was rather a question of how one was to be afforded, who was to choose her, and how the delicate situation of a young unmarried woman alone in a house with a man who was neither married nor unmarried, was to be handled. His mother was terrified that her susceptible son would fall in love, or be compromised by some unscrupulous schemer. He saw the dangers himself. 'Unless I liked a Governess I couldn't live with her and if I did – O fie. The flesh is very weak, le coeur sent toujours le besoin d'aimer.'[41]

There was no lack of applicants. Thackeray begged Mrs Carlyle not to send round her candidate, Fraulein Bölte: 'I have governidges calling at all hours with High Dutch accents and reams of testimonials . . . And I don't want a Gerwoman; and all our plans are uncertain.'[42] He, and still more his mother, would have been shocked to know that Amely Bölte had, only a month earlier, startled the Carlyles and their guests by being, as Jane Carlyle put it, 'quite rabid against marriage . . . all Thinkers of Germany she says have arrived at the conclusion that *Marriage* is a highly *immoral* institution as well as a dreadfully disagreeable one'.[43]

As it turned out, Mrs Carmichael-Smyth's choice, Bess Hamerton, became the first of a long series of governesses. The Hamertons were family friends who had been good to Isabella, visiting her at Puzin's, and Bess had already acted informally as a companion to old Mrs Butler. She was an Irishwoman, without formal training or special skills, but it was not her competence which concerned Thackeray; like most men of his generation he assumed that anyone who was more or less a lady could teach little girls as much as it was necessary for them to know. His stepfather was the first to point out Anny's abilities, and to suggest that she deserved to be carefully taught under her father's supervision – something Thackeray was always too busy to do. His reservations about Bess were rather to do with her social background and her ability to make friends with the children. Anny took against her from the first, and in less than six months Thackeray had asked her to leave. He tackled this difficult task as tactfully as possible, but Bess felt lasting bitterness, and it caused a serious breach between Thackeray and his mother. Writing to her to explain his decision, Thackeray complained of Bess's vulgarity, and her inability to understand Anny's 'delicate soul'.[44]

He was meeting his mother's long-distance attempts to rule his household with increasing firmness. He now saw too, and frankly pointed out, the problems that would arise were they all to live together permanently; that he and she would be competing for first place in the household, and in the children's affections. He followed up his dismissal of the governess by countermanding his mother's banishment of Mrs Gloyne, Isabella's attendant, who was coming in by the day to nurse and be a companion to the aged Mrs Butler, now living with them at Young Street. There seems to have been some idea in Mrs Carmichael-Smyth's mind that Mrs Gloyne had designs on her son: indeed, she seems at this time to have been obsessed with the fear that he would become emotionally entangled.

Thackeray assured her that the next governess, Miss Drury, was plain enough not to be dangerous. But by October 1847 she too had gone, and Thackeray, who was reading (and deeply impressed by) *Jane Eyre*, may have felt that plainness was not a sufficient defence against gossip. The famous dedication to him of the second edition caused him endless embarrassment because of the parallels, of which Charlotte Brontë was quite unconscious, with his own life. Miss Drury was succeeded by Miss Alexander, again plain, not too young, kind, 'but not by any means wise or fit to guide Anny's mind'.[45] By June 1848 Thackeray was writing, 'Poor Alexander must go.'[46] His mother resumed charge of the girls from time to time, when Thackeray was ill, or travelling, or when the governess problem was more than usually acute. Sometimes when they were with her they went to school, which Anny loved, in spite of her father's prejudices. The most satisfactory of the governesses, Miss Trulock, provided a longer than usual period of stability. But it was not until Amy Crowe, the daughter of an impoverished friend of Thackeray's from the Paris days, came to live with them in 1854, and became a loved older sister to the girls, and almost a third daughter to Thackeray, that the problem was finally solved. By then they were too old for a resident governess anyway.

The girls had, in addition to the governesses, lessons from visiting masters, and they attended lectures; but this haphazard and intermittent education meant that Anny never properly developed her considerable intellectual powers. She became a prolific novelist, with a gift for the vivid portrayal of isolated scenes, but no power of organization. Her brother-in-law, Leslie Stephen, who loved and admired her, was nevertheless exasperated by this lack of mental discipline, and wrote that 'she has not two facts in her head, and one of them is a mistake'.[47]

Minny figures far less in Thackeray's letters than her more turbulent and demanding elder sister. Writing to their aunt, Jane Shawe, Thackeray said he was afraid Anny was going to be 'a man of genius: I would far sooner have had her an amiable & affectionate woman – But little Minny will be that, please God.'[48] Minny seems to have been a quiet, rather passive girl, whose interests remained childish. At the age of twenty she was still more interested in kittens, and rescuing flies from drowning, than in young men. There were early fears, happily false, that she might have inherited Isabella's mental instability; she grew up to be quite normal. She was sweet, gentle, unambitious, rather pretty, with a quiet sense of humour. She seemed to embody the type of woman Thackeray found ideal, and Leslie Stephen thought her a perfect wife. He wrote of her that 'her simplicity was the simplicity of a child and she remained, in some ways, a child throughout life . . . to picture her to myself is now, more than ever, like looking into the very soul of a sweet child . . . To know her and her sister was to strengthen my regard for the father . . .'[49] Yet letters she wrote after her father's death show a capacity for shrewd and witty commentary on the people she met; and Thackeray respected her judgement, and feared her criticism of his lectures on the Georges. She seems an enigmatic, shadowy figure, touched by tragedy. Her only daughter Laura was mentally retarded, and Minny herself died young, pregnant with her second child.

Because of the peculiar circumstances of the household, Thackeray was closer to his daughters than many Victorian fathers. Though he still spent much time in all-male company, often at his clubs, he began to refuse some of the many invitations he received, because he was dining with his daughters, or taking them to the theatre, or some other treat. Anny remembered the Young Street household as a happy, if quiet one. Of course Thackeray never gave up the bachelor pleasures of dining in male company, eating and drinking too freely, and spending evenings in more dubious company than that of two little girls and their governess. But the introduction of a child in his novels tends to be the signal for a softening of the emotional tone. Characters are often judged by their treatment of children; if all Becky's other sins were to be forgiven her, her behaviour to her son would not be.

This in itself is not remarkable; it is the stock attitude of the nineteenth-century novel. What does seem strange is that Thackeray never really portrays a child from the inside. With all his experience of suffering as a child himself, and in spite of his closeness to his daughters, he seems to avoid the description of childish sorrow and pain. *Pendennis* is quite unlike *David Copperfield*, or *Great Expectations*, or *The Mill on the Floss*; novels which are at their greatest in their intimate pictures of the hopes and terrors of childhood. Pendennis springs fully armed from his creator's head as a lovesick adolescent; little Rawdon and little Georgy are minor characters who exist mainly to make clear the attitudes of the adults; even Clive Newcome and Philip Firmin, though they are shown as schoolboys, do not really come alive until they are young men. The childhood of women characters is even more obscure; the reader feels that, as Becky says of herself, they have been women since they were eight years old.

Yet Thackeray really loved children, and not only his own. Since his schooldays he had befriended those younger and weaker and even more vulnerable than himself. He was a far better and more accessible father than Dickens, who made such a public parade of being a father, but whose obsessional concern for order and tidiness, and driving ambition, had a disastrous effect on his family. Whenever Thackeray went into a family, he at once sought out the children, talked to them, watched them, spoiled them, giving them money and things to eat. 'Most of my Thackeray incidents seem more or less to relate to food,' Henriette Corkran confessed.[50] She remembered being saved by his intervention from a disgusting soup that the French *bonne* was trying to force on her.[51] He loved taking schoolboys to the play, and reliving his own boyhood through watching their enthusiasm. He was an observer of children, and knew exactly the kind of nonsense that appealed to a child's sense of humour, and how easily a child's feelings could be hurt;

but he never tried to intrude on their thoughts and feelings; indeed he specifically cautioned parents against being intrusive. 'What ardent, imaginative soul has not a secret pleasure-place in which it disports? Let no clumsy prying or dull meddling of ours try to disturb it in our children.'[52] Childhood, so brief and so vulnerable, seemed a territory too precious to be invaded and exploited by the novel.

Chapter 7

Vanity Fair

The world is a looking-glass, and gives back to every man
the reflection of his own face.

Vanity Fair, Chapter 11.

Though *Vanity Fair* is Thackeray's undisputed masterpiece, it at first
sold so badly that there was a real danger that it might cease publication
after the third number. When Bradbury and Evans began to issue it in
monthly numbers on 1 January 1847, only a dozen chapters had been
written, and the novel, which had already been turned down by
Colburn – possibly by other publishers too – might have been
abandoned for ever. Thackeray knew it was good, the big novel he had
been promising himself he would write ever since his student days. The
critics at once perceived its originality. But it seemed as though he still
couldn't 'hit the public', at a moment that was crucial for his fortunes.
The day after the first number appeared in its 'gaudy yellow' cover,
Thackeray wrote to William Aytoun of *Blackwood's*, pressing for a
notice:

> I think I have never had any ambition hitherto, or cared what the world
> thought my work, good or bad; but now the truth forces itself upon me,
> if the world will once take to admiring Titmarsh, all his guineas will be
> multiplied by 10.[1]

By October, Thackeray was still writing to his mother that the novel
'does everything but sell'.[2] Only after the twelfth number was success
assured, and even then sales were only a fraction of those of *Dombey
and Son*, also appearing monthly. At this stage Thackeray's integrity as
a writer and social critic worked against his acceptance by the section of
society he knew intimately and described with a sharply observant eye
and ear. He was never to reach, or indeed aim at, the larger audience

143

which Dickens manipulated. Later Victorians absorbed Thackeray comfortably by putting him in the niche which he later invited, of 'a gentleman writing for gentlemen'. It is a judgement which tones down the asperities of *Vanity Fair* to a quite unrealistic degree.

For *Vanity Fair* is an uncomfortable, as well as a highly entertaining book; designedly so. The echoes of Bunyan and Ecclesiastes in its title are never allowed to be forgotten by the reader. By 1846 Thackeray had begun to see his role as a writer as correlative with 'the parson's own',[3] much as George Eliot was to see serious fiction as a secular substitute for religion. It was certainly a way of asserting the dignity of literature; perhaps also of establishing himself on the same moral footing as the clergyman who happened to be Jane Brookfield's husband. Writing to their old Cambridge friend John Allen in February 1847 to protest at Allen's part in refusing Brookfield an Inspectorate of Schools (a post he was later given) Thackeray said that he suspected that Brookfield's reputation had been harmed by his friendship with the writer for *Punch*: 'Now it is not Punch that has perverted Brookfield; but Brookfield has converted Punch!'[4] In letter after letter at this time Thackeray reiterated his seriousness of purpose, already uneasy that the satirical label that had become attached to his work implied a levity that he was far from feeling. His most famous statement about his intention in *Vanity Fair* was made to Robert Bell, who reviewed it favourably in *Fraser's*.

> I want to leave everybody dissatisfied and unhappy at the end of the story
> – we ought all to be with our own and all other stories. Good God don't I
> see (in that may-be cracked and warped looking-glass in which I am
> always looking) my own weaknesses wickednesses lusts follies short-
> comings? . . . We must lift up our voices about these and howl to a
> congregation of fools; so much at least has been my endeavour.[5]

However, this seriousness of purpose never betrayed Thackeray into writing a moral tract. *Vanity Fair* is a multi-layered book, which achieves its effect through ambiguity and indirection. Though the reader may feel a dissatisfaction and unhappiness with the human lot at the end of the book, as Thackeray intends: '. . . which of us is happy in this world? Which of us has his desire? or, having it, is satisfied?' – the sense of satisfaction which the book as a work of art gives us is all the greater because we feel the essential truth of the 'unhappy ever after' ending which reaches out into a grey-toned and believable future.

The novel seems to have been begun in a rather different spirit. The first working title, 'Pen and Pencil Sketches of English Society', suggests Thackeray's earlier style, and the kind of satirical approach that was channelled into *The Snobs of England*. The first draft of the early chapters was probably written during 1845, though Thackeray had been thinking about using the Napoleonic period for a novel, including the battle of Waterloo, as early as 1842, when he cross-questioned Captain Sibourne, who had written a history of the 1815 campaign, at Charles Lever's house near Dublin.[6] The first four chapters, in which Amelia and Becky emerge from the schoolroom, an early version of Chapter 6, in which Becky has her first reverse, Becky's letter from Chapter 8, without the accompanying narrative commentary, and chapters 9 and 10, were all written considerably in advance of the rest of the novel.[7] Chapter 5, which introduces Dobbin, was added later, at the stage when Thackeray began to change George Osborne from an amiable but rather characterless young man, to one altogether more unpleasant and culpable. The title of chapter 5, 'Dobbin of Ours' is a parodic reference to Charles Lever's novel of the Napoleonic period, *Tom Burke of Ours*, and introduces the mock-heroic theme which permeates the first half of the novel. The drawing for the capital C which opens the chapter shows two little boys in a nursery battle, with wooden swords and paper hats; the chapter recounts a bloodier school encounter of the kind Thackeray repeatedly wrote about, where a kindly older boy was roused to fight the school bully in defence of a younger one. The pattern is set for Dobbin's later actions, while the drawing comments reductively on the idea of heroism at any level.

The novel's second working title, 'A Novel without a Hero', was retained as the subtitle of *Vanity Fair*. It indicates a shift in the direction of Thackeray's ideas which is of considerable significance for the final shape of the book. Thackeray had abandoned his early enthusiasm for Carlyle; but he still took his ideas seriously enough to feel the need to defend the art of fiction against Carlyle's attack on it in his essay 'Biography', of 1832, and to attack the idea of the Great Man proposed in *Heroes and Hero-Worship* of 1840.

Carlyle's 1832 essay disturbed Thackeray, and he returned to it several times. The passage in *Pendennis* that points out the 'distinct universe' peculiar to each individual consciousness denies Carlyle's contention that it is possible, through biography, to enter into another person's inner world. Where Carlyle saw each individual as 'a mirror both scientific and poetic ... to us', Thackeray saw the mirror as warped and cracked at best. Carlyle's lofty dismissal of the novelist as a flawed biographer, his work as a 'Long-ear of a Fictitious Biography',[8] is specifically taken up as a challenge in *Vanity Fair* and intricately woven into the fabric of the novel. The original cover illustration for the monthly numbers shows the clown-preacher who is the narrator of the story standing on his Swiftian tub, gloomily haranguing a mostly cheerful and inattentive audience. Both the preacher and the members of his audience, down to the Amelia-figure and her baby in the foreground, have asses' ears. In the background are the two national monuments that had been the subject of *Punch*'s ridicule since they had first been proposed; the statue of Wellington (strategically placed so that its subject could admire it out of the drawing-room windows of Apsley House), and the Nelson column, which had only been erected after innumerable delays. In Thackeray's sketch Nelson is in place at last, standing on his head; the Iron Duke is mounted on a donkey.[9] So much for the Military Hero.

one - /

In the new frontispiece drawn for the 1848 two-volume edition, the clown-narrator sits on the ground, leaning against the puppet-box, looking into the cracked looking-glass. The wooden sword by his side again emphasizes the ludicrousness of military glory. But it is in an addition to the original version of Chapter 8, after the moralizing narrative comment on Becky's witty letter from Queen's Crawley, that Thackeray makes his most overt comment on Carlyle. The narrator accepts 'the long-eared livery in which his congregation is arrayed', while describing the story he has to tell as a 'history' and insisting 'one is bound to speak the truth as far as one knows it, whether one mounts a cap and bells or a shovel-hat; and a deal of disagreeable matter must come out in the course of such an undertaking.' He goes on to narrate two contradictory anecdotes about the relationship between fiction and the truth or falsity of feeling it can evoke, which suggest that the line Carlyle draws between history and biography on the one hand, and the 'Long-ear of a Fictitious Biography' on the other, is a good deal too simple to have much meaning in the complicated world of Vanity Fair.

If a man is not a hero to his valet, Carlyle wrote in *Heroes and Hero-Worship*, 'it is not the Hero's blame, but the Valet's; that his soul, namely, is a mean *valet*-soul!'[10] In *Vanity Fair*, as in so much of Thackeray's writing, the servants are sharper-eyed than most at seeing the exact truth about the would-be heroes and heroines: the valet-soul of Isidor does not prevent him from summing up his master, Jos Sedley. Indeed, what emerges in their relationship is their likeness to each other. Becky is always found out first by the servants' hall: 'the awful kitchen inquisition which sits in judgement in every house, and knows everything'. Only Dobbin and Amelia, who make no attempt at heroism, are loved by those who serve them.

Vanity Fair contains a sustained criticism of romanticism, an attack on the attitude to life and literature that Thackeray had found personally distasteful since his Weimar days. It seemed to him a cover for a

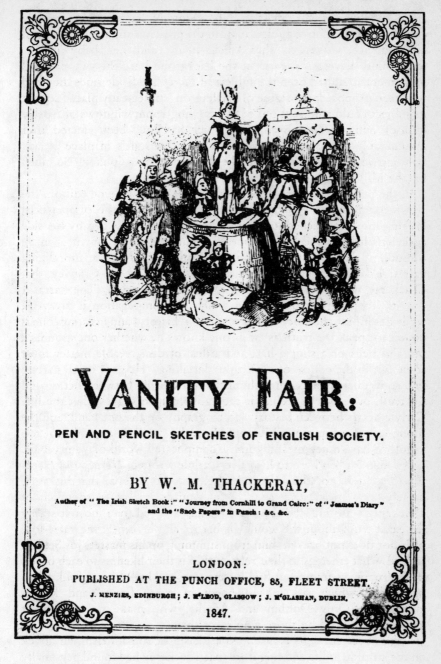

VANITY FAIR:

PEN AND PENCIL SKETCHES OF ENGLISH SOCIETY.

BY W. M. THACKERAY,

Author of " The Irish Sketch Book :" " Journey from Cornhill to Grand Cairo:" of " Jeames's Diary "
and the "Snob Papers" in Punch : &c. &c.

LONDON:
PUBLISHED AT THE PUNCH OFFICE, 85, FLEET STREET.
J. MENZIES, EDINBURGH ; J. M'LEOD, GLASGOW ; J. M'GLASHAN, DUBLIN.
1847.

The preacher in Vanity Fair

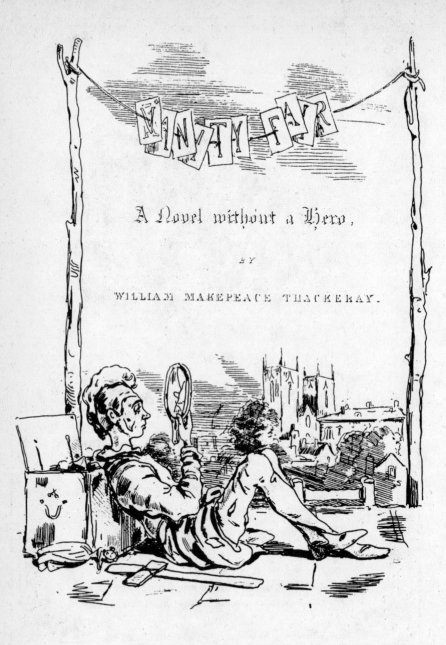

The cracked looking-glass

profound cynicism and disregard for the feelings of others, wrapped up in an apparent search for self-realization. He wrote of Byron: 'That man *never* wrote from his heart. He got up rapture and enthusiasm with an eye to the public';[11] and *The Second Funeral of Napoleon* was written to expose the sham of the military hero, as well as the sham of the ceremonial it described. The cult of the hero is central to the romantic attitude; and the story of Becky Sharp, the outsider who attempts by strength of character and intelligence alone, without any advantages of wealth or birth, to climb the highest positions in society, only to find that each success leaves her equally bored and discontented, is a wry parody of the *bildungsroman* of the period in which the novel is set. The initial drawing for Chapter 64 shows Becky as Napoleon returned from Elba, gazing across the Channel at England, with thoughts of conquest. By this stage in her history, all vestiges of heroism have fallen from Becky, who is in a period of seedy decline.

A portion of the novel under its second title was set up in proof by Bradbury & Evans as early as the summer of 1846. Serialization was supposed to begin in May 1846, but was delayed, perhaps because the publishers were less than wholeheartedly enthusiastic about the book. But the success of *The Snobs of England*, and of Thackeray's first Christmas Book, *Mrs Perkins's Ball*, finally assured its appearance. 'I have always been told that it was "Mrs Perkins's Ball" which played the part of pilot or steam-tug to that great line-of-battle ship "Vanity Fair", and which brought it safely off the shoals,' Anny recalled in her biographical introduction to the novel.[12] The final title came to

Becky as Napoleon

Thackeray while he was at Brighton in the autumn of 1846. 'I jumped out of bed, and ran three times round my room, uttering as I went, "Vanity Fair, Vanity Fair, Vanity Fair",' he told his new friend Kate Perry.[13] The discovery of the title, with its didactic and religious implications, gave the book an extra dimension which turned it from an entertaining, but formally conventional, piece of social satire, into a novel in which the repeated destruction of form becomes an essential way of mediating the reader's response to the fiction, and ensuring that any complicity with the characters can't last for long, however beguiling their wit or recognizably and realistically human their actions.

It was at this third stage of the novel's creation that Thackeray developed more fully the intricate web of narrative commentary which is woven around the characters and the action. By developing the strategy, already familiar from his earlier work, of using highly individual, even idiosyncratic, narrative voices, he separated the author or, rather, what Wayne Booth has christened 'the implied author'[14] from the narrator. The latter becomes a character in his own right, though a confusingly self-contradictory one, existing in an artistic no man's land, somewhere between the reader and the characters in the story. Thackeray himself points to this separation of 'author' and narrator in the preface 'Before the Curtain' written for the 1848 edition, where he makes a distinction between the 'Author' of the work and the 'Manager of the Performance'. But he also refers in the preface to the 'man with a reflective turn of mind' who walks through the Fair as an observer, and to 'poor Tom Fool', who is clearly the same person who looks at his distorted image in the frontispiece. The confusion this creates in the reader's mind – who *is* the narrator, the reliable and omniscient voice who will tell us the story and also what to think about it? – is quite deliberate. His lifelong fascination with the theatre, and the relationship between illusion and reality, already present as early as *Flore et Zephyr*, emerges once more in the unnamed but ever-present cast of characters who surround the 'real' characters of the story of *Vanity Fair*. These are, in fact, all different faces of the 'Manager of the Performance', who is an actor-manager of the old school, a true pro who is a bewildering quick-change artist. He can appear to hold one opinion with sincere conviction at one moment, and at the next add another twist to his argument which brings it crashing to the ground. Sometimes his views coincide with those of the 'author', sometimes not.

With this acrobatic harlequin performance going on in the foreground, the story, and the characters in it, appear to gain in solidity by contrast, so that when the 'Manager' describes them as puppets, and claims that it is he who manipulates them for our entertainment, we react indignantly. Ever since the novel first appeared, critics have gone to the lengths of claiming that we know more about his characters than Thackeray does, or that he 'lies' about them, or that he has somehow lost control of his own book: 'The Art of Novels *is* to represent Nature: to convey as strongly as possible the sentiment of reality . . .'[15] Thackeray wrote, objecting to the grotesque and theatrical in Dickens's early novels. In *Vanity Fair* he takes care to make those elements the property of the narrator, and not of the characters.

The meaning that *Vanity Fair* has held for most readers is contained in the narrative's insistence that there are no inviolable standards of good and evil available in this world. Not all the book's readers have approved of this: Harriet Martineau, who much admired *Esmond*, was not alone in being unable to read *Vanity Fair* 'from the moral disgust it occasions'.[16] Good not only does not triumph over evil, except in the most marginal and limited ways, it is apparent that it cannot. Becky, an adulteress and murderess, is not assigned any terrible fate at the end of the novel, nor is one projected for her outside the book. Writing to the Duke of Devonshire, who had inquired about the futures of his characters, Thackeray assigned Becky 'a small but very pretty little house in Belgravia' and a circle of respectable friends who consider her 'a *most injured woman*'.[17] Becky's punishment is no more than the boredom and weariness that she feels after each successive triumph, which may not seem to differ materially from the boredom and weariness that Dobbin feels at the end of his story. It is hard to imagine this being permitted in the moral universe of any other English nineteenth-century novel. We may even feel that Becky, with her energy and inventiveness, and her capacity to accept the down-turns of fortune with good humour, comes off best after all, since even the least ambiguous spokesmen for the 'humblemindedness' Thackeray admired – Dobbin and Lady Jane Sheepshanks – do not obtain happiness through behaving correctly. It is the moment of rebellion in each, Dobbin's when he rounds at last on Amelia, and Lady Jane when she refuses to have any more to do with Becky, that the reader admires. Yet those rebellions, though they do produce results, do not bring happiness either. Though *Vanity Fair* is, in its own distinctive way, an exemplary and didactic novel, it does not convey its message through simple cause and effect exposition.

It works, rather, through a duality at every level of the writing, by presenting two points of view which appear to offer a choice, but which, more often than not, require the reader to make an attempt at synthesis. There is, first, the historical duality. As an historical novel, set a generation back, yet still within the lifetime of the author and many of his readers, *Vanity Fair* builds up, through an accumulation of significant detail, an authentic picture of the world that immediately preceded the Victorian era, so that its readers could see their own world coming into being in its pages. The battle of Waterloo was a crucial event: without the defeat of Napoleon England would have become a struggling island-fortress, or a conquered dependency of France. By setting his characters' private lives in the context of the vast historical events of their time, which have a devastating impact on the Sedleys and the Osbornes, Thackeray also suggests, though he does not explore it fully in this novel, another duality, that of private domestic happiness struggling in the face of public indifference or hostility.

Thackeray was of the same generation as the children in the novel, young George and young Rawdon; his mother (who survived until 1864) was the same age as Amelia. Thackeray's father, like George Osborne, died in 1815, though of a fever in India, rather than with 'a ball in his odious bowels'.[18] The phrase is Thackeray's private version of George's end, in contrast to the novel's more conventional, though dramatic, 'lying on his face, dead, with a bullet through his heart'.[19] The narrator, when he has any age at all, appears to belong to the same generation as the main characters. When his omniscience gives way to the partial and external knowledge of an observer – one who nevertheless claims, with Carlylean extravagance, a knowledge he cannot possibly have – he links the past of the action and the present of the narration together.

> It was on this very tour that I, the present writer of a history of which every word is true, had the pleasure to see them first, and to make their acquaintance. (*Vanity Fair*, Chapter 62, *Works*, 11, p. 793)

This double vision is maintained in the apparently casual use of trivial details: Rawdon's impromptu will refers not just to a gun but 'my double barril by Manton'. Joseph Manton was the best (and most expensive) gunsmith in Regency London; Byron was one of the many who practised his aim in the shooting gallery behind Manton's shop. But a couple of pages later the narrative brings the possession of objects up to date with a deliberate reference to a firm that did not exist in 1815:

> If Messrs. Howell and James were to publish a list of the purchasers of all the trinkets which they sell, how surprised would some families be: and if all these ornaments went to gentlemen's lawful wives and daughters, what a profusion of jewellery there would be exhibited in the genteelest homes of Vanity Fair! (*Vanity Fair*, Chapter 30, *Works*, 11, p. 369)

Similarly, the row which Amelia has with her mother over the use of Daffy's Elixir, a popular eighteenth-century opiate, still in use in Thackeray's time, but old-fashioned enough to be discredited, makes her momentary flash of rebellion an important and sympathetic issue to the modern woman of 1847. The novel is full of such specific allusions, to the names of actors, opera singers, shops, popular songs, and the brand-names of widely advertised products. Thackeray learnt the trick of specificity long before, in the days when he learned the journalistic trade from Maginn and his associates at *Fraser's*, but in *Vanity Fair* it is never used at random. The narrative is full of hints to the reader to apply the story to contemporary society. In the first edition there was a disingenuous footnote to Chapter 6 explaining that the illustrations do not show the characters in the correct historical costumes, because 'I have not the heart to disfigure my heroes and heroines by costumes so hideous', with a little vignette showing how they would really have been dressed. It could be, of course, that the pressure of turning out text and drawings on time each month would have been made intolerable by the added burden of historical accuracy. It is more likely that the historical inaccuracy of the illustrations was making a point by blurring the line between past and present, alternately insisted upon and denied by the narrative.

In addition to the stereoscopic vision of past and present, there is a doubling of narration, which first describes what the characters are and do and feel; and then comments on the description in ways which make one doubt its reliability. In the very first chapter, the introductory description of Amelia sets up her supposed 'accomplishments' – always derided by Thackeray – in exaggerated terms which make it clear she

'I have not the heart to disfigure my characters'

cannot possibly possess them, against straightforward qualities of love and gentleness he expects us to value more. Yet the narrative immediately casts these qualities in doubt by making fun of her friendships: 'She had twelve intimate and bosom friends out of the twenty-four young ladies.' The condescending narrative comment that she was 'a dear little creature' and an extended description of her sensibility over trifles make it clear that she is a sentimental little goose, capable of feeling, but quite undiscriminating in what she feels about. Having persuaded the reader to despise her, the narrator then introduces a prototypical reader, Jones, against whom the real reader immediately reacts; helped, in the first edition, by the illustration of this club bore:

> All which details, I have no doubts, JONES, who reads this book at his club, will pronounce to be excessively foolish, trivial, twaddling, and ultra-sentimental. Yes; I can see Jones at this minute (rather flushed with his joint of mutton and half-pint of wine), taking out his pencil and scoring under the words 'foolish, twaddling' &c., and adding to them his own remark of '*quite true*'. (*Vanity Fair*, Chapter 1, *Works*, 11, p. 8)

This use of double irony is fundamental to the narrative. By adding an extra twist to the usual irony of saying the opposite of what is really meant, the narrator leaves the reader wondering whether he does in fact mean exactly what he says. Then he may shift ground yet again. The

Jones reading Vanity Fair

question most often asked about *Vanity Fair* – are we meant to admire or condemn Becky Sharp? – ignores the subtle ways in which our response to her is constantly being changed by the quirks and doublings of the narrator. The reader of *Vanity Fair* is forced to remain active and alert. The world of the novel is real and solid enough, but the reader is not drawn into it, as into a dream or fantasy. The novel is not intended to enchant; instead it has a compensating energy, an atmosphere of intelligent alertness which reaches out to the reader without enveloping him.

The narrative commentary may seem didactic; but when we examine it closely, in relation to the straightforwardly narrative passages, we are always thrown back on our own judgement, without being allowed to rest comfortably on received opinions. Even where the narrative withholds comment, a stock situation is often seen in a new light, so that assumptions must be questioned. The devoted sick-nurse, for example, smoothing the pillow of the dying parent, child, or husband, is a cliché of the Victorian novel. Thackeray takes a sidelong glance at such preconceptions. He had tried to nurse his own wife, and had been forced to admit that a paid nurse does the work infinitely better, and more cheerfully. So Becky becomes, for entirely self-interested motives, an impeccable nurse to the rich hypochondriac, Miss Crawley:

> She passed as weary a fortnight as ever mortal spent in Miss Crawley's sick-room; but her little nerves seemed to be of iron, and she was quite unshaken by the duty and the tedium of the sick-chamber ... During the illness she was never out of temper; always alert; she slept light, having a perfectly clear conscience; and could take that refreshment at almost any minute's warning. (*Vanity Fair*, Chapter 14, *Works*, 11, p. 164)

Taken on its own, this might seem admirable; Becky is always presented as more practically useful than Amelia, as well as more intelligent. But the leisurely unfolding of the novel allows us to see repeated instances of the way in which she uses situations to her own advantage. After her initial attempt and failure to catch Jos, neatly symbolized by the green silk purse she is netting, which stands for her attempt on the Sedley money and her envy of it, Becky learns fast how to turn situations to her own advantage. She sets out to captivate Rawdon, and succeeds in making him fall genuinely in love with her. In the superficial terms of Vanity Fair she is a good wife to him, using her devious intelligence to keep them both afloat, and until the final moment of catastrophe he admires and respects her. Amelia's tearful dependence on George simply annoys him: at the Duchess of Richmond's ball 'her appearance was an utter failure (as her husband felt

'Mr Joseph entangled'

with a sort of rage)'.[20] But Becky ultimately destroys Rawdon; and she
has a deleterious effect on all the men who fall for her charms except
Lord Steyne, who is even more corrupt than she is. Her 'good-nature',
which the narrative repeatedly insists on, is, it becomes clear, a kind of
moral indolence, and disappears as soon as her interests are threatened
in any way.

The dual view of women which is expressed in the parallel lives of
Becky and Amelia, and also, to a lesser extent, in the minor female

characters, is another of the novel's powerful ambiguities. On their first appearance in the world, Becky and Amelia represent, at a primitive level underlying the narrative sophistication, the pairing that dates from the Weimar experiences. Becky is the clever, gifted intellectual, the Jenny/Ottilia cannibal, who devours men while remaining thin and predatory. Amelia on her first appearance in the story is described as rosy, round-cheeked and healthy, and always good-humoured; she begins by fulfilling the Melanie/Dorothea role, though of course the way in which her character develops takes a quite different direction. But the basic opposition of the female as devourer, and as nurturer, is embedded in the book in terms of childlike simplicity of which Thackeray was probably hardly conscious.

Yet whenever the reader is tempted to oversimplify, seeing Amelia as exemplifying heart, for example, and Becky mind; or casting Amelia as the passive, loving satellite that Thackeray acknowledged he preferred a woman to be, and Becky as the manipulative and organizing female he privately confessed he disliked and feared, the narrative adds some qualification. Amelia's obstinate stupidity in refusing to acknowledge Dobbin's love, and her deification of George, who had made her miserably unhappy during their few weeks of marriage, are set against her capacity for self-sacrifice and her lack of pretension. She brings out the best in those around her – even, at times, in Rebecca, who is finally the agent of her necessary disillusion with George. This frees her to love Dobbin, though not to achieve unqualified happiness with him. The ambivalence of the narrator's farewell to Amelia: 'Grow green again, tender little parasite, round the rugged old oak to which you cling!'[21] elides from the picture of a sensitive plant to that of an ivy, throttling the life out of the oak. It is hardly a comfortable picture, in spite of the affectionate terms in which it is phrased. If Becky is a mermaid, feeding on drowned corpses, Amelia is a parasite sucking the life from the man she clings to. Both are cannibals. Yet the test is finally that we know Amelia has the capacity for love, and the insight to know the truth of her relationship to Dobbin; she exists in a different emotional world from Becky's busy hypocritical charities:

> The Destitute Orange-girl, the Neglected Washerwoman, the Distressed Muffin-man, find in her a fast and generous friend. She is always having stalls at Fancy Fairs for the benefit of these hapless beings. (*Vanity Fair*, Chapter 67, *Works*, 11, p. 877)

Those capital letters, and the beautiful, ambiguous placing of 'hapless' make it quite clear that Becky's charity is only one more way of self-assertion.

The different ways in which women react to a situation which they are powerless to change – the male province of warfare, which we know Thackeray considered barbarous and outmoded – is examined in the Waterloo chapter, 'The Girl I left behind me'. Mrs O'Dowd, hitherto presented as a ridiculous character with a broad brogue and social pretensions which make even the polite and reticent Dobbin choke with suppressed laughter, is now shown combining practicality and love in her preparations for her husband's comfort in the field. The plate 'Venus preparing the armour of Mars', with its mock-heroic insistence on the comic aspect of the O'Dowds, is balanced against the narrative comment which, at the level of practical good sense, implicitly criticizes Amelia:

> And who is there will deny that this worthy lady's preparations betokened affection as much as the fits of tears and hysterics by which more sensitive females exhibited their love, and that their partaking of this coffee, which they drank together while the bugles were sounding the turn-out, and the drums beating in the various quarters of the town, was not more useful and to the purpose than the outpourings of any mere sentiment could be?

'Venus preparing the armour of Mars'

The narrative doesn't rest there, however, in a simple opposition of sense and sensibility. Practicality is taken a stage further in the presentation of Becky's calm selfishness, and the ironic narrative comment on it:

> Knowing how useless regrets are, and how the indulgence of sentiment only serves to make people more miserable, Mrs Rebecca wisely determined to give way to no vain feelings of sorrow, and bore the parting from her husband with quite a Spartan equanimity.

This prepares the way for a reaction in favour of feeling; and the scene which follows – one of the great moments of the book – exists on an entirely different level, where questions of usefulness, everyday feelings of affection, cease to have meaning.

The O'Dowds and Becky are seen in pictures as well as words, Becky comfortably in bed after Rawdon's departure; but Thackeray wisely did not attempt to draw Amelia at this climactic moment of her life. She is seen, through the eyes of the man who truly loves and values her, proleptically mourning her husband's death. Objects have throughout the chapter had a characterizing significance. The Major's wicker-covered 'pistol' flask of brandy, Rawdon's old uniform, worn so that Becky can sell his new one if he is killed, fill out the picture of the people they belong to. Now they become symbolic of the betrayal of innocence: Dobbin might be present at the scene of a rape. For the second time the sight of Amelia's grief makes him feel a criminal, as it had when he forced George into marrying her. Her face:

> haunted him afterwards like a crime, and the sight smote him with inexpressible pangs of longing and pity. She was wrapped in a white morning dress, her hair falling on her shoulders, and her large eyes fixed and without light. By way of helping on the preparations for the departure, and showing that she too could be useful at a moment so critical, this poor soul had taken up a sash of George's from the drawers whereon it lay, and followed him to and fro with the sash in her hand, looking on mutely as his packing proceeded. She came out and stood, leaning at the wall, holding this sash against her bosom, from which the heavy net of crimson dropped like a large stain of blood.

This image of Amelia's capacity for deep feeling, written in deliberately heightened language, is contrasted with George's eagerness to be off, conveyed in short clauses as the thoughts succeed one another in his head, and the young man's eagerness, callous though it is, is shared by the reader through the forceful, direct language:

'Thank Heaven that is over,' George thought, bounding down the stair, his sword under his arm, and as he ran swiftly to the alarm-ground, where the regiment was mustered, and whither trooped men and officers hurrying from their billets, his pulse was throbbing and his cheeks flushed; the great game of war was going to be played, and he one of the players. (*Vanity Fair*, Chapter 30, *Works*, 11, pp. 361–73)

We know from *Snobs* as well as from private statements in his letters how much Thackeray disliked the professional army, and disapproved of 'the great game of war'; yet the excitement here, rightly conveyed through the immature George's feelings, rather than those of the experienced O'Dowd or the gentle Dobbin, is irresistible. Nevertheless, the force of the scene with Amelia, and her near-madness after George's departure, which shakes even the imperturbable Becky, is strong enough to remain with us throughout the book, qualifying our irritation with Amelia for her selfishness towards Dobbin. The clear case put by the narrative against the romantic stereotype of the woman who gives her heart for life cannot quite overcome the strength of this moment, and of the later scene, which reinforces it, when Amelia gives up her son to his grandfather, and the child behaves with his father's selfishness.

'You know you are only a piece of Amelia – My Mother is another half: my poor little wife *y est pour beaucoup*,' Thackeray wrote to Jane Brookfield, apologizing for naming Amelia's maid 'Payne' after hers.[22] Mrs Brookfield resented any identification of herself with the character, whom she found dull and selfish. Certainly the picture of her that emerges from her published letters seems very unlike Amelia. Her letters to Thackeray are those of a tease, alternately keeping him off and drawing him on. A letter of February 1847 begins with distant formality but ends 'You left a great blank behind you – not to be filled up at all';[23] and she was an intelligent, sharp-tongued, critical woman. Yet Thackeray thought there was some resemblance, and said so to his mother. He was implying that there was some parallel with Amelia in Jane's situation in her marriage. He saw her as devoted against all reason to a husband whom he felt was unworthy of her. 'I am afraid my dear Mrs Brookfield will die. She sinks and sinks and gets gradually worse . . . She never says a word but I know the cause of a great part of her malady well enough – a husband whom she has loved with the most fanatical fondness and who – and who is my friend too – a good fellow upright and generous kind to all the world except her.'[24] The published letters exchanged between Jane and William Brookfield during the 1840s do not confirm this idea. It seems the affectionate, bantering correspondence of a couple who are still close to each other after some years of marriage, in spite of the disappointment of having no children. Thackeray was more aware of this than he always cared to acknowledge. 'How many people are you? . . . (you are) quite different to us all . . . and you make gentle fun of us all round to your own private B. and offer us up to make him sport. You see I am making you out to be an Ogre's wife and poor William the Ogre to whom you serve us up cooked for dinner.'[25] The old spectre of the devouring woman, which had always haunted him, is transmuted here into that of the collusive and obedient wife of the devourer.

Whether consciously or not, Thackeray does seem to have used Jane Brookfield as a physical model for his drawings of Amelia, which are closer to the innumerable portraits he made of her than to the description of Amelia in the text. The drawings of the real woman, as of the character, are insipid and unsatisfactory, vitiated by idealization. At this stage in their relationship Jane was 'a sort of angel' to Thackeray; his mind's eye holds a picture of a fantasy, and it is this that is transferred to the paper.

The part of Amelia that can be accounted for by Thackeray's view of his mother is contained in the touching, but infuriating, aspects of her

The ogre's dinner

maternal brooding; expanded and deepened in his next novel into the character of Helen Pendennis. Amelia's obsession with her dead husband is not to be found in Mrs Carmichael-Smyth, who married her Dobbin all too soon for her little son's comfort. She did retain a romantic image of Richmond Thackeray all her life, and was talking of him to her granddaughters on the night she died. No doubt she also talked of him to her son, who reminded her so much of his father when they were reunited in England. Thackeray's discovery that he had a black half-sister (her daughter was a not entirely welcome visitor to England in 1848), may have induced some disillusion with the romantic stereotype of the dashing father on a white horse. Georgy is allowed to keep his illusions, only gradually adding to them the reality of a true affection for 'old Dob', which, with its uneasy mixture of respect and veiled contempt, mirrors Thackeray's early feelings for his stepfather, more accurately perhaps, than the softened picture of the relationship between Clive Newcome and the Colonel.

'My poor little wife *y est pour beaucoup.*' The relationship of Isabella to the writing of *Vanity Fair*, as well as to the character of Amelia, is complex. The whole question of what men do to women in the society that Thackeray has under review, and why women allow, or even provoke them to do it, is the outcome of seven years' brooding on the brief but crucial period of his marriage. The writing of *Vanity Fair* seems to have freed Thackeray from the spectre of Isabella and his guilt about her, rather as the writing of *To the Lighthouse* finally freed Virginia Woolf from her long-dead mother. The references to Isabella in his letters are more elegiac after 1848, as if she had become a part of his past, assimilated and embalmed in memory. He came to feel that she was happier if he did not visit her and rouse her out of her dream-world to painful reminders of their relationship and her duties as a wife and mother. He stopped taking the girls to see her, and it was only after his death that Anny re-established contact with her mother, and continued to visit her regularly until Isabella died. Though he used different aspects of her life and character in *The Newcomes* and *Philip*, the character of Amelia is his farewell to the living Isabella, and the mixture of affection, pity and irritation that she is meant to arouse in the reader is a true reflection of Thackeray's own unresolved feelings. The 'parasite' aspect of a childlike character, too fearful of the real world to be able to face reality on her own, selfishly dependent on the 'rugged old oak' to which she clings, is balanced by the 'quality above most people whizz: LOVE – by wh. she shall be saved'.[26]

It is an unsatisfactory and partial view of womanhood for most readers, and was so even when the novel first appeared. But it is an accurate and touching portrait of a real woman, stultified by her upbringing and education, unable in times of trouble to do anything practical to help herself or those she loves except by the negative action of depriving herself of her son, and almost of life itself. Yet, though the separation between the negative but loving Amelia and the active, intelligent, yet finally destructive Becky should be clear, there is more overlapping than at first appears. Amelia may be in part based on Isabella Shawe; but Becky Sharp is given her physical appearance. Like Becky, Isabella was tiny, red-haired and thin. 'Your little red-polled ghost pursues me everywhere, the phantoms of some of your songs are always in my ears,' Thackeray wrote during their engagement.[27] Becky also shares Isabella's musical ability and taste. Her well-trained voice, like Isabella's, charms all who hear it. Being Becky, she makes use of this gift to further her own ends, matching the performance to the audience and choosing her songs to project the right image. She sings sentimental ballads for Jos, religious songs by Mozart for the unhappy Catholic Lady Steyne. Amelia lacks Becky's artistic gifts, and is made to seem more of a cipher by contrast. She learns to appreciate music fully for the first time only at Weimar, in Dobbin's company; and we recall that it was Dobbin who bought back her piano for her at the sale of the Osbornes' possessions.

Becky has the spirit of a knowing and world-weary woman in the body of a child; part of Isabella's original charm for Thackeray had been her childlike freshness and *naïveté*. Her appearance and inner reality were in harmony with each other, where Becky's attractions, insisted on by the narrative, though denied by the hideous portrayal of her in the illustrations, are a cover for the ugliness of her soul. After Isabella's madness took hold, it must have seemed at times to Thackeray that she had become a different person. 'He told me that mad people, no doubt, have peculiar ideas; but if you live much with them, you begin to think "they're very rational",' Richard Bedingfield recalled.[28] Isabella was not always passive and withdrawn: at times she played 'nasty tricks' and was troublesome to her attendants.[29] Part of Thackeray's longing for simplicity in women is due to a fear of the devious and manipulative elements that may be lurking under the surface. 'I like this milk-&-water in women – perhaps too much, undervaluing your ladyships' heads, and caring only for the heart part of the business.'[30] By a deliberate apportioning to Becky of some of Isabella's attractions, the balance is perhaps better held in the author's mind between the female alternatives, and the issue made more complex for the reader.

Becky is the living proof that if virtue is not its own reward in 'Vanity Fair', neither does vice bring its own punishment. In fact, she possesses most of the generally accepted masculine virtues. She is clever, quick-witted and resourceful, courageous in her calm acceptance of reversals, and in her refusal to give up trying to make her way in a world which repeatedly rejects her. Her mistakes, in the earlier part of the novel at least, arise mostly from inexperience and impetuosity, and serve to endear her to the reader. But she has had the misfortune to be born a woman; and her upbringing and worldly circumstances, though not her fault, do not entitle her to behave in an 'unwomanly' way. Her denial of the attributes of her sex, as the nineteenth century saw them, always lead her in the end to restlessness, dissatisfaction and boredom. As Thackeray admitted, she is in some ways very close to her creator, in whose writing the cry 'Vanitas vanitatum!' is increasingly heard over the remaining fifteen years of his life. 'I think I could be a good woman if I had five thousand a year,' Becky muses, and the narrator comments:

> And who knows but Rebecca was right in her speculations – and that it was only a question of money and fortune which made the difference between her and an honest woman? If you take temptation into account, who is to say that he is better than his neighbour? (*Vanity Fair*, Chapter 41, *Works*, 11, p. 532)

The comment is of course intended to provoke an indignant denial from the reader, as it did from G. H. Lewes in his review of *Vanity Fair*; but an uncomfortable feeling, too, that there is something in it. Thackeray made exactly the same suggestion about himself; only considering that he needed ten, rather than five thousand a year. There is an unstated but clear parallel between Thackeray, the fiction writer, and Becky, the creative artist who concentrates her energies on the making of a persona to present to the world for her own advantage. Perhaps, Thackeray seems to be conceding, Carlyle was right about the writers of contemporary fiction after all:

> there is no *Reality* in them . . . Nothing but a pitiful Image of their own pitiful Self, with its vanities, and grudgings, and ravenous hunger of all kinds, hangs forever painted in the retina of these unfortunate persons.[31]

In the character of Becky, Thackeray created the embodiment of Carlyle's idea of the modern writer; but he simultaneously denied Carlyle's gibe by creating one of the great characters of English fiction.

The illustrations to *Vanity Fair* were designed to be an integral part of the book. Though Thackeray was dissatisfied with them, calling them, 'tenth or twentieth rate performances having a meaning perhaps but a ludicrous badness of execution',[32] they do add another layer of meaning to the story, and require to be 'read' with as much care as the text. The modern reader is at a disadvantage here. The only edition currently in print which contains all the illustrations reproduces the Oxford text of 1908, in which the illustrations are so much reduced that it is often impossible to make out the significant detail present in the first edition. For the 'ludicrous badness of execution' Thackeray blamed the engravers as well as his own incompetence, with some justice. Some of the original drawings for *Vanity Fair* have survived, and make one regret that modern methods of reproduction were not available in 1847.[33] The watercolours in particular have a charm which is almost always missing from the full-page etchings and smaller wood-blocks.

The illustrations are of three kinds. Each number was accompanied by a full-plate steel engraving illustrating some episode in the text. Often Thackeray takes the opportunity to make clear a point which is only hinted at by the narrative. 'Miss Sharp in her Schoolroom' shows the neglected pupils quarrelling, and so comments silently on Becky's method of instruction:

> She did not pester their young brains with too much learning, but, on the contrary, let them have their own way in regard to educating themselves; (*Vanity Fair*, Chapter 10, *Works*, 11, p. 106)

'Miss Sharp in her Schoolroom'

'*Becky's second appearance as Clytemnestra*'

By a similar strategy, the engraving 'Becky's Second Appearance in the Character of Clytemnestra' confirms the narrative's broad hint that she murders Jos for his insurance money.

The smaller, wood-block drawings consist of illustrations in the body of the text, which again are often used for amplification and commentary, as well as straightforward illustration. In Chapter 2 there is a cut of the young Becky entertaining her father's disreputable friends with the dolls presented to her by Miss Pinkerton. She holds them like puppets, foreshadowing the way in which she will manipulate other people throughout the novel.

The third category of drawings, also wood-cuts, consists of the elaborated capital letters which introduce almost every chapter. These are modelled on the capitals in *Punch*. They are emblematic comments on the action of the chapters they introduce, and often serve to draw the reader's attention to some aspect of it. Chapter 4, for example, has Becky sitting in the curve of a capital P, dangling a fishing-rod into the water for a very fat fish, which helps to undercut the narrative

Becky as manipulator

Becky angling for the fat fish

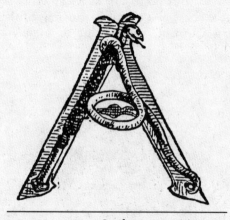

Snake

commentary's sympathy, in this chapter, for a motherless girl who has to angle for a husband by herself. The capital for Chapter 14, in which Becky is such an admirable sick-nurse, shows a snake winding itself round the letter A. Other capitals work in the same way. Chapter 21, in which George Osborne refuses to marry the mulatto heiress, Miss Swartz, is introduced by a cut of a girl playing with a black doll, which, by suggesting that Miss Swartz is a puppet in the hands of the white characters, adds a sympathy for her which is largely lacking in the text. Chapter 30 – the Waterloo chapter – shows a blind man about to fall into the water, so combining a pun with a double commentary, on the author's confessed inability to describe military scenes and the appearance of the hitherto private characters on the scene of a grand

The black puppet

'Waterloo'

public event. Both author and characters are getting into deep water. In the illustrations which show outdoor scenes, such as this one, there is almost always a church tower or spire in the background; often, also, a house or group of houses. These are silent reminders to the reader of the eternal verities of home and religion which *Vanity Fair*'s inhabitants neglect. Added emphasis is given by the church in the background of the frontispiece, identified as that of Ottery St Mary, where Thackeray spent his boyhood.

The writing of *Vanity Fair* was finished on 28 June, and Thackeray took the children to *The Rivals* to celebrate, though he felt 'very melancholy and beat'.[34] The two-volume edition came out on 18 July, his thirty-seventh birthday. Thackeray was rather reluctantly persuaded to give a party for fifty people to celebrate the two events, and then, leaving the children with Miss Alexander's family at Richmond, he went for a short holiday to the continent. *Vanity Fair* was at last a commercial success. The volume edition sold a thousand copies before publication, but Thackeray, though gratified to be 'all of a sudden a great man'[35] took time to recover from the reaction on finishing it. In one of his long, carefully composed letters to Mrs Brookfield he revealed humorously how difficult it was to shake himself free of the story:

> I am going today to the Hotel de la Terrasse (at Brussels) where Becky used to live, and shall pass by Captain Osbornes lodgings where I recollect meeting him and his little wife who has married again somebody told me: but it is always the way with these grandes passions. Mrs Dobbins or some such name she is now: always an overrated woman I thought – How curious it is! I believe perfectly in all those people & feel quite an interest in the Inn in wh. they lived.[36]

However, travelling had, as usual, a good effect on his spirits, and he wrote from Brussels to his mother that 'the water is already flowing into the basin again'.[37] At Spa he began work on *Pendennis*, in which he was to quarry his own experiences for fictional purposes more closely than ever before.

Abroad

Chapter 8

Pendennis

It is strange to take one's place and part in the middle
of the smoke and din, and think every man here has his secret *ego*
most likely, which is sitting lonely and apart, away
in the private chamber, from the loud game
in which the rest of us is joining!

Pendennis, Chapter 70.

Vanity Fair won Thackeray public recognition. But it was not the sort of book to gain easy popularity, and however much he might decry public taste and seek to educate it to something more complex than a sentimental sympathy with criminal heroes, or a fascination with the manners and intrigues of the upper classes, Thackeray needed his books to be liked. The mass popularity that Dickens had achieved by now ensured huge sales. Thirty thousand copies of the first number of *Dombey and Son* were sold, and his Christmas book for 1846, *The Battle of Life*, though *The Times* called it the very worst of 'the deluge of trash' offered to the public that Christmas, had sold twenty-three thousand copies on publication day. Thackeray could not afford to ignore the financial rewards of popularity on this scale, and in addition to his own raids on the Christmas market, *Mrs Perkins's Ball* and *Our Street* (which had sold modestly compared with Dickens's), when writing *Pendennis* he deliberately set out to create a likeable, though flawed, protagonist, as a focus for the reader's sympathies.

Pendennis began to appear in monthly numbers in November 1848, in the same yellow covers as *Vanity Fair*. The serialization of *David Copperfield* started six months later, and Thackeray, with characteristic generosity, at once acknowledged the greatness of Dickens's new book. 'Get David Copperfield,' he wrote to William Brookfield early in May, 'by Jingo its beautiful – it beats the yellow chap of the month hollow.'[1] To Jane Brookfield he said that Dickens's newly simplified style showed that he had been taking a lesson from the author of *Vanity Fair*; also that reading *Copperfield* had put him on his mettle again: 'All the mettle was out of me, and Ive been dreadfully & curiously cast down this month past.'[2]

Pendennis *frontispiece*

Neither novel was in any strict sense autobiographical, but both made use of what Dickens called 'a very complicated interweaving of truth and fiction'.[3] Dickens, able at last to confront more directly the trauma of his childhood sufferings, and to make it public through fiction, created a first-person narrative which heightened and exaggerated his real experiences, so that the semi-autobiographical David becomes another of the oppressed children who recur as almost mythological figures in his earlier novels.

Thackeray, also using some of the facts of his early life, took a different course, playing down his own hardships and reverses, making his hero's entry into the world just difficult enough to be interesting, but avoiding any revelation of his family tragedy. The narrative, instead of the bewildering multiplicity of voices of *Vanity Fair*, employs a single, reliable third-person narrator. This deliberately sets a distance between reader and character, encouraging the reader to take on the role of an indulgent older relative or friend, rather than to identify with the central figure. It was one way, for Thackeray, of legitimizing the use of reality in fiction. In the person of the older, disillusioned Warrington he gently mocks the over-intense, romantic autobiographical revelation of Pen's novel 'Walter Lorraine', his self-dramatizing account of his early adventures.

Pendennis, by implication, is a very different kind of book. However, the personal element, even so softened and disguised, plays an important part in the charm that the story exerts on the reader. Anny wrote that it always seemed more like hearing her father talk than any other of his books.[4] The narrative is often very similar to the tone of his long, carefully composed letters to Jane Brookfield, who had by now superseded his mother as the person to whom he wrote most frequently and intimately. Thackeray himself, writing the early chapters, began to distance himself affectionately from his hero:

> He is a very good natured generous young fellow and I begin to like him considerably. I wonder whether he is interesting to me from selfish reasons and because I fancy we resemble each other in many points, & whether I can get the public to like him too?[5]

Thackeray sets out to win the reader's affection for his protagonist, even as the narrative is pointing out his faults. There is little of the uncertainty and ambiguity about character and motive which readers and reviewers had objected to in *Vanity Fair*: the irony is straight-forward, the story follows the familiar and reassuring pattern of a young man learning, through repeated mistakes, the correct way to act in the world. The world of *Pendennis* is not, of course, presented as an ideal one, but it is not rejected totally as an inadmissible model, in the way that the Fair through which the 'man with a reflective turn of mind' had wandered had been. In the preface which he wrote for the first volume edition of 1850, Thackeray claimed to be showing as much of the real world of his times as the prudery of the public would allow:

Since the author of 'Tom Jones' was buried, no writer of fiction among us has been permitted to depict to his utmost power a MAN. We must drape him, and give him a certain conventional simper. Society will not tolerate the Natural in our Art. Many ladies have remonstrated and subscribers left me, because, in the course of the story, I described a young man resisting and affected by temptation. My object was to say, that he had the passions to feel, and the manliness and generosity to overcome them. You will not hear – it is best to know it – what moves in the real world, what passes in society, in the clubs, colleges, mess-rooms, – what is the life and talk of your sons. A little more frankness than is customary has been attempted in this story: . . . If truth is not always pleasant, at any rate truth is best. (*Pendennis, Works*, 12, pp. xxxvi–xxxvii)

However, the suggestion that a frank and manly writer is struggling with the forces of Bowdler and Mrs Grundy is disingenuous. By comparing himself with Fielding (even while deprecating the extent to which he is forced to be different) – a comparison the critics were quick to take up – Thackeray appears to be offering the equivalent for his times of Fielding's honesty about his hero's failings and those of the world in which he moves. To some extent he does do this. Pen is quite happy – or for a while persuades himself he is happy – to take money from a woman, as Tom Jones does from Lady Bellaston; but times have changed, and Blanche's fortune comes with a wedding ring attached. Moreover the straightforward openness of the eighteenth century, and the savage purity which lay behind the twisting and turning narrative of *Vanity Fair*, are replaced by a more genial and compromising tone of voice in Thackeray's *Bildungsroman*. A closer literary relative is Waverley, who, like Pen, suffers from a desultory and inadequate education, and is a romantic who learns to abandon romanticism during the course of his adventures.

The lessons the hero is confronted with are moral, rather than practical ones: though Pen does learn, as the young Thackeray had, a way to earn his living in the faintly raffish world of London journalism, his entry into this milieu is improbably smooth and easy. Thackeray's denial of his own early struggles, and the superior tone adopted in *Pendennis* to the world of journalism, led to a 'dignity of literature' controversy with Forster and other journalists who had struggled up by their own efforts, and were now trying to raise the status of the profession. Forster – a rigid moralist who originally perpetrated the phrase about the protection of the young from immorality that Dickens immortalized (only slightly altered) in the mouth of Podsnap in *Our Mutual Friend*, 'would it bring a blush into the cheek of the young person?' – felt Thackeray was being unfair to the profession in his portrayal of Captain Shandon, who edits the 'Pall Mall Gazette' from the Fleet Prison, and is not above begging small sums from his friends which are at once used to buy drink. In fact Shandon, who is of course modelled on 'bright broken Maginn', is a watered-down version of Thackeray's old associate, of whom he had noted on his death that he would make 'a famous subject for moralizing'.[6] Shandon, in deference to the susceptibilities of a mid-century readership, is faithful to his wife; Maginn, as Thackeray knew from his early personal experience, was notorious for 'drink and the girls'.

Apart from giving Pendennis an easier time than he had himself, Thackeray's picture of literary London in his youth is vivid, and, within the limits imposed by Victorian censorship, accurate. Journalism was still dominated by clever but unstable Irishmen whose status remained low. Gentlemen did not admit to being employed in Grub Street, and though an increasing number of them were writing, occasionally or regularly, for the journals, the almost invariable rule of anonymity made it possible for them to conceal this from their friends or employers. But in the decade between Thackeray's early struggles and the writing of *Pendennis* much had changed. Thackeray maintained that writers should be content to rely on the response of the public for status and financial reward: the obvious retort, which the bland presentation of Pen's gentlemanly dalliance with the press could only reinforce, was that it might be all right for him, but there were many others less fortunate who still needed and deserved help. Thackeray was invariably generous to individual journalists and their families, as the Crowes and the Corkrans, friends of his early days in Paris whom he helped over many years, testified. It was the organized charity of the Royal Literary Fund, and the idea that authors were in a different category from other men that he objected to. 'Hearts as brave and resolute as ever beat in the breast of any wit or poet, sicken and break daily in the vain endeavour and unavailing struggle against life's difficulty . . . who is the author, that he should be exempt?'[7]

In his portrayal of Pendennis, the over-impetuous, proud, young man, very conscious of his gentlemanly status, Thackeray makes various adjustments to reality – perfectly permissible in a novel – by which he began to create an image for himself in the public mind which acted as a shield from inquisitive intrusions on his privacy. Pen is, in many ways, close to Thackeray's younger self; but he is a simpler, luckier man than his creator, and the various dark secrets which the book contains are not his, but those of the characters surrounding him. Protected by his twin guardian angels, his mother and Laura, he is never in any real moral or practical danger, even when he appears to be about to sell his soul for ambition and money. Pen escapes, as Thackeray did not, from undergraduate excesses without impaired health (a venereal infection would have been unmentionable, of course). His gambling mania does not lead to irretrievable financial embarrassments, and he is only threatened by an improvident marriage, not faced with the consequences of an actual one. Pen is ploughed at his first attempt to take a degree, but returns to try again, and succeed. Thackeray never took his degree at all. The possession of a degree is of no more practical use to Pen than it would have been to Thackeray; but it is important in supporting the work ethic which was becoming the paradigm of Victorian middle-class masculine virtue. 'Men must work, and women must weep' – women must also, if they are to win Thackeray's overt approbation in his fiction, love unselfishly, passively and whole-heartedly.

'A Few Little Bills'

Laura's loan of five hundred pounds to set Pen up in the world strengthens the bond between them, and is promptly repaid; Thackeray took far longer to pay back his cousin Polly the same amount, and the entanglements of family finances after the collapse of *The Constitutional* led to years of wrangling between the Carmichael-Smyth brothers. He eventually found his cousin and adoptive sister so intolerable and their household so gloomy and eccentric that he no longer allowed his children to visit her. Thackeray's own period of keeping house with the Carmichaels convinced him they could never get on together: Mary was too disorganized, too pretentious, and worst of all, of so jealous a temperament that she spent her time brooding over imagined slights or insults to herself or her children. There was certainly never the close bond between the cousins that, for Pen and Laura, eventually overcomes all other entanglements and ends in marriage. According to Thackeray's account, Mary Carmichael's chief feeling for him, at least in adult life, was one of jealousy of the preferred and adored only son; a feeling Laura might reasonably have for Pen, but is too angelically good ever to entertain for a moment.

However, the darker side of Thackeray's own life does not go entirely unrepresented in the novel, though it takes a disguised form. It has often been pointed out that while Pen is a portrait of the young Thackeray, his sardonic and reductive mentor Warrington stands in for the older Thackeray, the ironic observer who has withdrawn from active participation in life to stand on the side-lines, advising and warning. 'Bluebeard', as old Lady Rockminster calls him, has a real skeleton in his cupboard, a vulgar and disreputable wife whom he keeps hidden by the sacrifice to her of his small income. He is therefore as effectively barred from making a serious relationship with Laura as if she were already married to Pen. It is an altered version of Thackeray's own situation at the time he was writing *Pendennis*, married and not married, and in love with a woman he could never hope to possess.

Pen's experience and Thackeray's do overlap with a frankness surprising for its date in one of the most important and psychologically interesting strands of the book, the exploration of the loving but uneasy relationship of an only son with his passionate, possessive, widowed mother. Perhaps *Pendennis* can be seen as containing Thackeray's attempt to write out of himself the intense relationship, half real, half fantasy, that had persisted since his childhood separation from his mother. 'When I was a boy at Larkbeare, I thought her an Angel & worshipped her. I see but a woman now, O so tender so loving so cruel.'[8] The climax of this relationship in the novel concerns Helen Pendennis's unwarranted assumption of Pen's seduction of Fanny

Bolton. This seems to have been based on an equally unfounded accusation by Mrs Carmichael-Smyth. Though Thackeray said, at the time he was writing *Pendennis*, that he hoped his mother would have behaved exactly as Helen Pendennis had done if he had got entangled with a 'naughty woman', he expressed it rather differently to Mrs Sartoris in 1855. In a letter which is frank about his dislike of her sister Fanny Kemble, while apologizing for his too open expression of it, he explains his sympathy for Fanny's husband, Pierce Butler, who had been accused of having an affair with the governess.

> the story of Jane Eyre, seduction, surreptitious family in the Regents Park, &c wh. you may or may not have heard, all grew out of this confounded tradition, ... & as the calumny has been the cause of a never-quite-mended quarrel and of the cruellest torture & annoyance to me, whenever I hear of poor gentlemen & poor governesses accused of this easy charge, I become wild and speak more no doubt from a sense of my own wrongs than theirs.'[9]

Pendennis contains a candid and searching portrait of the woman Thackeray now saw clearly, and, by conveniently killing off the character, enables Pen and Laura to forget the cruelty and enshrine the angel of his boyhood vision. But since they are already adults, there is something mawkish about the solution. David Copperfield's childhood loss of his mother makes his nostalgia for her and his attachment to Dora, in many ways so like her, entirely credible. Pen's substitution of his 'sister' Laura, his mother's choice for him, has always seemed unsatisfactory. Old Lady Rockminster spoke for many of Thackeray's readers in preferring 'Bluebeard' as a husband for her protégée. Laura and Pen are too much overshadowed by Helen's ghost in the closing chapters of the novel; one senses Mrs Carmichael-Smyth (who did not care for her fictional portrait) being placated by an attempt to reinstate the childish worship.

The characterization of Laura is, for a modern reader, perhaps the greatest barrier to an appreciation of the novel. Though Laura's situation in relation to the hero is based on that of Mary Graham, it is the character of Blanche Amory, with her literary pretensions, false sensibilities, and desire to dominate provincial society, that owes something to Thackeray's view of his cousin. The unbelievability of Laura has its roots elsewhere, and plays a larger part in weakening the novel's structure than the coarsely melodramatic treatment of the villain Altamont, which has sometimes been objected to. He, resuscitated from Thackeray's *Fraser's* days, given the name of one Yellowplush

Helen, Arthur and Laura (private version)

character, and the habits and tastes of another (Deuceace), slots easily
enough into the comic *demi-monde* of Captain Costigan and the
Chevalier Strong. Laura is meant to be taken seriously. (Whether the
fact that her name, Laura Bell, was that of a notorious *demi-mondaine*,
is meant to be a sardonic joke is questionable. The coincidence was
pointed out – in print at least – only after Thackeray's death.[10] He
certainly knew about the courtesan who had a liaison with a Nepalese
prince, Jung Bahadoor, who figures in Thackeray's comic poem 'Mr
Molony's Account of the Ball'. She was the subject of some of the
bawdy songs sung, after midnight when the innocents like Clive
Newcome and his father had left, at Evans's Supper Rooms, one of
Thackeray's regular haunts. If it is a joke, it is one that would have been
appreciated only by male readers; another example of the gulf that is
shown, in the novel, to exist between male and female worlds.)

In *Vanity Fair* the balance of interest between the two girls is not
evenly held, and Thackeray was perhaps trying to correct this by giving

Laura a succession of rivals, rather than a single permanent opponent, so that he might not again be accused of making vice more interesting than virtue. The reader's interest in her plight should be strengthened; yet she is as tiresome a female figure as Thackeray ever drew. Some of the first readers of *Pendennis* felt this, though others complained that she was 'too good' for Pen and should have been allowed to marry Warrington. Her 'goodness' is mostly passive and self-abnegatory: she early learns to 'suffer and be still', like one of Mrs Ellis's Women of England. But, given Laura's origins, and Helen's attitude to her, this is a plausible reaction, and could still have been made interesting. Amelia does not lose credibility as fortune's blows rain on her. Laura does, in spite of some moments of rebellion. She refuses Pen's first, insultingly half-hearted proposal, knowing that he is offering marriage only to please his mother. She supports Helen in her scornful dismissal of Fanny Bolton from Pen's bedside, and is, for once, included in the narrative's condemnation of the cruelty of respectable women to their less fortunate sisters. She falls briefly in love with Warrington; though this is never given more than the status of a passing fancy, and seems less poignant than Fanny's infatuation with Pen. There is the potential for a serious portrait of an independent-minded young woman in the novel, yet all the opportunities given by the plot are passed by. It is not until the creation of Ethel Newcome that Thackeray showed he could in fact create a 'good' young woman with a mind of her own.

The lack of impression Laura makes on the reader can partly be blamed on the language in which she is described. Thackeray is too concerned to force his reader's compliance by narrative commentary; and whereas a description of Pen as 'our young friend Arthur Pendennis' works because of the edge of irony it contains, given the reader's knowledge of Pen's faults and foibles, 'our Laura' seems merely a coy attempt to circumvent the difficult business of making a virtuous character come alive. (When Henry James does something similar, referring to Maggie Verver in *The Golden Bowl* as 'our young woman', the phrase is carefully placed to reawaken the bewildered reader's sympathies for a character whose portrait is by no means unambiguously drawn.)

Laura's reality is not strengthened, either, by a distinctive tone of voice. Other characters in *Pendennis* are memorable for affectations, as Blanche is, with her over-emphases and schoolgirl French; or for slang, up-to-the-minute like Foker's, or out-of-date like the Major's; or for various kinds of substandard English, such as the Irishisms of Emily and Captain Costigan or the cockney of the Boltons. Much of the interest and humour of the novel comes from the verbal clashes registered by

Thackeray's acute ear, and the way in which characters are placed by their speech. Laura is too respectfully treated, and her quiet tone is only really effective in the passages of dialogue with Blanche, where it gains authority from the contrast with the affectations of the authoress of 'Mes Larmes'.

> 'Tell me everything. I already love you as a sister.'
> 'You are very kind,' said Miss Bell, smiling, 'and – and it must be owned that it is a very sudden attachment.'
> 'All attachments are so. It is electricity – spontaneity. It is instantaneous. I knew I should love you from the moment I saw you. Do you not feel it yourself?'
> 'Not yet,' said Laura; 'but I daresay I shall if I try.' (*Pendennis*, Chapter 22, *Works*, 12, p. 275)

Here Laura gains the reader's sympathy by her reticence and sense of humour, but a modern reader's assent is not easily won by passages like this:

> A smile heavenly pure, a glance of unutterable tenderness, sympathy, pity, shone in her face – all which indications of love and purity Arthur beheld and worshipped in her as you would watch them in a child, as one fancies one might regard them in an angel. (*Pendennis*, Chapter 71, *Works*, 12, p. 915)

'Why fails my pencil'

The clue to the failure of Laura lies, I believe, in the development of Thackeray's relationship with Jane Brookfield from 1847 onwards. When he tried to draw her face he confessed he came nowhere near a likeness. He wrote her a poem 'A Failure', implicitly connecting his inability with the hopelessness of their relationship.

> Each individual feature lies
> Within my heart so faithful writ
> Why fails my pencil when it tries
> Continually to copy it?
>
> What's life but this? – a cancelled sheet
> A laugh disguising a defeat,
> Let's tear and laugh and own it so.[11]

Her tone of voice, and the complexities of her character seem also to have eluded him. Because of the peculiar nature of their situation, in which he was licensed, for a while at least, to adore his friend's wife, while knowing that he could not expect anything but sisterly friendship in return, this third great love of his life was the most unreal of all. The little boy who temporarily lost his mother, and so embalmed an unnaturally idealized picture of her in his heart, corrected that portrait gradually in adult life. His letters, and the portrayal of Helen Pendennis, show that he had become quite clear-sighted about her possessiveness, and the melancholy religiosity which she developed after settling in France. The young man who found himself a child-bride untouched by the compromises of the world, and lost her again to a perpetual childlike twilight, finally gave up his dream of recovering her as his own youth disappeared. But the middle-aged man who fell in love with an impossible object, a pure, virginal, married woman, who became a substitute for those earlier dreams, never entirely recovered from his adoration of her, and its outcome. The passage about Laura's childlike and angelic qualities is very close in tone to the many references to his feelings for Jane Brookfield in his letters from 1847 to 1850.

He called her 'Madonna', and his dear sister, and assured her husband, in an apology for an occasion in 1847 when he had displayed 'uncouth raptures' and Brookfield had for the first time objected to the warmth of his feeling for her, that he loved her with exactly the same pure love as he felt for his daughter Minny.[12] He exaggerated her illnesses in the early years of her marriage, attributing them in part to marital disharmony, but at the same time taking them so seriously that he feared she would die.[13] Whatever the nature of her illness was, it obliged her to lie about on sofas a good deal during 1847 and 1848. In one letter she apologizes for her handwriting, which, never very tidy at the best of times, is here execrable, and explains that she has to lie completely flat.[14] This suggests the possibility of a threatened, or actual, miscarriage. In December 1848 Thackeray sent her a copy of Dickens's story 'The Haunted Man', because, though he hadn't read it all through himself, his mother thought Jane would find it personally affecting.[15] The story has an account of a woman's grief for her stillborn child. 'When I think of all those hopes I built upon it, and the many times I sat and pictured to myself the little smiling face upon my bosom that never lay there, ... I can feel a greater tenderness, I think, for all the disappointed hopes in which there is no harm.'[16]

Far from dying prematurely, Jane survived to bear three children, and outlived Thackeray, her husband, her daughter, and many of her contemporaries, to become an extremely tough old lady. Henriette Corkran remembered meeting her 'tramping about in rain, hail and snow, or seated in omnibuses'.[17] After Thackeray's death she published several mediocre novels. Two of them, *Only George*, published in 1866, and *Not Too Late*, which appeared two years later, have plots which are reminiscent of the Brookfield/Thackeray triangle. In the first the girl marries the wrong man, but widowhood conveniently restores her to the arms of 'George', whose character is described in terms which suggest Thackeray's. In the second, the girl is engaged to a curate whose violent and gloomy jealousy match traits that Thackeray complained of in Brookfield.

In later years Jane made more direct use of Thackeray's infatuation for her, selling, in 1887, many of his letters to her, for publication in

Jane Brookfield on her sofa

expurgated versions. The correspondence with Scribners, the original publishers, makes it clear that this was for the sake of the couple of hundred pounds it brought her, hardly a fortune even then, and though she wrote of 'sacrificing her personal feelings'[18] and claimed to believe that the letters would appear only in the United States, it was inevitable that they would be published in England as well. Her action shocked Anny, and would have horrified Thackeray. To read his letters to her, and to Kate Perry and Jane Elliot, the sisters who became his confidantes after the break with the Brookfields, when he could no longer communicate with Jane directly, and then to read those of hers to him which have survived, and hers to her husband, is to be aware of an immense emotional gulf.

She seems to have encouraged Thackeray's devotion to her by cautiously hinting that her marriage was unhappy. In October 1848 they spent a few nights under the same roof, at her family home, Clevedon Court, near Bristol, for the first and only time, and something occurred – probably no more than an intimate conversation and a chaste embrace – which was a turning-point in Thackeray's feeling for her. He wrote her a letter in French afterwards, of which the English transcript in *The Letters and Private Papers* is a slightly watered-down version. In it he recalls, in highly emotional terms, her 'chère (petite) voix qui m'appeloit dans la nuit à Clevedon', and sees himself as one of the damned, and her as an angel taking pity on him.[19] Writing to Jane in April 1850, when he had been rereading the early chapters of *Pendennis*, he recalled his sufferings:

I remembered allusions wh. called back recollections of particular states of mind. The first part of that book was written after Clevedon in '48 – que de souffrances![20]

In January 1849 Jane's uncle Henry Hallam protested at Thackeray's intimacy with her. Their brother-and-sisterly relationship was becoming an embarrassment for the family, and though there was no suggestion of impropriety, Thackeray was, none too gently, warned off. He reacted indignantly, again claiming the entire innocence of his feelings. Nevertheless, it was a terrible shock when he was told in July 1849 that she was pregnant. He managed at last to be happy for her sake, and to hope that she would find in motherhood the happiness that was no longer present in her marriage. But the pregnancy forced him to recognize that she was not a sexless angel, but a married woman with a newly strengthened bond with her husband.

The child, born in February 1850, was a daughter, Magdalene. She grew up to strengthen the links between the Brookfield and Thackeray families by marrying one of the Ritchies, and becoming Anny's sister-in-law; by then Thackeray was long dead, but he would have appreciated such an ending to the story. Her name was an extremely unpopular one in an age when it was a synonym for a prostitute: one wonders whether her father, who apparently chose it, was expressing his liberal attitude to 'fallen women', or making an ironic point about Thackeray's 'Madonna' worship. Thackeray was prevented from seeing Jane and the baby for more than two months. Refused admittance to the house, he fled abroad, as was his habit in moments of emotional crisis. It was not a final break, 'the chain pulls tighter the farther I am away from you,' he wrote from Paris,[21] but he was forced to acknowledge his jealousy of Jane's husband and to face the sexual content of his love for her. From this point the eventual explosion became inevitable, though, by the exercise of caution on both sides, it was delayed for a further eighteen months.

Throughout these personal upheavals, Thackeray continued to force himself to the writing and illustrating of *Pendennis*. Apart from the effect of the Brookfield entanglement on the character of Laura, there is a more generalized struggle within the novel with the imprisoning forces of convention. *Pendennis* contains a series of exciting and disturbing situations, all potentially disruptive of the social order. The narrative repeatedly presents the reader with the possibility that the world of the novel – which, if not identical with that of the reader, is cognate with, and parallel to it – may be changed by the deliberate action of a character. But each time the outcome is evasive: the social order is re-established, and the subversive character is, in one way or another, punished for the attempt. At the outset, the adolescent hero is threatening to 'ruin' himself and his family by an unsuitable marriage to an older woman, of a lower social class, who is an actress in a second-rate touring company. The episode is one of high comedy which serves to introduce two of the novel's best characters: Major Pendennis, who handles the situation with a worldly tact which the reader whole-heartedly admires, and Captain Costigan, the most fully developed of Thackeray's ebullient Irish drunks. The verve and humour with which the story is told, which start the novel off at a high level of enjoyment, conceal, for the moment, the questions about the social structure of nineteenth-century England which Thackeray has very much in mind. Here the possibility that a man might marry (rather than just have an affair with) an actress is dangled before the reader; later in the novel

Major Pendennis to the rescue

'The Manager from London'

Emily Costigan does achieve total respectability by a marriage to a nobleman. From the outset she is presented as a thoroughly respectable, good-humoured, good-hearted girl, though a stupid and uneducated one; she is a development of the earlier Ravenswing. Yet it is made clear that narrator and reader are expected to agree that it would be a disaster for Pen to marry her.

Costigan and Major Pendennis

Such possibilities are raised throughout the novel. The possibility that a servant – albeit a rather grand servant – can fall in love with a lady (rather a dubious lady) – as the chef Mirobolant does with Blanche Amory. Or the possibility, raised and then denied by the preface, that an author can show in a novel what really goes on in the world of men from which 'decent' women are excluded, including the seduction of working-class girls by young men-about-town. This leads on to the possibility that young gentlemen may, even should, marry such girls. Most dramatically presented is the possibility that a servant can dare to turn the tables on a bullying, mean employer, as the Major's valet Morgan does, and triumph over him. Finally, at the level of emotional rather than external action, there is the possibility that a mother's love is not always as straightforward as it seems and can be corrosive and destructive when it treats an adult as if he were still a child, or worships him as a god:

> that anxiety with which brooding women watch over their son's affections – and in acknowledging which, I have no doubt there is a sexual jealousy on the mother's part, and a secret pang. (*Pendennis*, Chapter 24, *Works*, 12, p. 298)

The statement in *Vanity Fair* that 'Mother is the name for God in the lips and hearts of little children'[22] (bitter rather than sentimental in its context, since it refers to little Rawdon's worship of Becky) is implicitly reversed in Helen's attitude to her far from godlike son.

However, all these potential alterations of the status quo are dealt with and reversed before they get out of hand. Emily Costigan is awarded an effete elderly nobleman as a husband, and the implication is that they deserve each other. The curate, Smirke, is punished with ridicule for his effrontery in aspiring to marry Helen Pendennis, as is Mirobolant for his attachment to Blanche. Mirobolant is based on the famous and much-respected Alexis Soyer, whom Thackeray knew personally, who was responsible for transforming the arrangements for feeding the troops in the Crimea; yet he is portrayed as a stage Frenchman, a nineteenth-century comic stereotype. In each case Pen's self-righteous horror is gently mocked, but seen as a correct, if exaggerated, reaction.

The relationship of Major Pendennis and his servant Morgan is carefully built up throughout the novel to show how little there is to choose between the two men, who work as a team to bring about the Major's devious plans. The Major assumes complacently that Morgan does not know anything he is not supposed to know, while Morgan is secretly at work on his own behalf. 'Morgan Pendennis', as he is known in the exclusive servants' club which parodies his master's (and whose meetings are held, appropriately enough, in the Wheel of Fortune public house), even speaks with the Major's old-fashioned slang and pronunciation, identifies himself with the Major's toadying and tuft-hunting, and, to the outside world, speaks of the Major as 'we': 'We've been intimate with the fust statesmen of Europe. When we go abroad we dine with Prince Metternich and Louy Philup reg'lar.'[23] His patience under the Major's petty tyranny evokes at least a qualified sympathy from the reader, and his moment of triumph in Chapter 67, 'In which the Major is bidden to stand and deliver', when he reveals that he is considerably richer than his master, and even owns the house in which the Major is a lodger, is exhilarating.

I've bought the place, I tell you, with my own industry and perseverance. I can show a hundred pound, where you can show fifty, or your damned supersellious nephew either. I've served you honourable, done every-think for you these dozen years, and I'm a dog, am I? I'm a beast, am I? That's the language for gentlemen, not for our rank. But I'll bear it no more. I throw up your service; I'm tired on it; I've combed your old wig and buckled your old girths and waistbands long enough, I tell you. Don't look savage at me, I'm sitting in my own chair, in my own room, a-telling the truth to you. I'll be your beast and your brute, and your dog no more, Major Pendennis 'Alf Pay.

Morgan triumphant

The reader agrees with the Major's immediate reaction: 'Morgan's speech had interested him, and he rather respected his adversary, and his courage in facing him.' But while it is quite in character for the Major to decide fairly rapidly that Morgan must be brought low, and quite in character for Morgan to attempt to blackmail his ex-employer, it seems unconvincing for Morgan to be shown up as an abject coward, easily terrified by a pistol which, as the Major reminds him, he knows perfectly well hasn't been loaded 'these fifteen years'. The courage he has shown in the preceding scene simply doesn't allow for so rapid a change. But the truth of the character has to give way to the needs of the plot: Major Pendennis, obsolete, immoral and ridiculous old snob though he is, still has a part to play as the hero's uncle, quite unconvincingly reformed on the last page by the sickeningly pious Laura:

> Major Pendennis became very serious in his last days, and was never so happy as when Laura was reading to him with her sweet voice, or listening to his stories. For this sweet lady is the friend of the young and the old; and her life is always passed in making other lives happy. (*Pendennis*, Chapter 74 *Works*, 12, p. 976)

The slackness of this writing, with its meaningless repetitions of 'happy' and 'sweet' is a long way from the ironic and ambivalent farewell to Amelia and Dobbin in *Vanity Fair*. Morgan, whose parliamentary ambitions seemed more ridiculous to Thackeray and his readers than they would have done after the Second Reform Bill, is given a more lively send-off, neatly placed as a radical agitator in the phrase, 'in the present political movement has pronounced himself like a man and a Briton'. In the last sentence of the book, a page later, the reader is asked to 'give a hand of charity to Arthur Pendennis, with all his faults and shortcomings, who does not claim to be a hero, but only a man and a brother'. The juxtaposition of the two phrases, both originating in the Abolitionist propaganda poster showing a slave asking, 'Am I not a Man and a Brother?' would have been significant in *Vanity Fair*, where Thackeray, as an old *Fraser's* writer, uses the phrase as Maginn and his contributors had done, in a way which makes clear it has become a cliché and a joke. In *Pendennis* it seems as though the irony is unintended.

Thackeray was aware of the unevenness of the writing in *Pendennis*, and often referred to dissatisfaction with the book in his letters. He had an excuse for the shortcomings of the latter part of the book which was nothing to do with his personal unhappiness. At the end of August

1849, when he was writing Number XI (Chapters 33 to 36), he made a rapid visit to Paris to see Mrs Halliday, his father's sister, who was dying, stayed to comfort her old husband, and visited the Ritchies and Bess Hamerton: 'If there has been one virtuous man in Paris it is Madam's most obajient servant,' he told Jane Brookfield.[24]

A few days after his return in the middle of September he developed a dangerous illness, almost certainly cholera, then reaching epidemic proportions throughout the country. He told one correspondent that the doctor thought it had been 'intermittent fever' (or malaria) but treatment with quinine did him no good.[25] He was alone in the house, except for the servants. The children were on an extended visit to Wales with their grandparents, in one of the gaps between governesses. Their absence saved him from the attentions of the homoeopathic doctors favoured by the Carmichael-Smyths and distrusted by Thackeray, though at least one homoeopath, Dr John Drysdale of Liverpool, apparently achieved spectacular successes with cholera patients in the 1849 epidemic. Thackeray himself believed that he owed his life to the care of Dr John Elliotson, the maverick doctor whose experiments with hypnotism had caused his expulsion from the Chair of Medicine at University College, London, and brought him the friendship of Dickens. John Forster, putting aside their literary and personal differences, brought him to Thackeray's bedside. Thackeray, in gratitude, dedicated the interrupted novel to the doctor, and included him in it as 'Dr Goodenough' who saves Pen's life and is the only person round the sick-bed to appreciate and sympathize with Fanny Bolton.

Thackeray was severely ill for ten days, but well taken care of by his servants, and friends supplied invalid food and visited him regularly. By the beginning of October he was well enough to complain that the doctor had taken his soup away, and by the time his mother had been informed and had rushed ahead of the children and her husband, arriving by 17 October, he was out of danger, though still extremely weak. 'How thin and changed, with what great wan eyes my father looked at us when we reached home and were allowed to go up to his room to see him in his bed,' Anny remembered.[26] By 22 October he had the courage to fly to Brighton with his manservant, who wheeled him out on the pier in a Bath-chair. He always insisted that 'Dr Brighton' did him good, and he gradually recovered his strength.

He came back to London at the beginning of November, and was soon at work again, in spite of the troubles and gloom which the presence of his mother in the household seemed to bring as she grew older. This time she was laid up with severe rheumatism, 'restless and moaning', devotedly attended by her husband. Thackeray saw more of

Helen and Arthur (public version)

the children than he had ever done before, and rejoiced that Anny, now twelve and a half, was 'almost a young woman, and will soon be a capital companion for me'.[27] He was still not completely well, and from this time until his death suffered increasingly from bouts of illness. In December he complained to Jane Brookfield of having done 'a poor drivelling days work' on *Pendennis*, which had been interrupted first by the illness, and then by the writing of *Rebecca and Rowena*, begun during his convalescence and timed to catch the Christmas market. The burden of work still included his pieces for *Punch* and other miscellaneous journalism as well as the novel, and the presence of the printer's devil sitting in the hall became more and more oppressive. 'My

The author in difficulties

young ones said to me just now Papa how will you get through your plates and your Punch and your Xmas book and your Pendennis?' he complained as he was writing the penultimate number in October 1850.[28] The last dozen chapters of *Pendennis*, though they still contain good things, betray a sense of exhaustion and a lack of enthusiasm that is not surprising in the circumstances.

He finished the final double number on 26 November 'very tired and weary & solemn minded'.[29] But almost immediately he was at work again, preparing the lectures on *The English Humourists of the Eighteenth Century* that he had arranged to give the following May. He was also thinking about 'a better subject for a novel than any I've yet had'.[30] The sadness of attending Harry Hallam's funeral at Clevedon, soon to be used as the setting for *Esmond*, was succeeded by a cheerful Christmas party at the Wiltshire house of Sir John Cam Hobhouse, the friend of Thackeray's *bête noire* Byron. Peacock was one of the party; 'a whiteheaded jolly old worldling', whose novels Thackeray admired. 'It is eating and idling all day long: but not altogether profitless idling.'[31] Though he was sorry to be away from his family and Jane Brookfield, the old-fashioned country-house world was a useful way of getting into the mood of the eighteenth century, the setting for his writings of the

following year. 'If you live with great folks, why should you not
describe their manners?' he wrote apologetically to Mrs Gore.³² He was
coming to appreciate that there might be literary material for him, too,
in the company of the great, even if his radical and evangelical
upbringing still caused him twinges of unease as he enjoyed the good life
it provided.

Pendennis was published by Smith, Elder in two volumes in
December 1850 as soon as the last number had been issued. It appeared
simultaneously with Thackeray's Christmas book for that year, *The
Kickleburys on the Rhine*. The critics were enthusiastic about the novel
and took the opportunity to sum up Thackeray's achievements, ranking
him with Dickens. The Christmas book, a loosely narrated comic
account of the English middle classes abroad, was not so well received.
Thackeray was again accused of cynicism; satire was considered
inappropriate for a Christmas offering, and more than one reviewer
called the story 'unhealthy'. *The Times* reviewer attacked him unmerci-
fully for snobbery, carelessness and unjustifiable cruelty: 'playfully
fastening his satiric fangs upon the familiar prey, he dallies with it in
mimic ferocity like a satiated mouser'.³³ Thackeray made the tactical
error of writing a preface to the second edition, 'Of Thunder and Small
Beer', pointing out the disproportion between his slight piece and the
weight of the attack on it. The tag of cynicism which now seemed to be
attached to everything he wrote increasingly annoyed him. It was unfair
that he, who had tried for truth before all, and considered his calling as
serious 'as the parson's own', should be so persistently mislabelled. He
began to spell out the message more simply, and to abandon the
ambiguity and indirection of his earlier method.

Increasingly, in his letters and his conversation, he expressed a
disillusionment and weariness with 'the novel business'. Writing –
novel-writing as well as the ephemeral pieces for *Punch* and the other
journals – now began to seem just another way of making money, and
of gaining social acceptance. Such worldliness shocked Charlotte
Brontë, whose earlier hero-worship of Thackeray had been somewhat
dented by her meeting with him in 1849 and 1850. She had been upset
by his unthinking betrayal of her authorship of *Jane Eyre*, when it was
still a secret to the world at large, and distressed by his 'cynicism' in
conversation, though she still thought him 'great, interesting, and
sometimes good and kind'.³⁴ She was grateful to her publisher George
Smith for discouraging Thackeray from sending her a copy of
Pendennis: 'To have spoken my mind would have been to displease.'³⁵
She felt that he was now betraying his great gifts, spending the time
when he should have been struggling with his work on a meaningless

social round. The eagle who wrote *Vanity Fair* had become, she felt, the tame pet of countesses and marchionesses.

His anxiety over money, and reasonable fears of premature death induced by his illness, led Thackeray to consider other ways of putting something by for his children and their mother. Carlyle's lectures (Thackeray had attended the series *Heroes and Hero Worship* in 1842), provided a respectable precedent, his favourite eighteenth-century writers a promising subject. At one of the worst moments of his life, with Isabella showing the first signs of madness, he had managed to write a lively piece on Fielding. Now, through the early months of 1851, he immersed himself in the history and literature of the eighteenth century, with his historical novel always at the back of his mind.

Chapter 9

Esmond: The Power of the Past

At certain periods of life we live years of emotion
in a few weeks – and look back on those times, as on great gaps between
the old life and the new. You do not know how much you
suffer in those critical maladies of the heart,
until the disease is over and you
look back on it afterwards.

Esmond, Book II, Chapter 1.

The six lectures on the *English Humourists of the Eighteenth Century*
were given at Willis's Rooms, in a gilded saloon more often used for
Almack's balls. Charlotte Brontë was scornful of the surroundings and
the fashionable audience, but thought the lectures well composed and
delivered.[1] Thackeray's ease and simplicity were surprising, since he
had always been a poor public speaker ever since his undergraduate
failure, and regularly broke down when making after-dinner speeches.
In private, though reserved with strangers and people he did not like, he
could be an amusing conversationalist. He now managed to put this
aspect of himself across to his audiences. Bagehot recalled how, in his
lecture on Sterne, he reduced his audience to helpless laughter by his
way of reading the novelist's early sentimental letters to his wife, and
then later ones of a very different tone.[2] Not all his auditors were
enthusiastic, however. Carlyle fidgeted, looking at his watch, through
what seemed to him a superficial and unimpressive display.[3] Forster,
reviewing the lectures in the *Examiner*, dismissed them as 'literary
entertainment', a judgement Thackeray of course attributed to social
envy.[4]

For a modern reader, the lectures have not worn well. They now
seem anecdotal and scrappy, deliberately designed to discuss the
subjects' lives and not their writings, and displaying more personal
prejudice than literary judgement. The authors discussed become
fictional characters, waiting to play their parts in the next Thackeray
novel. Though lip-service is paid to the idea of *autres temps autres
moeurs*, his chosen authors are all seen through the prism of accepted
Victorian morality, and admired or condemned for their degree of

conformity to it. Thackeray is pandering to the expressed tastes and opinions of his visible, fashionable audience far more closely than he had ever done when writing for an invisible one. Even so he was not always immune from attack. His tolerant attitude to Fielding's novels was thought 'dangerously wrong' by Charlotte Brontë. She wrote, obviously with Branwell in mind: 'Had Thackeray owned a son, grown or growing up, and a son brilliant but reckless – would he have spoken in that light way of courses that lead to disgrace and the grave?'[5] Elizabeth Gaskell reported overhearing a strong objection to the same lecture when it was given in Manchester, as 'calculated to do moral harm'.[6] However careful Thackeray attempted to be, the accusations of levity and cynicism followed him still.

The chief interest of the lectures now lies in their discussion of other writers in terms of Thackeray's own literary and moral preoccupations. Swift is a 'week-day preacher'; but the Horatian Thackeray dislikes his fierce, Juvenalian satire, and he is attacked for his treatment of women and children. Steele, who, like Addison, was educated at the Charterhouse, is perceived as one of Thackeray's good-hearted but erring schoolboys: 'Kind, lazy, and good-natured, this boy went invariably into debt with the tart-woman, ran out of bounds, and entered into pecuniary or rather promissory engagements with the neighbouring lollipop vendors and piemen.' Steele is turned into an eighteenth-century Pendennis or Clive Newcome. He is also commended for being 'the first of our writers who really admired and respected women', and consequently overvalued as a writer. But the gulf between the eighteenth and the nineteenth centuries is still perceived as wide. Thackeray cannot bring himself to quote the brilliant but 'immoral' Congreve, and asserts: 'You could no more suffer, in a British drawing-room, under the reign of Queen Victoria, a fine gentleman or fine lady of Queen Anne's time, or hear what they heard and said, than you would receive an ancient Briton.' Thackeray, about to write the 'autobiography' of a 'fine gentleman' of Queen Anne's time, seems to be almost wilfully gagging himself in advance. His view of 'manly Harry Fielding' as he persistently calls him, is a reductive one, which sees Fielding as 'himself the hero of his books' and grossly underestimates the subtlety of his art. It has less of interest to say about his predecessor than the article of 1840.

The London lectures over, Thackeray went abroad for a holiday with his daughters, their first extended trip alone with him, and one which Anny recalled with enthusiasm in her reminiscences. They were away for six weeks, and Thackeray celebrated, rather glumly, his fortieth birthday. They travelled through Germany, Switzerland, Italy, Austria,

Anny and Minny

and came home via Weimar, where Thackeray nostalgically showed his children the scenes of his youth and introduced them to his old tutor, Weissenborn, and to Frau von Goethe. They also saw the former Melanie von Spiegel, now grown unrecognizably fat and middle-aged. Thackeray, wiser than Dickens with Maria Beadnell, stole away without making himself known to her.

The girls, Anny in particular, whom he described as 'a fat lump of pure gold – the kindest dearest creature as well as a wag of the first order'[7] were now old enough to be real companions. 'O may she never fall in love absurdly and marry an ass!' he prayed. Minny, aged eleven, was more unpredictable and 'Beckyfied'. But in general the three of them got on excellently, away from 'that baseness of London'. Travelling as a paterfamilias had its problems, though. He found it necessary to hurry away from 'the impure atmosphere' of Baden, and was 'shy' of people who were 'queer-looking or queer-speaking' – the very people who had so often provided the raw material of his fiction. The 'poor devil' of ten years back had been very different. 'He was a better fellow than the one you know perhaps,' he wrote to Jane Brookfield. 'I was a boy, 10 years ago, bleating out my simple griefs in the Great Hoggarty Diamond.'[8] This long, chatty, intimate letter – gently complaining at not having heard from her, even for his birthday – was to be the last he was to write her before disastrous and complicated griefs overtook their relationship.

In *Pendennis* Thackeray had worked external aspects of his life, available to anyone who took the trouble to inquire into his early years, into a good-humoured and entertaining novel. *The History of Henry*

WMT as Cupid

Esmond was in part an expression of his wish for literary respectability and the kind of status enjoyed by his boyhood hero, Scott. It was his intention to raise the genre of the historical novel from the depths to which it had fallen in the hands of Ainsworth, Bulwer Lytton and the prolific G. P. R. James. *Rebecca and Rowena* had been an affectionate and not very serious pastiche; *Esmond* was intended to rival *Waverley*. But the troubles brewing up in his personal life were to change the book irrevocably, and, paradoxically, the historical novel which had no obvious relationship to his own circumstances reveals far more of his inner life (as he acknowledged himself to those who knew him well) than the preceding *Bildungsroman*. In a letter to his mother he called his hero 'a handsome likeness of an ugly son of yours'.⁹

Esmond marks a watershed in Thackeray's creative life, as the break with the Brookfields did in his personal one. He might continue to speculate wistfully on the possibility of an eventual marriage with Jane, if Brookfield and Isabella were both conveniently to die, but he knew it was an impossible fantasy. Even at the height of his misery he retained a certain objectivity about his feelings. 'Very likely it's *a* woman I want more than any particular one . . . The want of this natural outlet plays the deuce with me. Why can't I fancy some honest woman to be a titular Mrs Tomkins? . . . What can any body do for me? Nobody can do nothing: for say I got my desire, I should despise a woman; and the very day of the sacrifice would be the end of the attachment.'¹⁰ For the last decade of his life his mood was elegiac, and his personal satisfactions domestic, or small-scale and temporary. *Esmond* was the last novel with which he consistently took pains, and tried something new. After that, though there are still flashes of the old fire, his fiction tends to work over old themes, and reuse old characters, with skill and charm, but with an increasing sense of *vanitas vanitatum*. Trollope, who admired Thackeray's skill in adopting an eighteenth-century tone in *Esmond*, felt, rightly I think, that he never quite succeeded in dropping it again.[11]

He returned to London in the third week of August, to find the Brookfields seriously at odds with each other, William Brookfield treating his wife, so Thackeray considered, as no gentleman ought to treat a lady, with contempt and abuse. It seems that Thackeray was present at some of their quarrels, and took Jane's part, which, since he was himself the underlying cause of their estrangement, made things worse and led inevitably to the row between himself and Brookfield, at which Jane was present. This seems to have taken place on or about 22 September. A painfully intense letter in French survives from this period. Ostensibly addressed to Kate Perry, his channel of communication with Jane when he could not write direct, it expresses the extent to which his love occupied the whole of his life and thoughts, day and night. He knows she does not love him; but at least she allows herself to be loved by him.[12] After the final row, it was to Kate Perry that he wrote on 23 September. He told her that Brookfield had 'spoken out like a man', and that the affair was at an end. He had deliberately attacked Brookfield in exaggerated terms, to make Jane side with her husband, and admitted he had said something (unspecified) 'quite unjustifiable'.[13]

As usual, Thackeray fled the scene, going to Matlock, where he visited Chatsworth, and met both the Duke of Devonshire and his head gardener Paxton, designer of the Crystal Palace, and was shown round the house. 'I had a great mind to say "Show me the Bluebeard Closet where the dead wives and the murdered secrets are: you must have a Bluebeard Closet – everybody has one." '[14] He had never been good at hiding his emotions; now he found it quite impossible, and his mother and Anny were very well aware of what was going on. Since there had been no physical relationship, he felt himself innocent of blame, and even unjustly injured by Brookfield's intervention. In many letters to his women correspondents, not only to his mother, Jane Elliott, and Kate Perry, but to those who were not so close, such as Mary Holmes, Lady Ashburton, Lady Stanley, and later on Mrs Baxter in New York, he poured out his grief and self-justification. Through all this, he was writing *Esmond*, conscious of the extent to which his state of mind was being reflected in the story. 'I am writing a book of cut-throat melancholy suitable to my state,' he told Lady Stanley,[15] and to his mother he wrote with premature optimism a few weeks later, 'I shall write it better now that the fierceness of a certain pain is over.'[16]

The raw, unmediated emotion of the early part of the novel still has a powerful effect on the reader, all the more poignant when one knows the situation that gave rise to it. Towards the end of the first volume, his obsession with the idea of unhappy marriage and the wrongs that wives suffer from tyrannical husbands begins to unbalance the book; it was perhaps fortunate that the novel was not published serially, for readers would surely have lost interest as the story lost impetus. The letters to Kate Perry show his emotions raging backwards and forwards: in one Jane is an angel who has given up everything for her husband: 'Youth and happiness and now her dearest friend – what a friend – and to what a man – a fellow that says to her face he ought to have married a cook, and treats her like one.'[17] But at another moment he feels that he has been played with and made a fool of by a woman who never had any real feeling for him. 'I was packing away yesterday the letters of years. These didn't make me cry. They made me laugh as I knew they would. It was for this that I gave my heart away.'[18] And while still protesting the purity of his love, he had to admit, 'I have loved his wife too much to be able to bear to see her belong even to her husband any more.'[19]

At the end of October a meeting was arranged by Lady Ashburton, who invited the Brookfields and Thackeray to her country house, The Grange, where after some 'parleys' the two Williams shook hands. 'Friends of course we're not; but bear each other.'[20] The formal encounter marked the final ending of the intimate phase of the relationship. Soon afterwards the Brookfields left England to spend the winter in Madeira. Brookfield was thought to be tubercular, though Thackeray had his doubts; at all events the trip came at a convenient moment for all concerned. (In February Thackeray reported to his mother that 'Brookfield has got immensely better, and read a play of Shakspeare to a delighted audience at Funchal ... There are other comedies being acted too comedies upon comedies.')[21] When they returned the following May, the acquaintance was cautiously resumed, but it was never to be on the old footing again.

Thackeray set off on the first of his highly successful lecture tours: to Oxford and Cambridge first, then to Scotland, writing *Esmond* as he went. He was scornful of these 'tightrope walking' performances. He liked to be admired by his equals, or betters, but never threw himself into public performance with the emotional fervour of Dickens. He read, rather than declaiming, without gesture, and with his voice only just raised above a conversational tone. He was determined that his

The lecturer as tightrope walker

manner should be gentlemanly, even if he felt secretly that the pursuit was not.

He had hoped to have the novel finished by January, but the lecturing interfered with writing, and he was not done with it until the end of May, though there were, this time, no illustrations to cope with. *Esmond* was the only novel by Thackeray not to appear serially, and not to be illustrated. It was also the first of his novels to be partly dictated, to Eyre Crowe, now his secretary, and to some extent to Anny. Smith, Elder paid him £1,000 for the initial rights, more than he had ever been offered before, terms which delighted him. They also agreed to his stipulations about the way in which it should be presented. Thackeray wanted it to look as much as possible like a genuine eighteenth-century novel, and Smith managed to find an old type-face with the long s, and produced it in three handsomely bound octavo volumes. The text of the novel, too, is a careful pastiche of eighteenth-century style and spelling: words and phrases – 'musick' 'recal' 'says she' – are used to give a period flavour, but sparingly, so that they do not hold up the story or distance the reader too much from the characters. There are some anachronisms and inaccuracies, but Thackeray took care with his research. He lamented that he could not spend another six months on the novel; and in a double-edged phrase said that 'there's a deal of pains in it that goes for nothing'.[22]

The real objection to his historicity lies not in lack of research, but in the suffocating blanket of Victorian respectability which weighs down the eighteenth-century action. Esmond is a Victorian gentleman rather than one of the age of Anne; Rachel a middle-class 'angel in the house' instead of the wife of a powerful Stuart aristocrat. Thackeray himself came to feel that Esmond was, as he said to Trollope, a prig. Nineteenth-century readers who could not stomach *Vanity Fair* found

Esmond much more to their taste. Harriet Martineau thought it '*the* book of the century, in its department'.[23] There was some outrage expressed at the near-incestuous union of Rachel and Esmond at the end of the book – George Eliot found it, for this reason, 'the most uncomfortable book you can imagine'.[24] Charlotte Brontë objected again to his 'bitter satire' and wished he would concentrate more on 'human nature at home' and leave political and religious intrigues alone.[25] Even now Thackeray could never be quite Victorian enough to suit all his readers.

The novel sold well initially, but a 'slasher' of a notice in the 22 December issue of *The Times* 'absolutely stopped' its sales.[26] The reviewer, Samuel Phillips, first mounted the familiar general attack on the novelist's 'cynicism', and then went on to call Thackeray's decision to 'convey himself to a strange climate and to take absolute leave of his choicest characteristics' suicidal. Phillips considered the novel dull, and took pains to point out all the historical inaccuracies. Phillips, in common with other readers, found the ending induced 'unaffected disgust'. Thackeray never forgave him for his 'careful dampers' in *The Times*; when Phillips died in 1854 he wrote to John Blackwood that if he had cringed to 'that poor Hebrew' and asked him to dinner he would have 'served a warm blanket next time instead of a wet one – but I never could abide the man or speak to him'.[27] *Esmond* survived Phillips's attack, and consolidated Thackeray's reputation in the way he had hoped it would, but he never made as much money from it as he felt he should have done.

Esmond, like *Waverley*, has an eponymous hero who is first seduced into supporting the Jacobite cause, and then disillusioned with it. Each man ends, after many adventures, a loyal subject of the Hanoverian dynasty, integrated into society as a private individual who has renounced military glory. Scott, writing of the recent past 'sixty years since', vividly brought to life events almost within living memory. Thackeray went further back, and the culminating scenes of his novel concern an (invented) abortive attempt to restore Prince James Edward, 'The Old Pretender', to the throne on the death of Queen Anne in 1714. Just as Waverley is an outsider, an Englishman who finds it difficult to interpret the feudal and tribal world of eighteenth-century Scotland, so Esmond, the supposedly illegitimate son of an English aristocrat and a young Frenchwoman, is a character always on the fringes of a society where honour and birth are intimately bound up together. It is another variation on Thackeray's theme of the lost inheritance, for of course Esmond *is* legitimate, though only by chance. This time the abnegation is voluntary: Esmond could have taken his rightful place in the world, but chooses to give it up to the members of his family to whom he owes so much kindness.

Esmond is a book full of secrets, and full of clues for the alert reader to pick up; often these are expressed in symbolic and metaphorical writing in the same way as in *Vanity Fair* (in *Pendennis* this is mainly confined to the illustrations). So, for example, in the powerful scene in which Esmond burns the papers that establish his legitimacy and right to the title, he notices that: 'On the Dutch tiles at the Bagnio was a rude picture representing Jacob in hairy gloves, cheating Isaac of Esau's birthright. The burning paper lighted it up.'[28] In attempting to stop the duel in which his patron and kinsman is killed, Esmond's right hand is wounded; he is forced to use his left – a symbolic gesture towards the bend sinister he is voluntarily accepting.

Secrets are imposed on Esmond early in life, and he learns to keep them in an unchildlike way. First the secret shame of his own birth, then the half-understood secrets of the intrigues in which his Jesuit tutor Father Holt is involved. Father Holt is a shape-changer, a half-magical figure to the child through whose eyes he is first shown to the reader, though a later perspective is added, in a way characteristic of the double vision of the book's narrative, which shows him to have been comically inept at intrigue. Father Holt tries to persuade Esmond to adopt the Old Faith, held by his father's second wife. Catholicism is represented by this rouged and rackety ex-mistress of James II and the kindly but devious priest, and religion and the Jacobite cause are bound up together for the boy in the secret comings and goings of Holt from Castlewood, in which he is innocently implicated. A new world of clarity and innocence seems to open before him when Castlewood is taken over by its new owners, young, handsome and Protestant. The twelve-year-old boy gratefully attaches himself to these godlike creatures, in particular to the young mother, only eight years older than himself, who includes him unhesitatingly in the family. This moment of acceptance opens the book, and proves to be of the greatest significance to the working out of the story.

However, the secrets persist, and are not so easily shaken off. The Castlewood women are renowned for their affairs with royalty; the men for sordid amours and drunken quarrels. Only Esmond and his beloved 'Mistress' and mother figure, Rachel Castlewood, stand apart from the rest of the family, she for her unworldly purity, contrasted with her own daughter's ambitions for wealth and station, and he by a constitutional melancholy reinforced by his ambiguous position in the world. Even so it becomes clear to the reader that at a semi-conscious level there is another secret; that of Rachel's not entirely maternal love for her young kinsman, and her awareness of its sexual content. When Lord Mohun, who has been attempting to seduce her, is injured, and Castlewood calls out to her 'Here's poor Harry killed', she screams and swoons, thinking that it is Harry Esmond he means. She knows, though Esmond does not, that she is not as morally superior to the rest of the Castlewoods as she appears to be. Her ambivalence and guilt about her feelings add another dimension to the atmosphere of intrigue and secrecy and shame that surrounds Esmond in his early years. She effectively puts him in a double-bind, depending on his love and loyalty, and demanding his fidelity; yet pushing him away whenever the relationship threatens to become too exclusive. Esmond is placed in a position where fidelity and renunciation – in effect complete passivity – become his habitual response to the world.

He voluntarily gives up his wealth and title, and behaves in such a way that he cannot hope to win his mistress's daughter Beatrix, with whom he is obsessively in love. He gives up; but he cannot let go; the story is permeated by an obsession with the past like that of Thackeray's admired friend Tennyson; a dwelling on the shadow that it casts over even the happiest moments of the present. 'O Death in Life, the days that are no more.' The woman whom Esmond loved first of all as a boy, and with whom he finally finds happiness, is perceived always in terms of his earlier memories of her, never as the living presence beside him as he writes. 'To the very last hour of his life,' Esmond writes of their first meeting (projecting with assurance into the future, for it is not in the last hour of his life that he is writing), 'Esmond remembered the lady as she then spoke and looked'[29] and again: 'Harry remembered all his life after how he saw his mistress at the window looking out on him, in a white robe.'[30]

The often acutely painful nature of these memories is made to seem more intense by the narrator's strategy of writing of himself in the third person, as 'Esmond' or 'Harry'; and yet lapsing from time to time into the first person, sometimes using both in the course of the same sentence. The effect is of a man attempting to keep a tight hold on his emotions, distancing himself from his memories by thinking of himself as a fictional character. Esmond achieves no success as a writer; and it is made clear that his play, 'The Faithful Fool', is a boring failure. His one subject is himself, and his past life. Yet he cannot keep up the strategy of thinking of himself as another all the time. The shifts of person are introduced with such care and subtlety that it is easy to miss them, and their significance for the characterization. Chapter headings, for example, are all in the first person. Moments of deep emotion sometimes are too; the moment, for example, when Esmond stands by his mother's grave: 'I felt as one who had been walking below the sea, and treading amidst the bones of shipwrecks.'[31] These shifts have the effect of creating a character who is able to reveal his most intimate thoughts and feelings, but who also sees from the outside, describing himself, his appearance, virtues and failings as they would appear to an impartial narrator.

He can also justify, even praise, his own actions, and he does; his self-absorption is saved from becoming intolerable only by his strong self-doubt and melancholy. Those who have had unhappy childhoods do often see their past selves as separate from them, unable to integrate them into the personality of the adult, and yet for ever bound to repeat the narration of unhappiness, like some Ancient Mariner unable to comprehend the reality of present serenity. 'The unhappiness of those days is long forgiven,' Esmond writes of his early years with foster parents, 'though they cast a shade of melancholy over the child's youth, which will accompany him, no doubt, to the end of his days: as those tender twigs are bent the trees grow afterward; and he, at least, who has suffered as a child, and is not quite perverted in that early school of unhappiness, learns to be gentle and long-suffering with little children.'[32] The reference to Thackeray's own early unhappiness is direct and inescapable.

The novel is also concerned with questions of identity: Esmond is, in an inner sense as well as a worldly one, a self-made man. Believing himself to be illegitimate, treated almost as a servant in the house of the man who is in fact his father, much as Thackeray believed Swift to have been treated by Temple, he must painfully try to acquire a sense of his own value which does not depend on worldly position or wealth. He achieves this, though at considerable cost to his psychic health, by his love for the woman who is part mother, part adored but distant object of desire, whom he ambiguously refers to as his 'Mistress'. This adoration involves keeping himself in a subordinate, depressed position, for the danger of losing her favour seems, because of her own ambiguity and apparent caprice, very real. Esmond is, first, the unwitting cause of the disintegration of her marriage when he brings smallpox into the house. He had caught it while flirting innocently with a village girl, and Lady Castlewood's outraged reaction clearly has a sexual content: it is as though Esmond had 'the pox' rather than smallpox. Later she blames him, quite unjustly, for her husband's death. Again, it is revealed to the reader, though not to Esmond, that she feels considerable guilt at having secretly wished it, and that it would have been Esmond's death that would have been a tragedy for her. When the truth about his birth emerges, therefore, he suppresses it in order to sacrifice himself for the woman he loves and her family.

Esmond is a complex character at odds with his times, 'not quite clever enough, or not rogue enough' for them as he says, who finally chooses to remake his life in America; the only solution Thackeray could see for the surplus population of his own time if they wished for a decent life without servility. It is another way of refusing engagement in the 'real' world of the eighteenth century, by going back – or forward – to a simpler kind of society. His shocked reaction to the immorality of his age is believable enough in terms of his feeling of alienation from it. He is a man who moves from obscurity and dependence to honour and acceptance, through a career as a professional soldier. He is in many ways a new kind of man, bridging the gap between the society of rank and the society of class. His attitude to women, for example, is one that Thackeray admired in Steele, who appears in the novel as a character who has some influence on Esmond as a boy. He achieves respect for his achievements, and acknowledgement that he is a gentleman, from those who at first despised him for his illegitimate birth. But his narration is permeated with the sense that he has never had the recognition he was owed for the loving loyalty he has shown to the usurping members of his family.

The crowning action of the book is the failure to overthrow the Hanoverian dynasty on the death of Queen Anne. At the crucial moment the Stuart Prince is absent, 'dangling after Trix', and loses his throne on account of his passion for an unworthy woman. The parallel with Esmond himself is never stated, but is clearly intended. Through his loyal love for one Esmond woman, and his obsessive passion for another, Henry Esmond loses his rightful position in the world. Both mother and daughter are shown to be unworthy of the love he gives them; Beatrix in a more obvious way is a worldly and wayward girl determined to make her mark through a brilliant marriage or a royal liaison, too capricious and volatile to appreciate her gloomy kinsman. Her mother Rachel betrays him in more subtle ways, first by refusing to prefer him to her drunken, unfaithful and brutal husband, then by unfairly accusing Esmond of being responsible for his death, and finally by never quite setting him free to make a determined pursuit of her own daughter when Esmond falls in love with her.

The portraits of Rachel Castlewood and her husband undoubtedly owe something to Thackeray's feelings about the Brookfields at the time the novel was being written. Trouble begins between Castlewood and his wife when the husband discovers that his wife is his superior, in intellect as well as virtue, as Thackeray thought that Jane was superior to her William. Esmond elaborates on the lying and hypocrisy that go on in unhappy households, and the way in which women are made slaves 'in my time'. This section of the novel is as clearly addressed to the failings of Victorian husbands as the moral lessons of *Vanity Fair* are intended to convey *de te fabula narratur*. 'When he left her, she began to think for herself, and her thoughts were not in his favour.'[33] Again: 'There is no greater crime for a woman who is ill-used and unhappy, than to show that she is so.'[34] The marital disharmony of the Brookfields is in the forefront of Thackeray's mind, but his own wife's unhappiness before and after Minny's birth underlie the comments, and give them added poignancy. ''Tis strange what a man may do, and a woman yet think him an angel.'[35] Esmond's comment recoils on himself, and his own treatment of Rachel while he is infatuated with her daughter.

Rachel is not, however, simply a portrait of Jane Brookfield. The maternal aspect again owes much to Mrs Carmichael-Smyth. Rachel is jealous of all pretty women, and won't employ an attractive maid, an echo of Mrs Carmichael-Smyth's anxiety over the Thackeray governesses. Jane, to do her justice, was confident enough of her own attractions not to fear other women. Thackeray drew her with two of her maids, all three graces pretty in a conventionalized way. The unresolved anguish of remembered loss repeatedly stressed in Esmond's narration seems to

Jane Brookfield with her maids

combine the feelings of Thackeray's recent emotional upheaval with the child's loss of his mother years before, as Esmond's 'Mistress' becomes first the substitute for the mother he never knew, and eventually the wife whose calm and gentle love consoles him for the loss of her own daughter. Esmond is frank to the point of cruelty about his feelings for the one and the other. His love for Beatrix is a delight and a torment: 'I blush, even now, as I recal the humiliation of those distant days, the memory of which still smarts, though the fever of baulked desire has passed away more than a score of years ago.'[36] 'He could no more help this passionate fidelity of temper than he could help the eyes he saw with . . . She had but to raise her finger, and he would come back from ever so far.'[37] Her reasons for spurning him ring true too: 'You were ever too much of a slave to win my heart,' she tells him.[38] Some of Jane Brookfield's letters to her husband, though not those to Thackeray, suggest a similar scorn of the 'slaves' who formed her circle, even as she enjoyed their attentions.

Rachel Castlewood, on the other hand, is repeatedly described by Esmond as an angel, too good for the world she lives in. 'I am in hell, and you are the angel that brings me a drop of water,' he tells her, when she consoles him over his hopeless love for her daughter.[39] The phrase is taken directly from one of Thackeray's most impassioned letters to Jane Brookfield.[40] The transference from letter to fiction gives the curious sensation that one half of Jane is consoling him for his love for the other half. It is as though Thackeray's pure and spiritual love for Jane is represented by Rachel, and his unacknowledged lust for her by Beatrix. The effect of splitting love between the two women in the novel is disturbing for the reader, even if it was consolatory for the writer, and probably accounts for the shocked accusations of 'incest' by early readers and reviewers. At times Rachel is seen quite coolly. ''Twas happiness to have seen her: twas no great pang to part; a filial tenderness, a love that was at once respect and protection filled his mind as he thought of her.'[41] This is the tone of Thackeray's misleading letters to Brookfield. Though Rachel's husband's judgement on her: 'Do you fancy I think that *she* would go astray? No, she hasn't passion enough for that. She neither sins nor forgives'[42] is proved wrong by the eventual revelation of her secret love for Esmond, she remains a sentimental rather than a passionate heroine, and his feelings for her, though deep, are more filial than overtly sexual. His feelings for Beatrix are acknowledged to the end: 'Such a passion once felt forms a part of his whole being, and cannot be separated from it; it becomes a portion of the man of today, just as any great faith or conviction, the discovery of poetry, the awakening of religion, ever afterward influence him.'[43]

Esmond's feeling for Beatrix, the same distance in years from him as he is from her mother, expresses the obsessional aspect of Thackeray's feeling for Jane, almost degrading in its abject hopelessness, that emerges from his letters, especially those to Kate Perry. In his angrier moments he deplores this kind of love, and even blames her for it. The contrasted pair of women who appear so often in Thackeray's writing are here linked in the closest possible relationship to each other, and to the hero of the novel. Each is a fully realized character, distinct in appearance and personality, but the hero loves them both, and the preface to his memoirs, written by his daughter, makes it clear that he never entirely loses his feeling for Beatrix, and that Rachel continues jealous to the end, as resentful of Esmond's feeling for their daughter as of his lingering love for Beatrix. When *Villette* was published, Thackeray, who had been stung by Charlotte Brontë's accusations of immorality, commented that at least he never made his good women fall in love with two men at once, as Lucy Snowe does.[44] Yet Henry Esmond is permitted to love two women. The difference is that the two women are so intimately connected, in a way that the narrative symbolically acknowledges by making them mother and daughter.

The Elton family home, Clevedon Court, where one of the most significant moments of Thackeray's relationship with Jane Brookfield had taken place, was the basis for the Castlewood of the novel. It is a rambling, romantic house near Bristol (Thackeray relocated it in Hampshire), mediaeval in origin, but much altered and added to. The Eltons were comparative newcomers; the house and surrounding estate had been bought by Sir Abraham Elton, a successful Bristol merchant, in 1709. The sixth baronet, Jane's father, a classical scholar who translated Hesiod and wrote for the *London Magazine*, inherited Clevedon only in 1842, the year in which the Brookfields married.

The house made a deep impression on Thackeray, though he stayed there only once. It was bound up with his feelings for Jane at the most intense period of his love, and is, with 'Fairoaks' in *Pendennis*, the only building to have positive emotional significance in his writings. Other houses, such as the various pretentious and gloomy homes in *The Newcomes*, have characterizing significance of a negative kind, or are described in comic set-pieces; Sir George Thrum's respectable mausoleum in 'The Ravenswing' is one of the best of these. Castlewood is, in a quite different way, intimately connected with Henry Esmond's character and fate: when he renounces his name and inheritance, he renounces his house in the literal as well as the metaphorical sense. Though he makes his new start in the New World, his estate there is called by the old name, and he is haunted by his memories of the place, as well as of its inhabitants.

Thackeray himself could no more write the Brookfield affair out of himself in *Esmond* than his hero could shed his past by writing of it. In 1854 he was still 'going about without a leg, without an eye, without caring for anything',[45] and even in 1856, hearing that Jane was expecting her third child, he revealed that he was yearning still, though he wrote, 'That pretty well finishes matters, suppose the way ever so clear. Her children . . . would hate a sham father. There's something immodest in the marriage of an elderly woman with children.'[46] His Madonna had betrayed him by her fertility, and the readjustment took many painful years to complete.

Chapter 10

New Worlds for Old

As Professor Owen or Professor Agassiz
takes a fragment of a bone, and builds an enormous
forgotten monster out of it, wallowing in primaeval quagmires,
tearing down leaves and branches of plants that flourished thousands
of years ago, and perhaps may be coal by this time – so the novelist puts
this and that together: from the footprint finds the foot; from the foot the
brute who trod on it; from the brute, the plant he browsed on,
the marsh in which he swam – and thus, in his
humble way a physiologist too, depicts the habits, size,
appearance of the beings whereof he has to treat; – traces this slimy
reptile through the mud, and describes his habits filthy and
rapacious; prods down his butterfly with a pin, and
depicts his beautiful coat and embroidered
waistcoat; points out the singular structure
of yonder more important animal,
the megatherium of
his history.

The Newcomes, Chapter 47.

As he aged, Thackeray became increasingly self-deprecating and critical about his writing, often attacking his performance more savagely than any of his critics. Trollope, who got to know him only in the last years of his life, assumed that Thackeray, like himself, had always lacked self-confidence. But Thackeray's estimate of his fiction was more accurate than that of his public. It seemed that his readers only really began to admire his work when he was himself aware of a falling-off in his powers. He had always appeared older than his years; grey-haired at thirty, in his forties he looked, behaved, and spoke of himself as an old man. 'At 47 Venus may rise from the sea, and I for one should hardly put on my spectacles to have a look.'[1] He acknowledged Dickens's superior fecundity of imagination, and even admitted admiration for Bulwer Lytton for writing, at fifty, in *My Novel*, a book 'fresher & richer than any he has done'.[2] The word 'fogey' appears frequently in his next novel, *The Newcomes*; Thackeray himself begins to fall willingly into that category. If he could have afforded to, he would now have given up the 'novel business' altogether, and written history, or gone into public life; he began to talk more frequently of standing for Parliament. For the time being he still had to make a living for himself and his family.

However, a new possibility presented itself at this time which, though its effect on his writing was not very marked, was to alter his life and his prosperity. In May 1852, while he was still writing *Esmond* and doing his tightrope act round the country with the lectures, Thackeray was invited to give them in the United States. He accepted, though he was not eager to go so far from his children for six months or more; nor did he ever come to enjoy lecturing, or feel it was a wholly legitimate occupation. Had he known of it, he would have endorsed Carlyle's comment in a letter to Emerson: 'Item: Thackeray is coming over to lecture to you: a mad world, my masters.'[3] However, it seemed a practical and comparatively easy way to put aside some money for his family, and at the same time to attempt to get his books, which had been extensively pirated in the States, properly published there.

Esmond was finished on 28 May, and Thackeray spent a week with his daughters and the Carmichael-Smyths on the Continent, parting from them at Frankfurt. He spent two months travelling, alone not from choice, but because his mother did not want to be parted from the girls, and he found increasingly that it was impossible to share authority with her. He returned to London in August, and then went on a lecture tour, correcting proofs of *Esmond* as they came from the printers; very slowly, as there was a shortage of the eighteenth-century typeface in which it was set.

In October he wrote to Anny, who objected to being left with her grandmother in France, 'I must and will go to America not because I like it, but because it is right I should secure some money against my death for your poor mother and you 2 girls.'[4] Anny was locked in combat with her grandmother over religion, and her position was becoming impossible. In her father's absence she was continually subjected to Mrs Carmichael-Smyth's hellfire Evangelicalism, of which Thackeray deeply disapproved, as she knew. Yet he felt that the girls must be under his mother's guardianship while he was so far away, and the line he took, not very satisfactory from Anny's point of view, was to let her know that she had his moral support, while recommending her to read the books Granny gave her, and then 'come to your own deductions about them as every honest man and woman must and does'.[5] It was a difficult prescription for an intelligent but dutiful fifteen-year-old to carry out, subjected as she was to her grandmother's unremitting moral pressure and emotional blackmail, and the misery of that time was to surface later in her first novel, *The Story of Elizabeth*, where the heroine suffers from her mother's infatuation with a French Protestant pastor.

Minny, at twelve, took the controversy more coolly. 'We are to go to M. Monod,' she wrote to her father, 'and he is to preach us a sermon every week, and we are to copy it and I daresay I will make a hash of it.'[6] Much of Thackeray's correspondence with his mother at this time is concerned with the same subject, she writing to complain that the girls won't listen to her view that all Scripture, including every word of the Old Testament, is the word of God; he affectionately insisting that they must be allowed to believe the gentler creed which he had set out as long ago as 1840, in his ballad of 'Jolly Jack'.

Anny and Minny with their grandparents

Give each his creed, let each proclaim
   His catalogue of curses;
I trust in Thee, and not in them,
   In Thee and in Thy mercies!

Forgive me if, midst all Thy works,
   No hint I see of damning;
And think there's faith among the Turks,
   And hope for e'en the Brahmin.

Harmless my mind is, and my mirth,
   And kindly is my laughter;
I cannot see the smiling earth,
   And think there's hell hereafter.

                        (*Works*, 7, p. 128)

'You don't like the people I like nor the opinions I like nor the books I like – ... our minds are no more alike than our noses: and each must follow his own,' he wrote to his mother from Boston, early in 1853.[7] He felt that she made differences of opinion into matters of emotion and sentiment quite unnecessarily. He was impressed to find that families could live peaceably together in America while each member went off to worship in a different church; it was one of the manifestations of a more relaxed and informal way of life which he came to value.

Thackeray sailed from Liverpool on 30 October 1852. He received the finished copies of *Esmond* just in time to send them to friends. Hearing of the murder of his old friend Savile Morton, the lover of Lola Montez and innumerable other women, he commented that his life was 'one scrape'.[8] He himself, like Esmond on his Virginia plantation, was now distanced from such disreputable acquaintances. Eyre Crowe accompanied him, and was to act (not very efficiently) as his secretary on the American tour. Thackeray was fond of him, and felt he was one of the few people outside his family with whom he could bear to live at close quarters, but he was irritated by Crowe's incompetence and foolishness. Crowe nearly caused a riot in Virginia by sketching the scenes at a slave auction, and Thackeray, who took great care to keep out of controversy while in the States, was not pleased. Other passengers on the SS *Canada* were the young poet Clough, already a friend, and the American writer James Russell Lowell and his beautiful wife. Thackeray soon recovered from sea-sickness enough to draw some of his playing-card cartoons to entertain Mrs Lowell. Though Mrs Carmichael-Smyth had been convinced, as always, that some disaster would befall her son, and insisted on giving him a life-jacket: 'what a smell it du make in the cabin to be sure!'[9] the voyage was uneventful.

He was determined in advance to like the United States, which he was to find, as Auden did, 'so friendly and so rich'[10] and not to turn on his hosts and make fun of them, as Dickens had done after his first visit, ten years earlier. He hoped that America would provide new material as well as dollars, but he rejected firmly the many suggestions – one of them from the showman James T. Barnum – that he should write a book about his experiences there. Looking for things to like, he found them. The New World, energetic and democratic, did seem a place where a man could make his way by his own efforts, without resort to influential connections or patrons. 'The young blood beating in its pulses warms one, like the company of young men in England.'[11] Like many later visitors, he noted that most of New York seemed to be constantly being pulled down and rebuilt, 'Nobody is quiet here – No no more am I – the rush and restlessness please me.'[12] He even managed to talk himself, half-seriously, into falling in love with a girl of nineteen. The hospitality was often overwhelming; he was lavishly entertained and lionized wherever he went. The lectures came to seem less good

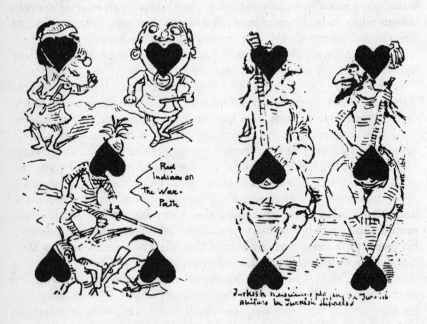

From a pack of cards

each time he had to deliver them, and at times he was almost terrified to go out in the street, in case he was hailed by one of the hundreds of 'acquaintances' whom he could not in the least remember. But he made real friends, too, and valued the acceptance and warmth he found in families where he could feel at ease. As always, he made himself a particular favourite with the children, sharing nursery dinners and finding presents to please the young people.

He went first to New York, where he was rather taken aback to find himself lecturing in a church, the First Unitarian Church of New York, whose pastor was the appropriately named Mr Bellows. He was slightly surprised, too, by the style of dress of respectable ladies, more like that of the French actresses of the Boulevard theatres than would have been acceptable at home. He was introduced to all the leading figures of the day, in New York and elsewhere; among them Emerson, Longfellow, the elderly Washington Irving, Charles Eliot Norton, Oliver Wendell Holmes. Two Presidents came together to one of his lectures at Washington; the President-elect with his retiring predecessor. He was impressed by his meeting with the blind historian, Prescott, and it was in Prescott's study that he saw the crossed swords belonging to two brothers who fought on opposite sides in the American Revolution, which gave him a germ of an idea for *The Virginians*. It is never entirely disagreeable to be lionized and Thackeray was repeatedly accused of enjoying it too much; but this crowded social life became increasingly irksome. It gave him no time to write, or take notes, hardly, even, time to write letters.

It was not the distinguished men of letters, however, but a representative, well-to-do family with a comfortable brownstone house on Second Avenue, that was to become most important to him in New York. The Baxters had a number of children, but it was their daughters Sally and Lucy, and their cousin Libby Strong, that Thackeray, missing his own girls, adopted most enthusiastically, particularly the nineteen-year-old Sally. 'I have been actually in love for 3 days with a pretty wild girl of 19 (and was never more delighted in my life than by discovering that I could have this malady over again),'[13] he wrote to his mother, and, perhaps with a wry pleasure in showing her the extent of his recovery, he told Jane Brookfield that he had 'found Beatrix at New York'. 'I can't live without the tenderness of some woman;' he went on, 'and expect when I am sixty I shall be marrying a girl of eleven or twelve, innocent, barley-sugar-loving, in a pinafore.'[14] The American girls, with their extra freedom of speech and action, were to influence the character of Ethel Newcome in the early chapters of his next novel; and though Thackeray would not have wanted his own daughters to dress or behave as they did, he was impressed by the extent to which Americans thought it important for their young ones to have fun. Writing to Mrs Baxter, who was in the end his favourite in the family, Rachel Castlewood to her daughter's Beatrix, he said that his own children had benefited from his observation of the way she treated hers.[15] He made the same point in *Philip*: 'I never saw people on better terms with each other, more frank, affectionate, and cordial, than the parents and the grown-up young folks in the United States. And why? Because the children were spoiled, to be sure!'[16]

His lecture tour took him to Washington and Virginia, where he saw slavery in action, and found little to condemn in the system except its inefficiency. He wrote to his mother, who had, like many English readers, been deeply impressed by *Uncle Tom's Cabin*: 'They are not suffering as you are impassioning yourself for their wrongs as you read Mrs Stowe they are grinning and joking in the sun.'[17] He took the point, made by those who defended slavery, that the poor in England were in effect often worse treated than a Virginian slave. 'Of course we feel the cruelty of flogging and enslaving a negro – Of course they feel here the cruelty of starving an English labourer, or of driving an English child to a mine – Brother, Brother we are kin.'[18] Acknowledging that the principle of slavery was wrong, he could not, from his brief experience of it in action, see any particular wickedness in the practice. His old acquaintance Fanny Kemble had been married to a slave-owner, Pierce Butler, and seen the effects of slavery over a number of years. She thought differently, and left her husband partly because of their disagreements on the question. Thackeray, with no personal knowledge of blacks, admired the equality of white America, but felt an instinctive revulsion from the appearance of the negro. 'Sambo is not my man & my brother; the very aspect of his face is grotesque and inferior.'[19] His reaction is in marked and depressing contrast to his open appreciation of most aspects of a country where he learnt to 'rub a deal of Cockney arrogance off'.[20]

The lectures were so successful that they were repeated in New York. Thackeray's health was good throughout his first American trip, and he survived the ordeal with nothing worse than fatigue, too many good dinners, and a bad cold. But by the end of March 1853 he was writing that the 'idleness of the life is dreary and demoralizing . . . the bore and humiliation of delivering these stale old lectures is growing intolerable'.[21] On 20 April, discovering that there were berths available on the Cunarder *Europa*, leaving that day, he took the opportunity to go. The haste of his departure avoided the farewells that he always hated.

By 2 May. he was back in London, and energetically taking up London life. He went to a ball at Lady Stanley's, renewed acquaintance with old friends, and visited 'the frying-pan' – Jane Brookfield, who now had a second baby, her son Arthur.[22] Ten days later he was in Paris with his parents and children. He found his mother as upright and handsome as ever, but his stepfather, who was seventy-two and had been ill during his absence, no longer a gallant soldier, but a quiet old man. The change is reflected in the description of Colonel Newcome in his last months. He walked with the children where he had walked with their mother years before, and visited his old friend Stevens the dentist, who had proved an irritating companion on the trip to Brussels in 1843.

The new grandeur of Paris, being rebuilt by Haussmann, impressed him, and he was happy for a time to visit old acquaintances and relations and listen to their stories and scandals. But he felt a stranger in his mother's house, pompous and awkward with her little circle of friends. Their small-talk soon became tiresome: 'From a twaddling society what can you have but twaddling? It's hard that there should be something narrowing about narrow circumstances.'[23] There was nowhere, now, where he was not a public figure, 'a heavy old Swell'. He wanted to be back at work. He also wanted to spend time travelling with the girls, perhaps to take them to Rome for Christmas. He could write the monthly parts of the new novel on the move, but in order to prepare the illustrations for the printers he would have had to be in London. It was decided that *The Newcomes* should instead have pictures by Richard Doyle, who had illustrated *Rebecca and Rowena*. Doyle, a Catholic, had broken with *Punch* because of the magazine's anti-Catholicism, and was badly in need of the commission. Thackeray did not always approve of his interpretations of the characters, and was impatient with his dilatoriness, but he admired Doyle's skill in doing easily what he himself had to labour over.

Thackeray returned to London for a busy month, without the girls. They had a good young governess in Paris, but she was 'much too young & pretty to come to a single man's house'.[24] He asked all his London friends to look out for another, with no success, and said he thought of writing 'The Adventures of a Gentleman in search of a Governess'.[25] He signed a contract with Bradbury and Evans for *The Newcomes*: £3,600 for a novel in twenty-four numbers, with another £500 from Harper and Tauchnitz. He packed up again, collected the children from Paris, and with a new manservant, Charles Pearman, but without a governess or maid for the girls, they set off for Germany.

He started work at once on *The Newcomes*. He was gloomy about it at first, feeling that it was a repetition of past performances, and that he was writing for money, rather than to enhance his reputation. But he also said, 'It torments me incessantly, and I wander about with it in my interior, lonely & gloomy as if a secret remorse was haunting me',[26] which suggests his creative energies were fully engaged in the writing. It was difficult for the girls, he knew. When he was absorbed in his work, and thinking of it even when he was not writing, he was a bad companion for them. Baden had 'a pleasant little society' for him, but the girls 'are too old and too young – too old for the children, & too young for the out young ladies – Come quick O model-Governess!'[27] He found occupation for Anny by dictating much of the novel to her, and the three of them wandered about through Switzerland and back through Germany happily enough, though Thackeray got a fever at Frankfurt. They arrived back in London, with four numbers written, on 1 September. The Young Street house had been lent to an impoverished young couple, W. W. F. Synge and his American wife, who had, in the manner Thackeray approved, married on 'nothing a year'; and for a while they all lived there together. But the household, with two masters, was soon at sixes and sevens, and Eliza the housemaid spoilt Charles Pearman – an ominous hint of trouble to come. By 1858 the invaluable Charles had made Eliza, respectable, honest, ugly and thirty-five, pregnant. After twelve years of devotion to the girls, she, as well as Charles, had to leave.

The lease of Young Street was a short one, and Thackeray bought a new house, 36 Onslow Square, though he did not move into it until 1854. It was the first property he had owned; a new terraced house, tall and thin. The girls had a floor to themselves, and a bathroom; an idea which Thackeray had brought back from the States. They all went to see the Brookfields, and Thackeray invented a new commandment for himself: 'Thou shalt not pity thy neighbour's wife.'[28] He was beginning to be able to be more objective about his infatuation. A quick trip to Brighton – the setting for some of the best chapters of *The Newcomes* – and they were off again to Paris, where they had their own apartment in the Champs-Elysées, and the girls could resume their studies with the pretty governess. But Paris still wasn't good for his work; obligations and distractions made it seem easier to write in a railway-carriage, or an inn. It was difficult to get the children away from his mother, but at last, at the end of November, they set off for Rome.

Even when they were settled in a palatial apartment in the Via della Croce, conveniently placed over a bakery, writing was not easy. Thackeray caught malaria, which was from then on to become one of his recurrent illnesses: for the last ten years of his life he was continually ill. Without a governess, the girls depended on him for company, and though he enjoyed seeing them 'as good and as happy as girls can be',[29] it was not always possible to find entertainment for them. Fortunately the Brownings and the Sartorises were in Rome, and Mrs Sartoris's sister Fanny Kemble. All were endlessly kind to Anny and Minny, and Thackeray even 'learned to admire but not to endure'[30] Fanny Kemble. She made a great impression on Anny, who remembered her eccentric style of dress and behaviour as liberating, if sometimes embarrassing.

Thackeray also made friends with an American poet and sculptor William Wetmore Story and his wife, who had recently lost their little son, and whose daughter Edith was also very ill. Thackeray took to visiting the stricken household daily, taking a chapter of a fairy story written and illustrated especially to read to Edith as she convalesced. This became *The Rose and the Ring*. Nearly fifty years later Edith remembered him vividly:

> There seemed no distance between us; and I can see him today as I saw him then – his large powerful frame dominated by his great head; the steadfast eyes and his gold spectacles in my child mind the only thing that showed he was not a real giant . . . It was a black day when the dear giant did not come.[31]

The Rose and the Ring, published at Christmas 1855, was Thackeray's last Christmas Book, and the only one really written for children. It is still read with pleasure by children today. The effect of living at close quarters with his own daughters, without the constraint of his mother's presence, or the distractions of London life, can be felt in the easy playfulness of the writing. The book is effective at a fairy story level, designed for the quite small 'Roman' children, Edith Story, Pen Browning, and others; but it also has elements of parody and reference intended for adolescents like Anny and Minny. There are Shakespearean echoes: Giglio, like Hamlet, suffers from a usurping uncle. Female 'accomplishments', always a target for Thackeray's satire, are made fun of. There are private jokes at the author's expense, too. The hero works so hard at university that he is able to make '*without any preparation*' a speech in blank verse lasting three days and nights, which enraptures all who hear it. The hero and heroine are given, like all Thackeray's important characters, 'a little misfortune' as a christening present by the Fairy Blackstick, and end up nicer and wiser in consequence.

The original impulse for the book was a set of Twelfth Night characters, King, Queen, Prince, Princess, and so on, that Thackeray drew for a children's party, and on which he built the tale for Edith Story. The spontaneity and fun of the watercolour sketches are reflected in the writing. It was one of the few enjoyable occupations of a winter

Giglio's speech

The Fairy Blackstick and Gruffanuff

King Valoroso   *The Queen*

that was a failure for him, though he was pleased that his daughters enjoyed it. As in Athens and Paris, he felt that great art was often a 'sham', and that the best thing about Rome was the sunset over St Peter's. He was often ill, and when he was well had to work constantly at the book to make up for time lost, uncharacteristically getting up before dawn to get the day's work done. He had little opportunity even to absorb the atmosphere of the artists' colony, the specific reason for his visit, which was to furnish the background for part of Clive Newcome's student life. Communicating with the publishers at long distance raised problems: often by the time he got proofs it was too late to correct errors. There was a muddle over additional material for the early numbers. He had to admit that he might as well have stayed in London to write the novel, and when he got the news of the death of his favourite aunt, Charlotte Ritchie, his first thought was to return to Paris to comfort her daughters. He got as far as giving up the Rome apartment, but thinking things over more calmly, decided to go instead to Naples, hoping his health would be better there. Two weeks later the girls caught scarlatina.

Fortunately there was a good English doctor, they had the illness mildly, and Thackeray was, very unusually for him, four months in advance with his writing. But in March he was writing despairingly that

'To be father and mother too is too much work for any one';[32] and as soon as the girls were well enough they set off for Paris. The book was finally finished at the end of June 1855. It had taken him two years to write.

Henry James specifically mentioned *The Newcomes* in his famous attack on the form of the nineteenth-century novel: 'What do such large loose baggy monsters, with their queer elements of the accidental and the arbitrary, artistically *mean*?'[33] Despite Thackeray's own misgivings about the book, which seemed at times to haunt him like a large stupid ghost, its organization is more subtle than James perceived. Bradbury and Evans were worried by the novel's slow beginning. But the leisurely pace of the opening sections is essential to establish the scope of the book. A convincing atmosphere of the crowded feeling of Victorian family life is built up by the amassing of detail: the seeming triviality of much of it is important to the effect that Thackeray is aiming at. Sophia Alethea Newcome's dreary Nonconformist religion, as well as her financial acumen, is to have a profound effect on her descendants. By describing her grand and gloomy house in Clapham in some detail, the narrative can show how she combines her allegiance to the Clapham Sect with a shrewd investment in land. References back to earlier novels, too, are more than authorly self-indulgence. It is enough for anyone who has read *Vanity Fair* to be told that the Countess of Kew is the sister of the Marquis of Steyne to know the way in which she is likely to behave, and it is of course Captain Costigan, an old acquaintance from *Pendennis*, who outrages the Colonel by singing bawdy songs in front of Clive in the Cave of Harmony. Such references are a form of narrative economy, rather than prolixity.

Thackeray chose to tell the story in the person of Pendennis because, 'under that mask and acting, as it were, I can afford to say and think many things that I couldn't venture on in my own person, now that it *is* a person, and I know the public are staring at it'.[34] The myriad masks of *Vanity Fair* have dwindled to one, and the complexity of Henry Esmond's position simultaneously inside and outside his history is replaced by the straightforward narration of an observer. The voice of the Pendennis who tells the story of the Newcome family is now that of a middle-aged fogey, conventional in outlook, and dependent on the judgement of his wife Laura, who is presented as a model of moral rectitude. Thackeray's friend Whitewell Elwin complained in his review of the book of Pendennis's 'exhibition of uxorious weakness',[35] and Thackeray explained that he intended to show that Pendennis was a weak character, led by women.[36] But the absence of another narrative presence to act as a corrective makes it difficult for the reader to interpret this. The presence of Warrington, who though he and Laura were in love with each other for a while in *Pendennis*, here invariably takes the opposite point of view from Laura, is not an adequate substitute.

As the full title, *The Newcomes: Memoirs of a Most Respectable Family*, suggests, it is the ramifications and interconnections of a middle-class family network that are under examination, rather than the fortunes of any one of its members. Thackeray may have been aware that his cousin Alicia Bayne, with whom he corresponded from time to time, was, with her mother, compiling *Memorials* of the Thackeray family; such family chronicles were anyway quite common. Clive is inadequate as a hero, as critics have complained, exactly because he is intended to be a pawn in the games played by his elders with the lives and happiness of their children, one of the major themes of the book. Though the situation of a young man at first indulged and spoiled by a widowed parent and then forced to come to terms with poverty and take seriously the art he had only played with is also that of *Pendennis*, Clive Newcome does not take the centre of the stage to anything like the same extent. The Newcome family, with all its complications of ancestry, 'high' and 'low' breeding by no means correlating with wealth and poverty, or with good or bad behaviour, becomes a paradigm for nineteenth-century society, and the novelist, like the palaeontologist, reconstructs the whole from the part.

One important preoccupation of the novel is an attempt to define, more searchingly than ever before, the idea of a gentleman. To what extent can a man be stripped of everything that has contributed to his self-esteem, and his importance in the eyes of the world, and still retain the magical quality which, according to Thackeray, is instantly recognizable? And to what extent are the two generally acknowledged 'gentleman-makers', blood and wealth, really necessary for the formation of one? By tracing the entirely believable and realistic connections through marriage of an entire family, Thackeray shows how it was possible for a socially acceptable young man to have two aunts, one who let lodgings and cooked the dinner with her own hands, one who was a member of the aristocracy, and for the lodging-house keeper to be rather the better lady of the two. The situation leads a stupid, effete member of the old aristocracy, Lord Farintosh, into comic bewilderment.

> I give you my honour there was a fellow at Lady Ann's whom they call Clive, who is a painter by trade – his uncle is a preacher – his father is a horse-dealer, and his aunt lets lodgings and cooks the dinner. (*The Newcomes*, Chapter 42, *Works*, 14, p. 565)

Colonel Newcome, the 'megatherium' of the history, is of course not a horse-dealer, but he takes pleasure in breaking in a pony himself for his favourite niece Ethel; he never has any shame in performing menial tasks, and spends his wealth not on himself, but to give pleasure to others. Thackeray, who always admired the old-fashioned simplicity of his mother's and stepfather's way of life, based the Colonel on Major Carmichael-Smyth, and Miss Martha Honeyman on his great-aunt Miss Becher. In his next novel, *The Virginians*, he explicitly made a distinction between the simplicity of an eighteenth-century lady who takes pleasure in making the pastry and carving for her guests, and nineteenth-century pretentiousness. He may have been conscious, too, of the contrast between the humble circumstances of the Brookfields when he first knew them, and their present state; for Brookfield, though never wealthy, had now become, like Charles Honeyman, a fashionable preacher.

The distinction between true and sham dignity, gentility and snobbishness, is one that the characters in *The Newcomes*, Ethel in particular, have to learn. Colonel Newcome is, if anything, more of a gentleman as a pauper than he was as a rich man, and his livery as a Grey Friars pensioner is shown to be as honourable as his army uniform. Thackeray, who had inveighed against uniforms of all kinds as snobbish impostures, here turns his ideas upside down, and asserts that the apparel need not proclaim the man if it is worn in an honourable and dignified spirit. Clive has inherited from his father an indifference to snobbish distinctions, and chooses to become a painter at a time when art was not, in England, considered a profession suitable for a gentleman. (Thackeray repeatedly points out that attitudes were different on the Continent.) His fellow-students and acquaintances naturally assume that his art is simply a rich young man's hobby; so, less expectedly, does his father. It is one of the inconsistencies that makes the Colonel so believable a character that he cannot always accept in his son his own unconventional simplicity and indifference to the rules of society.

Thackeray, as ever unsentimental about his hero's abilities, sets up a contrast between Clive, the gentleman amateur painter who has talent which can be improved with hard work, and his friend J. J. Ridley, the son of a butler, who has true genius, and works ceaselessly to develop it. To a modern reader the descriptions of J.J.'s portraits and historical paintings, genres in which he is supposed to succeed where Clive fails, are not appealing, and his 'sweet and fanciful' fairy pieces sound sentimental and trite. The attractive illustrations of Doyle, who may have been an inspiration for the character, seem closer to Clive's careless but more spontaneous caricatures and sketches, so that the force of the comparison is lost.

The story begins with the boyhood of Thomas Newcome, later Colonel Newcome, the son of the first marriage of a self-made man. Out of favour with his stern stepmother, he is glad to be banished to school at 'Grey Friars'. When he commits the final sin of falling in love with the Catholic daughter of a French *émigré*, he is packed off to India, as Anne Becher had been by her grandmother. The gentleman-makers have for him been the English public-school and the Army. The necessity to make his own way in the world has been a concomitant, though not a condition, of his final status. He, unlike his father, has married 'beneath' him in terms of his adult status (though not in terms of birth), into a *petit bourgeois* family; his wife, Clive's mother, dies – conveniently, for the Colonel only married her out of kindness.

The main action of the novel is set in motion by the Colonel's return from India, to be reunited with his son Clive, sent to school in England ten years before. The Colonel is quickly established as an innocent in the ways of the world, eccentric in appearance, and unconcerned with convention, whose behaviour is governed by a simple, old-fashioned code of morality.

> As they talk, the boy gives sidelong glances at his new friend, and wonders at the Colonel's loose trousers, long moustachios, and yellow face. He looks very odd, Clive thinks, very odd and very kind, and he looks like a gentleman, every inch of him. (*The Newcomes*, Chapter 6, *Works*, 14, p. 75)

Thackeray had been reading *Don Quixote*, and acknowledged that the Don, with some suggestions from his favourite eighteenth-century reading in the characters of Parson Adams and Dr Primrose, had been the inspiration for Colonel Newcome. Certainly the Colonel's lack of common sense, amounting at times to downright stupidity, recalls all three. It had always been Thackeray's creed that cleverness had little to do with goodness, and in the Colonel he combined Dobbin's gallant, military melancholy with Amelia's obstinate, stupid goodness to make the point that a gentleman need not be intelligent, or even a good judge of character. The Colonel is frequently, obstinately, wrong about people, seeing the world in black and white terms that lead him to overvalue and then to underestimate, swinging violently from love to hate. And yet – he is a gentleman. That fact is acknowledged even by those who dislike him, and reiterated throughout the book. Trollope spoke for contemporary readers when he wrote: 'It is not because

Colonel Newcome is a perfect gentleman that we think Thackeray's work to have been so excellent, but because he has had the power to describe him as such, and to force us to love him, a weak and silly old man, on account of this grace of character.'[37]

The Colonel's simple morality does not allow for changing social attitudes, and when he stands for Parliament he gets in because he promises, in all innocence, reforms which he will be quite unable to carry out. This has the same effect, without his knowing it, as the most shameless opportunism. Gentlemanliness, in its purest form, is seen as akin to Christianity in its essence, an unworkable code for everyday use, and yet an ideal to be upheld and striven for. The reader is made to believe it matters, even when the Colonel is at his most prejudiced and intolerable. It is as though Thackeray is making amends for the instinctive ambivalence and insistent questioning of the single-minded view of life that is at the heart of his earlier writing. He seems to have set himself the task of showing that it was possible for a good man to justify a way of looking at the world that was in direct opposition to his own. Yet he could not lose sight of the dangers that the kind of rigidity that now characterized his mother's outlook brought with it. Thackeray himself felt that the 'story seems to breathe freely' after the Colonel had been banished to India again.[38] The strain of defending the alternative position was beginning to tell.

Thackeray freely acknowledged that his stepfather, Major Carmichael-Smyth, provided a large part of the character of Colonel Newcome, together with many of the details of his life. Thackeray loved him dearly, and appreciated his simplicity and uprightness of character. But he also found him intensely irritating. Anny's account of the old gentleman's eccentricities and his inventions, intended to make their fortunes but doomed always to ignominious failure, like those of some nineteenth-century Professor Branestawm, is affectionate but hilarious.[39] Like the Colonel, the Major was almost criminally innocent in money matters, losing the family fortunes in the collapse of the Indian Banking Houses as Colonel Newcome does by trusting to the dubious finances of the Bundalcund Banking Company. But the portrait is not exact in every detail. Another major theme explored in *The Newcomes* is that of marriage, and the way in which young people were forced or manipulated into marriage for financial or dynastic reasons. The Colonel is shown to be culpable in his gentle insistence that Clive shall marry, if not the girl he really loves, then the one who is available and apparently suitable. Though he doesn't care about worldly advantage, the Colonel is as selfish in his way as Lady Kew: both put their own feelings first, rather than those of the children whose interests they are supposedly serving. The Colonel imagines that Clive's affections are easily transferable, and he doesn't take seriously Clive's other passion, for art. Thackeray, of course, married for love, without a penny, and his parents never questioned his decision (perhaps there is a hint in *The Newcomes* that it might have been better if they had), or his infatuation with art, or his struggles to live by writing, but did all they could to help him.

Thackeray's concern with the marriage theme was immediately prompted by watching Sally Baxter surrounded by her suitors, flirting with them all, and tempted by thoughts of making a 'good' marriage. His own daughters, too, were growing up, and the governess problem would probably, in a few years, be succeeded by the marriage problem. He hated the thought of losing them again, just when they were becoming real companions for him, and was secretly pleased that Anny, 'my dearest Fat', was plain and overweight and clever; not likely to be sought after too soon or too often.

As usual in Thackeray's novels, there is a pair of contrasted girls in *The Newcomes*; one dark, one fair; one clever, one stupid; one beautiful, one pretty and appealing. But Ethel Newcome and Rosey Mackenzie form a more subtle and interesting contrast than Laura Bell and Blanche Amory. Ethel is by no means a conventional 'good' heroine in the early part of the novel, but independent in thought and sharp-tongued; a further development of the line started by Becky and modified in Beatrix. When she satirizes the marriage market round which she is paraded by wearing a green 'sold' ticket taken off a painting at a private view, or when her forthrightness and wit eventually scare off her cousin, Lord Kew, her intended husband, the reader applauds her independence and unconventionality. Yet Ethel has been brought up to the idea that it is her duty to marry, and marry 'well'; society gives her no alternative, and the narrative gives her only the alternative of another kind of marriage, a love match. She is seriously tempted by the chance of a dynastic marriage to the fatuous Lord Farintosh, and submits to the humiliating pursuit that her grandmother undertakes, chasing the quarry from one country house to another. Only the shock of her brother's disastrous marriage, and his cruelty to the wife he does not love, brings her to the realization that she has nearly fallen into the same trap. Ethel does not really want to marry at all: the role of a Victorian wife and mother is too constricting for her undisciplined intelligence. Thackeray did not originally intend to pair her off with Clive, but to leave their love unconsummated and a regretful memory, like that of Clive's father for Mme de Florac. In order to fit her for the descent into marriage, she has to decline disastrously, in the later chapters, into a pious and 'humble-minded' shadow of her earlier self. At first she has a strong family resemblance to her grandmother, Lady Kew; by the end of the novel she is a clone of the egregious Laura Pendennis.

Rosey Mackenzie is both more and less than a foil to Ethel, a convincing and terrifying portrait of a woman who has succumbed totally to the pressures of Victorian expectations. She is symbiotically attached to her awful mother 'the Campaigner', who is one of Thackeray's most lively and cruel portraits of his mother-in-law, Mrs Shawe. Pretty, vapid Rosey has been programmed by her upbringing: she exists to please, and becomes an old man's pet to her uncle James Binnie and to Colonel Newcome. She is always ready to oblige, but has no capacity for deep feeling. Easily scared by her mother's violence she yet cannot be torn from her side, and is plastic and malleable to an extent that robs her of all personality. After having her ears boxed by her mother in the bedroom, she comes down, quite composed again, to sing, appropriately enough, 'Batti batti' in the parlour. Her only weapons are hysterics, and, after marriage, perpetual pregnancy: Mrs Mackenzie is for ever urging her to think of her 'condition'.

Rosey has, as much as Ethel, been brought up to the one purpose of marrying as well as she can. She goes through her tricks like a circus animal; sings her six songs; agrees with everything that is said to her; catches the expressions of those around her and laughs or looks sad as seems appropriate. She cannot be a proper wife to Clive, who feels she is more at ease with his father than she is with him, and for the first time in a novel by Thackeray there is the suggestion that, though it may be disastrous for a woman to be more clever than her husband, as Ethel would have been too much for Lord Kew to cope with, it may also be disastrous for her to be too stupid to be able to communicate with him intellectually at all. Clive's generation demands more of a wife than his father's did. Rosey cannot be a proper mother either; though she is constantly pregnant, she is not even effective as a breeding animal, and has little interest in the one child she does manage to rear.

Rosey Mackenzie is both an awful example of female education and conditioning at its worst, and a very distanced and bitter version, almost a caricature, of one side of Isabella Shawe. Isabella's dependence on her mother before her marriage, and her difficulty in thinking or acting for herself without succumbing to the pressures of stronger personalities, Thackeray's own mother and grandmother among them, are exposed in Rosey, with compassion, but without disguise. 'The overpowering mother had taken utter possession of this poor little thing . . . She sat under Mrs Mackenzie as a bird before a boa-constrictor, doomed – fluttering, fascinated; scared and fawning as a whipt spaniel before a keeper.'⁴⁰ Rosey and her sinister mother, whose behaviour in private and public are so dissociated as to make her seem insane, mark the extreme poles of female adaptation to a society which had rendered women powerless to rule their destinies in any straightforward way.

The arranged marriage of Barnes Newcome and Lady Clara Pulleyn, beginning in tyranny and ending in disaster, is another example of the helplessness of women. Thackeray's anger at the iniquitous unfairness of the marriage laws, which denied a divorced woman any right to her children, whatever the circumstances, is genuine. But it is dissipated into a conventional view of the disgrace of divorce for a woman, and the impossibility of happiness in a second marriage. 'All the sisterhood of friendship is cut off from her . . . She knows she has darkened the lot and made wretched the home of the man whom she loves best.'⁴¹ Only the marriage-market, he suggests, makes marriages that break up. The course of the Brookfields' love match might have shown him it was not always so simple. Perhaps he was comforting himself for the knowledge that Jane would never have run away with him by persuading himself that she would have been rendered even more unhappy by doing so.

The differences of opinion that Thackeray had been having with his mother over religion find expression in *The Newcomes* in a determined privileging of the religion of the individual heart and conscience over the religion of forms. On the one hand there is the satirical portrait of the opportunistic clergyman, Charles Honeyman, one of Thackeray's best comic characters, who calls forth some of the elegant, paratactic descriptive writing that is characteristic of *The Newcomes* at its best. Using short clauses, often separated by semicolons, Thackeray builds an elaborate rhetorical structure which is both ridiculous and vividly descriptive.

By his bedside are slippers lined with blue silk and worked of an ecclesiastical pattern, by some of the faithful who sit at his feet. They come to him in anonymous parcels; they come to him in silver paper; boys in buttons (pages who minister to female grace!) leave them at the door for the Rev. C. Honeyman, and slip away without a word. Purses are sent to him, penwipers, a portfolio with the Honeyman arms; yea, braces have been known to reach him by the post (in his days of popularity); and flowers, and grapes, and jelly when he was ill, and throat comforters, and lozenges for his dear bronchitis. In one of his drawers is the rich silk cassock presented to him by his congregation at Leatherhead (when the young curate quitted that parish for London duty), and on his breakfast-table the silver teapot, once filled with sovereigns and presented by the same devotees. The devoteapot he has, but the sovereigns, where are they? (*The Newcomes*, Chapter 11, *Works*, 14, p. 147)

Later Honeyman, bending with the wind of religious change, turns morning service in his fashionable chapel into a theatrical performance, nicely judged to appeal to the latest evangelical fashion, with the backing of a Jewish impresario whose wife and daughter provide the sacred music.

> Formerly he used to wear a flaunting scarf over his surplice, which was very wide and full; and Clive remembered when as a boy he entered the sacred robing-room, how his uncle used to pat and puff out the scarf and the sleeves of his vestment, arrange the natty curl on his forehead and take his place, a fine example of florid church decoration. Now the scarf was trimmed down to be as narrow as your neckcloth, and hung loose and straight over the back; the ephod was cut straight and as close and short as might be – I believe there was a little trimming of lace to the narrow sleeves, and a slight arabesque of tape, or other substance, round the edge of the surplice. As for the curl on the forehead, it was no more visible than the Maypole in the Strand, or the Cross at Charing. Honeyman's hair was parted down the middle, short in front, and curling delicately round his ears and the back of his head. He read the service in a swift manner, and with a gentle twang. When the music began, he stood with head on one side, and two slim fingers on the book, as composed as a statue in a mediaeval niche. (*The Newcomes*, Chapter 44, *Works*, 14, p. 582)

Opposed to this kind of play-acting, and the sham of 'family worship' in the cold, unloving household of Sir Brian Newcome, are passages in praise of the private devotion of individual women, Laura and Mme de Florac, and, in the later chapters, of the reformed Ethel. Even art becomes a form of religion, in the visionary attitude adopted by J.J., in contrast to Clive's more practical approach. The satire at the expense of the ecclesiastical hypocrite, uniquely Thackerayan, has worn better than the mawkish praise of the priggish Laura, which could come from any sentimental novelist of the period.

Few other Victorian novels attempt as inclusive a picture of early Victorian society as *The Newcomes*: it can stand comparison with *Bleak House* or *Middlemarch*. It is sometimes sentimental, and sometimes prolix – there are chapters in which, for all the richness of detail, there is very little that occurs to advance the story – but it is grossly undervalued today. It was highly praised by Victorian critics, many of whom thought it better than *Pendennis*. Carlyle thought that *The Newcomes* and *Esmond* were 'two of the *grandest* novels in the language'.[42] For all its faults, it seems astonishing that there has been no new edition since an Everyman reprint of 1962.

Chapter 11

The Toad under the Harrow

But now that the performance is over,
my good sir, just step into my private room, and see that it
is not all pleasure – this winning of successes. Cast your eye over those
newspapers, over those letters. See what the critics say of your harmless jokes,
neat little trim sentences, and pet waggeries! Why, you are no better
than an idiot; you are drivelling; your powers have left you;
this always overrated writer is rapidly
sinking to – &c.

'Thorns in the Cushion', *Roundabout Papers*.

For the last ten years of his life, Thackeray was writing against death, as anxiously as he had written 'for life' as a young man. Except when he was distracted by the familiar pleasures of society and club life, or the satisfaction he now gained from the company of his daughters, his harem of 'two little wives not jealous of each other',[1] money and illness came to dominate his thinking. He was now making enough from his writing to ensure a comfortable way of life for himself and the girls; the Onslow Square house was newly and expensively furnished, and the battered bits and pieces accumulated over the years since the Great Coram Street days were finally discarded. They kept a brougham (Anny was rapped over the knuckles for overworking the horse),[2] and Thackeray, in one of his fits of determination to take more exercise, bought a quiet cob from his neighbour Marochetti to ride himself – and managed to fall off it almost immediately. But this style of living meant that he saved little, and whenever he did have any money to spare he tended to give it away. He and Trollope lent W. W. F. Synge £900 each, for example (only £400 of which had been repaid to each of them at Thackeray's death).[3]

His letters during these years are full of references to friends and acquaintances in need, to whom he is giving a helping hand. When the Crowe family were in even worse trouble than usual, after the death of Mrs Crowe, he took Eyre's sister Amy into his household as a companion for the girls, now too old for a resident governess, and treated her like a third daughter. There were many others whom he helped on a regular or occasional basis: innumerable anecdotes testify to

233

Equestrian statue

his tactful generosity. He kept a 'floating loan' going; when he was repaid by one debtor, he immediately lent the money out again to someone else, and he took the edge off the obligation by saying always that he was only doing for others what had been done for him when he was young and in need. 'I wish I knew how to help your brother Fred – who hasn't got a brother Fred?' he wrote to Percival Leigh, who handled the publication of *The Newcomes* for him when he was in Rome.[4] However, his premonition that he would die early increased his anxiety over leaving enough at his death for Anny and Minny and their mother. When his *Punch* colleague Gilbert à Beckett died in 1856 without leaving a penny, and without having insured his life, Thackeray was shocked. 'Down from competence and comfort goes a whole family into absolute penury . . . – What is to happen to these people?'[5] Thackeray knew that if he had died in 1853 the same would have been true of his own family. À Beckett had gone the way of Laman Blanchard, William Maginn, and many others. Douglas Jerrold died in 1857, and Thackeray was a pall-bearer at his old adversary's funeral.

Kept in by the printer's devil

Dickens prevailed on him to deliver his lecture 'Charity and Humour' to raise money for Jerrold's widow and children. Dickens had been over-eager, it turned out, and Jerrold's son Blanchard was indignant that the hat should be passed round in this way, but it was symptomatic of the way in which literary men were expected to die paupers.

Faced with such examples, Thackeray continued to cast around for alternative ways of making a respectable living which would be less exhausting and more financially rewarding than the continual battle with deadlines and the uncertainties of popular taste. For a while he even feared that the Crimean War would affect the sale of novels, partly because of the economic crisis, and partly because the real news relayed by his friend William Russell of *The Times* seemed more compelling in its interest than any fiction could be. He thought for a while of starting a newspaper, modelled on the eighteenth-century *Spectator* and *Tatler*, to be called *Fair Play*. But another unlucky literary quarrel made him think better of it. He had written an article on the work of John Leech for the *Quarterly Review*, and in the course of praising Leech had suggested that Leech's cartoons were the only reason for *Punch*'s popularity.[6] This naturally infuriated his old friends and colleagues, and led Thackeray to feel that his carelessness and tactlessness would continually cause trouble on a daily newspaper, and that he had better leave the idea alone.

He again considered applying for a some kind of public post. This kind of undercover patronage for literary figures had, to some extent, taken the place of the private patron, and writers who would have considered it beneath them to accept the charity doled out by the Royal Literary Fund did not hesitate to accept sinecures of this sort. John Forster had been appointed Secretary to the Commissioners of Lunacy in 1855, and nobody thought it odd: Thackeray himself thought it good for the literary profession as a whole that members of it should be so recognized. He tried for a magistracy, and for the Auditorship of the Duchy of Lancaster, left vacant by the death of another literary man, Lockhart: '700 a year and nothing to do would suit me admirably',[7] but did not get either. His dreams of writing history or biography, of going into Parliament, or going back to studying art, were all luxuries that would eat up his capital, not add to it.

The best chance of improving his financial position quickly still seemed to be by lecturing in the United States, and though the frequent illnesses he now suffered made him dread going back there, he began, once *The Newcomes* was finished, to write a new series of lectures – only four this time – on the Hanoverian kings. Thackeray was never a respecter of royalty, and as early as 1845 he had written some short, scathing pieces for *Punch* on the four Georges, which contain in essence the subject matter and viewpoint of the 1855 lectures. Thackeray's feelings can be gauged from the epigram on George the First,

GEORGE THE FIRST – STAR OF BRUNSWICK

He preferred Hanover to England,
He preferred two hideous Mistresses
To a beautiful and innocent Wife.
He hated Arts and despised Literature;
But He liked train-oil in his salads,
And gave an enlightened patronage to bad oysters.
And he had Walpole as a Minister:
Consistent in his Preference for every kind of Corruption.

and that on George the Fourth – one of his favourite targets since the early Yellowplush days,

Georgius ultimus

He left an example for age and for youth
To avoid.
He never acted well by Man or Woman,
And was as false to his Mistress as to his Wife.
He deserted his Friends and his Principles.
He was so Ignorant that he could scarcely Spell;
But he had some Skill in Cutting out Coats,
And an undeniable Taste for Cookery.
He built the Palaces of Brighton and Buckingham;
And for these Qualities and Proofs of Genius,
An admiring Aristocracy
Christened him the 'First Gentleman in Europe.'
Friends, respect the King whose Statue is here,
And the generous Aristocracy who admired him. (*Works*, 13, p. 693–4)

Less respectful and more entertaining than the earlier set of lectures, *The Four Georges*, prejudiced though they are, and unfair in particular to George IV, are still good fun to read, and build up, with a Carlylean wealth of detail, a vivid picture of Court life and manners in the Georgian age, influenced in both style and content by the *Memoirs* of Horace Walpole. The picture is bowdlerized to some extent; when Thackeray says that the Countess of Suffolk was the only person who would have been worth meeting at the court of George II and quotes (not quite correctly) Pope's charming poem about her: 'I know the thing that's most uncommon',[8] he does not reveal that she was the King's mistress, though this is made clear enough in a passage in *The Virginians*.[9] Nevertheless he was outspoken enough about the habits of the Hanoverians to be alarmed to see a party of schoolgirls attentively listening when he gave the lecture on George I in Richmond, Virginia, and after the lectures had been given in England, he felt, for a while, that some of his aristocratic friends were angry at his abuse of the royal family. He was careful to include praise of Queen Victoria, very different in tone from his earlier coolness about her and the Prince Consort; but his attack on her uncle was felt by reviewers to be intemperate and unfair.

The first lecture sets the tone for the relaxed style of the series, with a reference to Thackeray's personal acquaintance with Mary Berry, who was, with her younger sister Agnes, a survival from the eighteenth century. Horace Walpole was enchanted by the sisters, and may even have proposed marriage to the elder. If so, she sensibly refused the elderly homosexual. He left them £4,000 each, and a house, Little Strawberry Hill, for their lifetimes. Mary Berry edited Walpole's writings. Harriet Martineau in her *Autobiography* describes the ancient pair, with their eighteenth-century rouge and pearl-powder and false hair, and their eighteenth-century oaths; quite unchanged in the very different society of the 1850s. The two were for Thackeray an invaluable link with the past, adding to his earlier experience of the less aristocratic old ladies of his own family, Mrs and Miss Becher, and Mrs Butler, to give him hints for the old women, survivals from an earlier age, who are affectionately if disrespectfully described in his novels. His next novel, *The Virginians*, contains another of these portraits. The Baroness Bernstein is Beatrix Esmond grown old and hideous, but still full of vitality and enthusiasm, as capricious as ever in her likes and dislikes. *The Virginians* makes use, too, of the background reading he had done for *The Four Georges*, as *Esmond* had grown out of *The English Humourists*.

The second trip to America, which occupied the autumn and winter of 1855–6, was less pleasant and even more exhausting than the first, though it achieved the primary purpose of making money. Thackeray thought of taking the girls with him, but decided that the kind of adulation that he received and the hectic social round would be bad for them, and that they had best stay quietly in Paris, near, but not with, their grandparents. They had an apartment in the same house as the Carmichael-Smyths, with the maid Eliza to look after them, so that they would not be too much exposed to their grandmother's authoritarian and gloomy ways. Though it was Anny who had suffered most during his earlier trip to America, Thackeray always worried about the effect on Minny of 'this doubt and trouble & gloom . . . my poor wife's youngest daughter mustn't be subject to too much of it,' he wrote to Charlotte and Jane Ritchie, thanking them once more for their kindness to his family in Paris.[10] Anny was now seventeen, Minny fourteen, and though they were still supposed to be studying French, German and music, Anny was considered more or less grown-up, and had already been to her first ball.

The Carmichael-Smyths were becoming old and frail, and the positions of dependency were beginning to be reversed. Thackeray was again trying to persuade the old people to settle near him in London. Their frequent illnesses meant that he wasted weeks of his time, when he should have been writing, travelling backwards and forwards across the Channel, and the girls lost the chance of a holiday with him in Scotland because they had to go to Paris to nurse their grandmother. But the Major was obstinately determined to stay in Paris, and though

Thackeray knew that being shut up alone with him exacerbated his mother's depression, there was nothing he could do. Fortunately the girls had their own friends in Paris as well as London now. The Brownings and the Sartorises were there, and the Dickens family spent the winter of 1855–6 just round the corner from them. Anny and Minny became close friends of Kate and Mamie Dickens.

Thackeray sailed for America on 13 October 1855, taking his servant Charles Pearman with him. Charles proved invaluable when Thackeray was ill, as he frequently was, but he could not provide companionship as Eyre Crowe had done on the earlier trip, and Thackeray worried about his evident loneliness and boredom. While he suffered from too much entertainment, his servant had too little, made no friends, and often had nothing to do. 'I don't call him my servant, I call him my companion. I found he didn't like the company downstairs (this was at a hotel) so I made him sit beside me at the *table d'hôte*,' he told an American acquaintance.[11] But the necessity of living at close quarters must often have been embarrassing for both of them. The word 'master' ought to be abolished, he wrote to his mother, criticizing her repressive treatment of a maid.[12]

Perhaps because of his precarious state of health, Thackeray found America less attractive than before. He was now plagued with three separate recurrent illnesses. His stricture grew worse over the years, and needed frequent and painful treatment from the urologist and surgeon Henry Thompson. He intended to have an operation, but put it off from year to year: Thompson was nervous of using the knife on the great author. Ever since the winter in Rome, he had suffered attacks of malaria, which were treated with quinine. He also had an intestinal disorder which he referred to as 'spasms'. These abdominal pains, with retching, sometimes accompanied by diarrhoea, were often severe enough to confine him to bed for several days, and caused him great suffering. They became increasingly severe and frequent, and he dosed himself fiercely, and probably inappropriately, with calomel, rhubarb, and 'blue pill' (mercury).

Much puritanical cant has been written, at the time of his death and since, about Thackeray's 'self-indulgence' being the cause of his illness, and ultimately of his death. He reinforced these attitudes by candidly admitting that he lacked self-control, and his disorder may have been exacerbated at times by over-eating and drinking, but it almost certainly had an organic cause. Though he was overweight at one time – he admitted to fifteen stone – he was a tall, big man, and such a weight would not in itself be dangerously abnormal for a man of six foot three. By the age of fifty, worn down by illness, he was quite thin, and had lost his appetite. The attacks seem by then to have had little, if any, connection with what he ate and drank. A Paris doctor told him in 1862 that he had a fatal complaint, presumably diagnosing a malignant intestinal obstruction. But cancer would have killed him within a year or two of the onset of his symptoms. They could have been caused by severe migraine: he suffered from headaches all his life. Another possibility is Crohn's disease (inflammation of the colon) for which no diagnosis was available until 1932; or he may have had reflux oesophagitis. He certainly also had undiagnosed hypertension. Many of his friends remarked his altered appearance in his last years, and though he bore his sufferings cheerfully, and tried not to let illness interfere with his life, the idea that he was simply a *bon viveur* digging his grave with his teeth cannot be substantiated.

By the time of his second visit to the States, his health was so precarious that lectures had to be postponed or cancelled on several occasions, and the touring became an ordeal. His earlier praise of the freedom and unconventionality of American customs and manners is replaced in his letters by observations closer to those of Dickens: graphic accounts of fellow travellers blowing their noses with their fingers, and shovelling food into their mouths with their knives. He was increasingly intolerant of dirt and noise and filthy meals in the taverns. His travels were occasionally lightened by comic episodes: he had a Pickwickian moment in a hotel when he started to undress in what he thought was his bedroom, only to be hailed by a female voice from the bed. On a Mississippi riverboat he found himself travelling with a giantess and a bearded lady 'who has a little boy of 3 who has also got very handsome whiskers and a little girl of 6 who seems to me rather pensive because her chin is quite smooth ... the Bearded Lady the Giantess & the English Lecturer all rowing in the same boat its pleasant to reflect on. O how sick I am of the House of Hanover.'[13]

His earlier complacency about slavery gave way to unease: a house he had visited on the earlier trip had been sold 'and I don't like to ask abt. the ebony child whom he tickled and nursed and brought up in luxury, and who I fear may be sold too'.[14] He saw now that the end of slavery was inevitable, but that the consequent competition of black and white labour in a free market would be disastrous for the black man. 'O it will be a terrible day, when 5 or 6 million of these blacks will have to perish and give place to the white man wanting work – but theres a long day for that yet, the West has to be filled ere the white mans hand turns against the black man ... perhaps in $\frac{1}{2}$ a dozen generations ... who knows whether the Great Republic may not colonize with its negroes the vacant British Isles?'[15]

The lectures were well attended, but attacked in the press, sometimes by journalists so ignorant that one interpreted a courteous reference to the Lord Carlisle of the time of George III as an attack on Thomas Carlyle. When Sally Baxter got married at the end of 1855, Thackeray did not go, giving as an excuse his fear that the journeys involved in getting to the wedding between lectures would be too much for him. He was homesick for his family, whose letters often took a long time to catch up with him on his travels, and alarmed to hear a rumour – which proved false – that Anny had fallen in love with a penniless consumptive curate. He wrote her a firm letter, which reads oddly from the man who had so often reiterated, in private and in his novels, his support and admiration for penniless love matches. 'You must no more think about a penniless husband, than I can think about striking work – these luxuries do not belong to our station.' She might as well think of marrying Charles Pearman '(what do I say? Charles is healthy & can make his 40£ a year)'.[16] Theory broke down when he was faced with the possible consequences in his own family. In *The Virginians* he reconstituted the fantasy: Theo Lambert, who is a sentimentalized version of Anny, nearly dies when she is not allowed to marry the man she loves, and cheerfully endures poverty with him until the inevitable happy ending.

The winter was a hard one; the trains on which he travelled often broke down because of the snow, and fires broke out on the river steamers. Thackeray wrote to tell Anny to be sure that Eliza had a fire. He was glad to spend some time in the warmer climate of the Southern States, but the constant travelling exhausted him. While he was away, *The Rose and the Ring* was published, and was an instant success, favourably reviewed everywhere. He had been less fortunate with another *jeu d'esprit* earlier in the year. His first and only attempt at writing a play, *The Wolves and the Lamb*, had been summarily rejected by the theatre manager to whom he sent it. Surprisingly, Thackeray's dialogue, so lively in the novels, fails utterly when it is not embedded in descriptive and analytic narrative, and he had to turn the play into a story, *Lovel the Widower*, in order to make something of it.

He was wholeheartedly glad to sail for England again on 25 April 1856 – no doubt Charles Pearman was too. Thackeray was ill throughout the voyage, and ill on his return home: he decided to spend three months improving his health, before getting down to writing another novel. In the meantime he gave the new series of lectures privately in London, to test out English reactions. He was reassured; his old schoolfellow Venables, who had attacked him in *The Saturday Review* for confusing the man and the monarch in the lecture on George IV, liked the first lecture, and 'Ld. Morley who belonged to the Court was not in the least scandalized.'[17] The lectures were a great success when he gave them publicly in London and when he toured England and Scotland with them from November 1856 to May the following year, and he made almost as much money with them as he had done in the United States. Still seeing himself as one day becoming a historian, he planned a larger work on the social history of the eighteenth century, incorporating the material used in the lectures. Consequently they were not published until 1860, when he used them in the *Cornhill Magazine*, having finally abandoned the larger idea.

In the summer of 1857 Thackeray satisfied the ambition he had cherished since canvassing for Charles Buller in 1832, by standing for Parliament. There was a by-election at Oxford in July and, with no preliminary canvassing in the constituency, and no more knowledge of politics than Colonel Newcome, he decided to stand as an Independent. It is a faintly ludicrous episode, even for the middle of the nineteenth century, when it was still possible to sit in Parliament on the grounds of being a gentleman and having enough money not to have to earn a living. Thackeray was not, and never had been, particularly interested in politics, unlike Disraeli, who was only secondarily a novelist. Even Lytton took his duties as a peer seriously, whatever Thackeray might think of his fiction. Thackeray was a professional writer; and his parliamentary ambitions were more of a fantasy than a serious possibility. The election cost him £850 which he could ill afford. The astonishing thing is that he lost by as few as sixty-five votes, though he thought that most of the electorate hadn't the faintest idea who he was, and though he made himself unpopular with some sections by refusing to uphold Sunday observance; he didn't see why people should not be free to amuse themselves innocently on a Sunday, as he had always done. He campaigned on a moderately liberal platform, for the adoption of the ballot, and the extension of the suffrage – though he was firmly against universal suffrage, claiming that it had led to tyranny rather than freedom in France.

He took his defeat good-humouredly, and turned back to the real business of his life. He had already started to think about a new novel in the previous summer, and had made several false starts. He had always said that the books people didn't write were the most interesting ones. After seeing Caroline Norton, whose marital troubles had contributed material for the divorce case in *The Newcomes*, and whose younger son had married an Italian peasant girl, he wrote to Jane Elliott and Kate Perry, 'That fellow would be a good character for a book – and his mother too if one could but say all one thought – but in England we are so awfully squeamish – Ah – if one's hands were not tied, there might be some good fun in that forthcoming Serial.'[18] *The Virginians* has a passage on the same theme: 'Suppose we were to describe the doings of such a person as Mr Lovelace, or my Lady Bellaston, or that wonderful "Lady of Quality" who lent her memoirs to the author of "Peregrine Pickle". How the pure and outraged Nineteenth Century would blush, scream, run out the room, call away the young ladies, and order Mr Mudie never to send one of that odious author's books again!'[19]

He got some way, so he told Whitwell Elwin, in a story which was to take up the character of J. J. Ridley from *The Newcomes*, showing him as a married man in love with another man's wife, but saved by the thought of his children from running away with her. 'This story,' said Elwin, who clearly knew the background of Thackeray's personal history, 'I begged him not to write.'[20] Finally he took refuge from the realities of contemporary life in the disguise of the historical novel. After jotting down some notes about the 1745 Jacobite rising, he returned at last to the theme of the Esmond family a couple of generations on, taking up the story of the twin grandsons of Henry Esmond in the eighteenth century, hinted at in the preface to *Esmond*, which he had started and abandoned in 1856. Serialization of the new book in the familiar yellow covers, this time illustrated once more by Thackeray himself, began in November 1857.

The Virginians is, far more than *The Newcomes*, a 'loose baggy monster', formless and diffuse. It is not a question, as it sometimes is for the reader of Dickens or Wilkie Collins, of getting lost in a maze of plot, sub-plot and counter-plot; rather that what plot there is is episodic and not strong enough for the length of the book, and that the narrative commentary has completely lost any ambiguity, and has ceased to make interpretative demands on the reader. Instead there is a great deal of straightforward moralizing, and the exiguous amount of action in each chapter is wrapped up in a blanket of sermonizing, often addressed specifically to 'young people'.

Thackeray himself knew that things were going wrong, and that it had taken him ten numbers to arrive at the point he should have reached in five. There is no attempt at historical pastiche, as in *Esmond*. There is a perfunctory mention now and then of family documents and letters, from which the story has been put together, but there is no pretence that the author is anyone but Thackeray himself. The narrative takes on the tone of a Victorian paterfamilias so wholeheartedly that it almost seems at times as though Thackeray is guying the role. But nothing in the working-out of the action, such as it is, suggests that this is really his intention, and the insertion of a thoroughly Victorian family, the Lamberts, into an eighteenth-century setting is further evidence of the exhaustion of his inventiveness. General Lambert's habits and conversation are, his daughter acknowledged in her introduction to the novel, Thackeray's own: they even read the same books and glean their classical allusions from 'old Burton, who has provided many indifferent scholars with learning'.[21] In the place of a bewildering multiplicity of contradictory voices, there is a single narrative voice, doubled by a character within the action who expresses the same beliefs and prejudices as the author. Then, without warning, the narrative voice is handed over to the one of Henry Esmond's grandsons who most resembles him. The last quarter of the novel resumes many of the narrative strategies that Thackeray had used to good effect in *Esmond*, but without the intensity of the earlier novel. George Warrington is more transparently based on Thackeray himself than Henry Esmond had been, so that the insistent voice of the depressed Victorian moralist, crying *vanitas vanitatum*, is heard yet again.

For the first time in his fiction Thackeray provides a pair of heroes, rather than his more usual juxtaposition of two girls. This is a potentially intriguing theme, and could have been used to investigate the complex psychological interweaving of the personalities of two brothers as Stevenson, always fascinated by the idea of the double, did in *The Master of Ballantrae*. George Warrington, the elder of twin brothers, is, like his grandfather, serious, melancholy and bookish. He is oedipally jealous of his widowed mother's interest in any other man; a convincing reaction to her open preference for his younger brother. He is implacable in hate and steadfast in love. Harry, the younger by half an hour, is openhearted, generous, foolish; the type that Thackeray so frequently admired in life and celebrated in his fiction. The two represent, in many ways, the two sides of Thackeray himself as a young man; the spontaneous, roistering, easily led youth full of generous enthusiasms, who gambled and fell in and out of love, and had daydreams of future greatness; and the wary observer, in the world of Bohemia but not of it, looking on at the antics of his immature other self.

The opening of the book promises well. In keeping with his earlier views on the historical novel, Thackeray provides a deliberately unheroic, but convincing, view of George Washington, which did not go down well with his American readers. The Warrington brothers are shown loyal to each other in spite of the pressure put on them by their mother's favouring of the younger and the seeming determination of all the other characters to set them against each other. But the apparent death of George, which clears the way for Harry to sample the pleasures and dangers of England, removes the possibility of interesting conflict until half-way through the book. Then George, the super-ego or conscience, returns from the dead just in time to save his unsupervised alter-ego from the consequences of his folly; and then takes his turn as unchallenged hero of the story, while Harry is relegated again to second place. The financial plight of the younger son is of course the basis of much eighteenth-century comedy; Thackeray reverses the situation; for though Harry, like other Thackeray heroes, fritters away his patrimony, George has to spend his paying Harry's debts and purchasing his army promotion, as well as expending money at his mother's command which she never gives back. The prodigal son not only gets the fatted calf, but the elder son's inheritance as well. Though Thackeray hints at some incipient conflict between the two, this is not allowed to develop. After a section in which the brothers face the corrupt London world together, Harry removes himself from the scene and redeems himself by becoming a soldier, leaving the way clear for the development of the reader's interest in George. The book virtually becomes two novels, not even as much interwoven as the stories of Becky and Amelia are, but existing for much of the time independently.

The two brothers are schematically opposed; Hogarth's Idle and Industrious Apprentices. Most of the amusing episodes belong to Harry, and to the first half of the book. He behaves in the way most typical of Thackeray's heroes, gambling; falling in love with an older woman, and as rapidly falling out of love with her again; becoming the spoiled favourite of an old woman, and then bewildered by her sudden loss of interest.

Whether as the Fortunatus of the fairy tale for whom nothing can go wrong, or as the pauper imprisoned for debt, Harry remains throughout the 'honest' impetuous good-hearted innocent, only superficially affected by the corrupt company he keeps. The old theme of the gentleman, and how he is to be recognized, is given a slightly different twist, since Thackeray's transatlantic journeys. The ignorant English are astonished to discover that a colonial can display polished manners, ride, shoot, and be a good judge of a horse. But the old themes are stated now, rather than investigated, and the blanket of narrative commentary is as heavy-handed as the 'editor's notes' had been in *Barry Lyndon*, in the days before Thackeray had full confidence in his narrative ambiguity. Now ambiguity has given way to coy references to his own times which make the point, all too obviously, that character doesn't change much, though manners may, and that manners owe more to hypocrisy than morals. 'No, madam, you are mistaken; I do *not* plume myself on my superior virtue. I do not say you are naturally better than your ancestress in her wild, rouged, gambling, flaring tearing days; . . . Only I am heartily thankful that my temptations are less, having quite enough to do with those of the present century.'[22]

George is potentially a far more interesting character than Harry, but Thackeray does not develop that potential. He comes back from captivity with the French – back from the dead as far as his relations are concerned – to find himself by no means welcome to his mother, who feels he, rather than her favoured younger son, is the usurper. It is reasonable that the volatile characters of fashionable London immediately switch their allegiance to the new-found heir, but Harry is the man of action who has been presented as more spontaneous and more engaging, and when the narrative also loses interest in him, the reader becomes confused. George, the charmless, melancholy intellectual who has little desire to shine in society or make his name in the world, who finds himself perpetually misrepresented and defamed, seems more like a *doppelgänger* than a character in his own right. It is as though Thackeray is making a half-hearted attempt to persuade his audience to repudiate the novelist and entertainer, in favour of the philosophical essayist and sober historian. It was perhaps because he was aware of this, and of a need to add immediacy, that Thackeray suddenly switched to letting George tell his own story, much of which is taken up with an overlong acount of a crisis in his wooing which recalls Thackeray's troubles in his engagement to Isabella.

Finally near the end of the book the two brothers find themselves fighting on opposite sides in the War of Independence. Thackeray seems to be presciently foreshadowing the Civil War in which many of his American friends, including the Baxters (Sally had married a Southerner) were to be caught up in 1861. The ideological question of slavery, the cause of that war, is ignored in the novel, and the blacks are treated in a jocular and superficial way, as boastful liars, childlike and lazy, who are well-treated, even indulged, by their masters. But they are granted personal attractiveness: the black valet Gumbo, though denied full humanity (even his name is that of a soup, and not of a person), is sexually attractive to the white maid-servants, who compete for his attention, and he is loyal to his master, not abandoning him even when his relations do so. He becomes one of Thackeray's familiar types, the servant who ultimately achieves the covert power that Thackeray felt that servants always wielded over their masters. The final illustration in the novel is of 'Sir George, My Lady, and their Master' – who is of course their servant, Gumbo.

While he was writing *The Virginians*, Thackeray was caught up in the silliest, and at the same time the most serious, public quarrel of his career, which came to be known as 'the Garrick Club Affair'. The

'*Gumbo astonishes the Servants' Hall*'

'Sir George, My Lady, and their Master'

occasion of it was trivial, an unpleasant gossipy article in *Town Talk* on Thackeray as a man and as a writer, by a young journalist, Edmund Yates, the son of the comedy actress whom Thackeray had adored as a schoolboy. It was probably Yates's claim that 'there is a want of heart in all he writes' which upset Thackeray most; but he claimed that Yates had abused his privileges as a member of the Garrick Club to publish details of his appearance and conversation, amounting to an abuse of private acquaintance. Yates refused to apologize, and asked Dickens's advice and help. Dickens, in the throes of his embarrassingly public separation from his wife, had confided in Yates, who had loyally supported him. He was already upset at a tactless remark of Thackeray's a month earlier, when the news of the Dickens's separation was the subject of club gossip. Hearing someone say that Dickens was having an affair with his sister-in-law, Thackeray said 'no such thing – it's with an actress'[23] thinking, so he claimed, that he was making things better. Dickens was in an exceptionally touchy state, and the undercurrent of rivalry between the two novelists surfaced in Dickens's defence of Yates. Thackeray, for his part, was said by several witnesses to have claimed that he was not concerned with Yates, but with 'hitting the man behind him'.[24]

Thackeray referred the matter to the Garrick Club officials. Though he had clearly over-reacted absurdly, the Garrick Club Committee upheld his complaint, and asked Yates to resign. This Yates refused to do, claiming that Thackeray himself had often made use of the characteristics and mannerisms of club members in his writing, notably in the 'Club Snob' section of *The Book of Snobs*, and in the character of Foker in *Pendennis*, based on the bouncy and offensively familiar Andrew Arcedeckne. This was true, and Thackeray added to the offence by attacking Yates in his next number of *The Virginians* as 'Young Grubstreet who corresponds with three penny papers and describes the persons and conversation of gentlemen whom he meets at his "clubs"'.[25] Finally Yates was expelled from the club. Since he could not afford the expenses of a Chancery suit against the Garrick, the affair fizzled out. Thackeray had won the battle, but at considerable expense of popularity among the people whose opinion mattered to him most. It is not clear why he was so sensitive over Yates's article, unless he genuinely felt that the young man, to whom he had always been kind, had been egged on by Dickens to attack him. He had remained friendly with Charles Lever after the much fiercer, and equally personal, attack in *Roland Cashel*, simply saying with calm dignity that it would do more harm to Lever than to him. The old rivalry and antagonism between Thackeray on the one hand, and Dickens and Forster on the other, had certainly been exacerbated by Dickens's treatment of his wife. The breach between the two novelists was not healed until shortly before Thackeray's death, though his daughters remained friends with the Dickens girls.

The many personal accounts of Thackeray in the latter part of his life which were published after his death are bewilderingly contradictory. There is no doubt that he made many enemies, and these saw him, as Yates did, as cold and haughty in his demeanour, not particularly brilliant or even interesting in company, and definitely something of a snob, ready to put down anyone who seemed to him unduly familiar with the great man. Disraeli's portrait of him as 'St Barbe' in his last completed novel, *Endymion*, is malicious, but quite recognizable. St Barbe is snobbish and envious, proclaiming that the aristocracy is doomed, and in the same breath complaining that the lords don't ask him to dinner. He despises his craft, complains how badly he is paid for writing, intrigues for public office, and talks of standing for Parliament, while quite unable to grasp any aspect of politics. Disraeli never forgave Thackeray for 'Codlingsby' and the *Pictorial Times* review. He must also have resented his review of *Sybil* in the *Morning Chronicle*, which complained that the novel was being used to convey a message unsuitable for fiction.[26] Even Trollope, who admired Thackeray as a writer and loved him as a friend, thought that he exhibited the 'self-consciousness and irritated craving for applause' shown also by Dickens and Macready.[27]

Thackeray himself lent credence to the unfavourable view of him in some of his published attacks of the 'Young Grub Street' type; even in *The Virginians* he was not content with the one snub, but returned to the attack in a way that was bound to make him unpopular:

> I am only half-pleased, for my part, when Bob Bowstreet, whose connection with letters is through Policeman X and Y, and Tom Garbage, who is an esteemed contributor to the *Kennel Miscellany*, propose to join fellowship as brother literary men, slap me on the back, and call me old boy, or by my Christian name. (*The Virginians*, Chapter 43, *Works*, 15, p. 443)

Yet in his family circle, or with friends who valued him for his generosity and openness, he seems to have been entirely different; kindly and indulgent, particularly to the young, always ready to help anyone in trouble; quietly amusing, though not elaborately witty; a loyal and steadfast friend to those of no particular distinction or literary understanding, who had some claim on his kindness or who had at any time been kind to him. His many old friends from Cambridge and Charterhouse days were added to over the years. Men such as Whitwell Elwin, the gentle, eccentric country clergyman who became editor of *The Quarterly Review* – Thackeray called him 'Dr Primrose' – and Dr John Brown, whom he met in Edinburgh when he first went to lecture there, each in his way a very minor literary figure, became his intimate and valued friends. They were treated with exactly the same courtesy as grander public figures such as Sir Henry Cole, friend of the Prince Consort, founder of the Victoria and Albert Museum and the moving spirit behind the 1852 Great Exhibition, who was also a personal friend; or the aristocrats with whom he was on intimate, rather than merely visiting terms. This is the Thackeray who emerges from his private correspondence, and from the reminiscences of his daughter. These friends all remark on his sensitivity and his almost womanly capacity for feeling both his own sorrows and those of others, and his ability to express emotion with unusual openness.

Yet another group of his friends – exclusively male companions – saw him as a perpetual Bohemian and *bon viveur*, a 'two bottle man' who cut short his life by self-indulgence in sexual pleasures as well as those of the table. In their company Thackeray became 'old Thack', unbuttoned, easy-going and ribald, sympathetic to younger men and fond of unconventional companionship which sometimes shocked his literary worshippers. Trouble seems to have arisen when those who were not within this magic circle behaved as though they were. George Augustus Sala, a much younger man who maintained a good relationship with Thackeray to the end of his life, was careful never to claim undue intimacy. He also made the point that Thackeray's sudden attacks of pain could make him seem cold and unfriendly, when he was in fact suffering too much to be able to carry on a conversation.[28] It must often have been difficult though, for those who did not know him well, to identify what made intimacy acceptable to him.

He was always an unusually confiding man with those he felt he could trust. Carlyle described him as 'very uncertain and chaotic in all points ... A *big*, fierce, weeping, hungry man; not a strong one.'[29] He told his women friends (often including those who were quite recent acquaintances) his emotional problems; the Brookfield affair was known in detail to so many of Thackeray's confidantes that one can sympathize with William Brookfield's continuing coldness to his old friend even when the 'affair' as such was some years in the past. He was touchingly open about his sensitivity to slights. He was uninhibited, too, in expressing his worries over his mother's increasing depression, and his occasional anxieties over the girls. With his male friends (and also, surprisingly, with his mother) he was ready to discuss his stricture, and his sexual frustration.

At the beginning of 1859, Thackeray was consulted by his publisher, George Smith, who wanted to set up a new monthly magazine. Smith wanted Thackeray to write one or two novels to appear serially in the magazine, and offered him £350 a month for the serial and book publication rights, a generous offer which he immediately accepted. Later in the year he suggested the magazine's title, *The Cornhill*, and accepted Smith's offer of the post of editor at a salary of a thousand a year. It was a decision he was to come to regret, even though his salary was doubled after the success of the first number. He had no right-hand man to take on the drudgery of the post: 'If there were only another Wills my fortune would be made!' he said, referring to Dickens's invaluable assistant editor.[30] As it was, his first enthusiasm was soon replaced by depression as the irritations and ceaseless labour entailed made him feel like 'a toad under the harrow'.[31]

Chapter 12

'Vanitas Vanitatum': The End of the Story

O my beloved congregation! I have preached this stale sermon
to you for ever so many years. O my jolly companions, I have drunk
many a bout with you and always found *vanitas vanitatum*
written on the bottom of the pot!

The Adventures of Philip, Chapter 2.

The first number of *The Cornhill Magazine* appeared on 1 January
1860. It was to be a 'family' magazine, priced at a shilling, and appearing
monthly. It was an instant success – the first issue sold 110,000 copies –
and it continued to appear as a literary magazine of high quality for over
a hundred years. George Smith, with Thackeray's help, had got the
formula right. Thackeray was jubilant, and feeling himself rich at last,
rushed off to Paris to celebrate, in a mood of jollity not very common
with him now. Whether he was the right person to be an editor was
soon to seem more doubtful. Harriet Martineau refused an invitation to
contribute: 'I don't fancy Thackeray as an editor . . . I doubt his power
of industry for *such* work, and I doubt his temper.'[1] Smith was later to
complain of his 'wayward and erratic judgement, which made him liable
as Editor to be influenced by totally irrelevant circumstances' – such as
whether the contributor was pretty or not.[2]

His help in setting up the magazine was certainly invaluable, for as
one of the foremost writers of the day he could approach other
established writers, many of them known to him personally, and be sure
of a response. Tennyson provided 'Tithonus' for the second number, in
spite of Thackeray's fear that Forster would try to stop him from
writing for the *Cornhill*; he was possibly influenced by Thackeray's
very genuine enthusiasm for *The Idylls of the King*: 'You have made me
as happy as I was as a child with the *Arabian Nights*, every step I have
walked in Elfland has been a sort of Paradise to me.'[3] Thackeray also
approached the Brownings; Carlyle, who wrote a friendly reply
regretting that he was too embroiled with Frederick the Great to think
of anything else; and Longfellow. Landseer provided a drawing. He

Letter to 'Dr Primrose'

welcomed those, too, whom he did not yet know except by reputation, like Trollope.

However, where Dickens had, with the backroom assistance of W. H. Wills, been a real success as an editor – his correspondence shows how much trouble he took with the contributions to each number of *Household Words* and its successor, *All the Year Round,* and to what extent he dictated the policy of the paper – Thackeray was dismayed at the amount of work entailed in producing the magazine each month, as well as writing his own contributions for it. He wrote a monthly essay, a 'Roundabout Paper', and also had the number of the current novel to produce. Added to the familiar pressure of monthly numbers, there were letters to contributors to write, rejecting, as gently as possible, unsuitable submissions, and the problem of keeping the paper within the rigid bounds of what seemed to him proper for 'family' readership. He described his very real difficulties with contributors who looked on him as a target for hard-luck stories in the 'Roundabout Paper' for the seventh number, 'Thorns in the Cushion':

Taking Time by the forelock

Here is the case put with true female logic. 'I am poor; I am good; I am ill; I work hard; I have a sick mother and hungry brothers and sisters dependent on me. You can help us if you will.' And then I look at the paper, with the thousandth part of a faint hope that it may be suitable, and I find it won't do: and I knew it wouldn't do. (*Works*, 17, p. 402)

One of the 'thorns' was the rejection of Elizabeth Barrett Browning's poem 'Lord Walter's Wife', an energetic plea for an end to the double standard in sexual morality: 'Though you write pure doctrine and real modesty and pure ethics, I am sure our readers would make an outcry.'[4] He also rejected Trollope's story 'Mrs General Talboys', because of its references to a man with illegitimate children. Trollope wrote a temperate letter pointing out the 'improprieties' in Thackeray's own writing, including *The Four Georges* and *Lovel the Widower*: both had appeared in the *Cornhill*.[5] However, the series by Ruskin which later appeared as *Unto this Last*, an attack on the accepted economic theories of Mill and Ricardo, was cut short not because Thackeray found anything to complain of in Ruskin's ideas, but because the *Cornhill*'s readers did.

Thackeray's editorial prudery does seem exaggerated, and old-fashioned for 1860, at a moment when so much was beginning to change in public attitudes; but he had suffered so much over accusations of immorality himself, that he was determined to avoid the risk of seeming to condone it in other writers. He had, too, in his later years, a serious and genuine sense of responsibility to young readers. Perhaps this went back to his own experiences of exposure to brutality and sexual explicitness in his schooldays. A 'family' magazine, read aloud to a circle of children, was not, he felt, the place for the harsher realities of mid-Victorian life.

Trollope was delighted to be offered £1,000 for a novel for the new magazine. He was astonished, however, that he was given only six weeks to produce the first number, and concluded, rightly, that Thackeray, who had been engaged to write serial novels for the magazine even before he was given the post of editor, had delayed starting until it was too late. *Framley Parsonage* became the major serial, and Thackeray's own short novella *Lovel the Widower*, adapted from his stillborn play *The Wolves and the Lamb*, ran for the first six numbers of the *Cornhill*. This postponed the necessity to produce a full-scale new Thackeray novel, though George Smith had seen this as being one of the main attractions of the new magazine.

The serialization of *Framley Parsonage* in the *Cornhill* was the turning point for Trollope as a writer. It consolidated his reputation and his finances, and introduced him to London literary life. It also brought him the friendship of Thackeray, whom he had admired, but never met until his tentative suggestion that he might be considered as a contributor for the forthcoming magazine was enthusiastically taken up. They met first at a banquet given by Smith to the *Cornhill* contributors to launch the magazine, and they were to be excellent friends for the remaining three years of Thackeray's life. Suggestions that Thackeray was envious of the success of other writers can, as Trollope himself pointed out, be contradicted by their affectionate relationship. *Framley Parsonage* was far more popular with the *Cornhill*'s readers than *Lovel the Widower*, which aroused vigorous protests for its suggestions that opera dancers had to be immoral to make a comfortable living, and was also dismissed by reviewers as an inferior and careless piece of writing.

The story of *Lovel* is simple enough. A demure little governess with a dubious secret in her past – she has been an opera-dancer, though remaining entirely respectable – seems to be hesitating between three suitors, the narrator, who knows her history and has helped her to her present position, the butler, who is really the hero of the story, and the local apothecary. But in the end she hooks her employer, Lovel the widower. It is a distanced and satirical parody of the romantic governess story, which takes a cool look at the stereotype. Bessy is more agreeable than Becky Sharp, but has an equally shrewd way of improving her chances in life. She is no Jane Eyre, though she too can say complacently at the end of the story, 'Reader, I married him.'

As a young writer, Thackeray had described a woman who moved the other way, from respectability to the jollier life of the *demi-monde*. In 'Shrove Tuesday in Paris' written in 1841, he painted a realistic portrait of a woman he knew, bored by the comfortable life of a governess in an English family, who returns voluntarily to squalor and poverty, but independence.

> She might have laid by a competence if she had been thrifty, or have seized upon a promise of marriage from young Master Tom, at college, if she had been artful; or better still, from a respectable governess have become a respectable step-mother, as many women with half her good looks have done. But no. A grisette she was, and a grisette she would be; and left the milords and miladies, and *cette triste ville de Londres, où l'on ne danse pas seulement le Dimanche*, for her old quarters, habits and companions. (*Works*, 3, p. 502)

The story of Mlle Pauline, whose 'type is quite unknown in England' Thackeray claimed, though Mayhew and others might have thought otherwise, would clearly not have been suitable for the *Cornhill*. Thackeray chooses instead to show what she might have been, as an artful, 'pure' English girl.

The main interest of *Lovel* lies in the way in which the story is told, using as a narrator a man who reveals, as Barry Lyndon does, a great deal more about himself than he is aware of. This goes back to Thackeray's earlier methods of narrative indirection. The narrator may, as he says himself, be telling the truth, or constructing a complete fiction: 'though it is all true, there is not a word of truth in it'.[6] He reveals himself as volatile, garrulous and cowardly, with a shrewd eye for similar failings in others. He is an observer, a representative of the novelist. His very name, 'Mr Batchelor', is an expression of his detached status, and he is essentially and crucially someone who fails to act. Thackeray, writing short fiction again, and having cordoned off the 'weekday preacher' who threatens to swamp the narrative content of his later novels by confining him to the monthly *Roundabout Papers*, can afford to revive the digressive, rambling and fanciful narrative of the early periodical pieces. Yet the story of Bessy Prior is placed in a solidly realized society, rapaciously acquisitive, and endlessly self-deceiving. The helplessness of the narrator parodies the helplessness of the novelist, who can endlessly create dissolving dioramas of fictional worlds, but can only affect the real one by pointing out the ambiguous nature of all reality, and the relativity of truth. The only straightforward character in the story is the butler, Bedford. He escapes from the tangled ambiguities of the narrative by refusing to speak or behave in the old 'flunkey' way; he has educated himself from his master's library, and acquired the advantages of his 'betters', while not losing the ability to take vigorous, physical action when he needs to. But as he is, in a quite literal sense, 'too good for this world' he is packed off to Australia at the end of the tale, to a continent where the concept of master and servant is ceasing to have any meaning.

By March 1860, Thackeray felt financially secure enough to buy a dilapidated Queen Anne house near Kensington Palace, 2 Palace Green. He intended to renovate it, but it proved to be in such a poor state of repair, that it had to be pulled down and a new house built on the site. Onslow Square seems never to have been entirely satisfactory; Thackeray didn't care for Brompton, the room which was supposed to be his study was noisy, and he worked in his bedroom. Palace Green, one of the first Victorian houses to be built in the 'Queen Anne' style, is a low but massive red brick building, 'the reddest house in all the town',[7] with the room that was Thackeray's study to one side, virtually separate from the rest of the house. It is now the Israeli Embassy. Thackeray, who shared the unpleasant anti-Semitic prejudices of his time, in spite of his friendship with individual Jews, notably Lady Rothschild, would have been surprised, to say the least. The house took two years to build, and cost him £6,000, a great deal of money at the time. Charles Carmichael told him he ought to call it 'Vanity Fair'.[8] But Thackeray maintained that it was a good investment, and he was proved right; after his death, less than two years after he moved in, it was sold for £10,000. 'Think of the beginning of the story of the little Sister in the Shabby Genteel Story twenty years ago,' he wrote to his mother, three months after taking possession, 'and the wife crazy and the Publisher refusing me £15 who owes me £13.10 and the Times to which I apply for a little more than five guineas for a week's work, refusing to give me more and all that money difficulty ended, God be praised, and an old gentleman sitting in a fine house like the hero at the end of a story!'[9] Though he did not live to enjoy this grandeur and comfort long, the house brought the different sides of his life, the domestic, the social, and the literary, together in a way that he had never achieved before.

'The reddest house in all the town'

The move was celebrated by two amateur performances of *The Wolves and the Lamb* – the only ones this static and unsuccessful drama ever had – before the furniture was moved into the large drawing-room of the 'W. Empty House'.[10] The first dinner in the new house was a magnificent entertainment for the *Punch* contributors, on 9 July. But though the splendid new study and library was designed to be a place where he could write comfortably, removed from domesticity without being cut off from his family, he still found it difficult to work at home. He told Whitwell Elwin that he wrote most of *Philip* at a tavern in Greenwich. 'There is an excitement in public places which sets my brain working.'[11]

The girls were now young women, with a social life of their own. Thackeray said they were more independent-minded than he was, and refused to be patronized by the 'great folks'. They still had no suitors, and were 'beginning to bewail their Virginity in the mountains',[12] though Anny felt Minny was still 'absurdly young for her age', more interested in playing with children and kittens than in young men.[13] Thackeray made no secret of his satisfaction that no one had appeared to take them away from him. Anny herself was finding consolation in writing. Her first published piece, an article called 'Little Scholars' on some charity schools she had visited, was published in the May 1860 number of the *Cornhill*, much to Thackeray's delight. He had tried to prevent, or at least delay, her attempts at writing; but now he felt that she was ready to begin, though still under his close supervision. Though she was twenty-three, it was he who suggested the title, and he corrected the spelling and punctuation as though she were still a schoolgirl. Anny, as always a serenely good daughter to her beloved father, had no feelings of resentment: she remembered the early days of the *Cornhill* as a golden time.[14] Two years later, however, she gave the manuscript of her first novel, *The Story of Elizabeth*, directly to George Smith, who accepted it for serialization in the magazine. Thackeray never even read it all through. When Smith sent him the proofs he said that he 'read some of them and then broke down so thoroughly I could not face the rest. She is such a dear girl.'[15] The novel was, absurdly, the unfortunate cause of the last of Thackeray's literary quarrels. It was given an adverse review in the *Athenaeum*, and Thackeray, wrongly identifying the reviewer, described him as 'a man who, in order to give him pain, had slapped his daughter's face',[16] and snubbed the unfortunate man at a club dinner.

Thackeray's last years were saddened by the deaths of friends and relations: Mrs Elliot died in 1859; his stepfather in September 1861; his cousin William Ritchie, younger than he by six years, in 1862, and, saddest of all because of her youth and his sentimental attachment to her, Mrs Hampton (Sally Baxter), who died of consumption in 1861, cut off from her parents and sister by the Civil War. He had at least managed to persuade his increasingly infirm parents to leave Paris in the spring of 1860, and they came to live round the corner from him, in Brompton Crescent. He no longer had to rush across to Paris, summoned by their real and imaginary illnesses, but the proximity of his invariably depressed mother was not always easy to cope with. Amy Crowe, after seven years as a member of the household, married a young relative of Thackeray's, Captain Edward Thackeray. After giving her away, Thackeray spent the afternoon in tears at Millais's studio.[17] But he made new friends, too. Kate Dickens, already a good friend of his daughters, had married Wilkie Collins's brother Charles, and the young couple both became very close to him. Thackeray wrote a poem for Kate, 'Mrs Katherine's Lantern', and had many conversations with her about her father. It was Kate, fond of Thackeray and more objective about her father than her sister Mamie, who brought about a reconciliation between the two touchy authors shortly before Thackeray's death. They met at the Athenaeum by chance, and, each softened by Kate's advocacy, spontaneously shook hands, Dickens shocked at Thackeray's altered appearance.

The *Cornhill* continued to exhaust and worry Thackeray, and he resigned the editorship in March 1862, just before moving into the new house. He was halfway through the serialization of *The Adventures of Philip*, his last completed novel. Though he had already released himself from the burden of illustrating the book, by engaging a twenty-one year old artist, Frederick Walker, to do so, he nevertheless needed to allow himself more time for writing, now that he was so often prevented from working by illness. He still kept a very firm control over the pictures, telling Walker what passages to illustrate, and how to do them; Walker did not always find him easy to work with.

The return to an earlier style in *Lovel the Widower* had not been popular with his readers, who preferred him in his now more familiar mood of Victorian moralist. Thackeray never tried such an experiment again. *Philip*, though it takes up the characters of the unfinished *Shabby Genteel Story* of 1840, is the most conventionally Victorian of his fictions, owing something in style to his new colleague Trollope, in characterization to Dickens. The villainous Dr Firmin is revealed by his appearance, and his 'stereotyped smile', with eyes and lips at odds with each other, is more reminiscent of Carker in *Dombey and Son*, than of any earlier Thackeray character. He comes to life in a recognizably Thackerayan way only when he removes himself from the scene: his letters from America, self-justifying, self-satisfied and outrageously hypocritical, though they don't really tie in with his grandiose presence earlier in the book, are wonderfully convincing and comic.

Philip is yet another version of the story of the rash but fundamentally good-hearted young man brought up to affluence and then plunged into poverty. Like much else in the novel, the familiar theme is here coarsened and exaggerated. Philip inherits a great deal of money, far more than any of Thackeray's other young men, from his mother, and the promise of more from his father. The loss of it is due not to misfortune, or his own extravagance, but to his father's wickedness. He wins it back, not through hard work, but by the creaking contrivance of a discovered will. In parts of the novel Thackeray makes a very direct use of his own early life, in the description of Philip's wooing of Charlotte Baynes in the teeth of her mother's aggressive disapproval and dislike, and these scenes are the best part of the book. Elsewhere there is a hardening into melodrama. Dr Firmin, the 'George Brandon' of *A Shabby Genteel Story*, becomes a pantomime villain, and Caroline, whom he tricked into a false marriage and then abandoned, becomes a pantomime angel with a cockney accent, nursing the sick and acting as surrogate mother to Firmin's son Philip.

Philip himself is a rude and boorish young man, whose class- and colour-prejudice jar unpleasantly on a modern reader. Where George Osborne could be scornful of Miss Swartz without being identified with the narrator, since he was not a hero, and the narrative ambiguities of Thackeray's style left the reader free to see the episode whichever way he wished, Philip's taunting and bullying of the mulatto Woolcomb are extremely distasteful, and the half-hearted attempts by the narrator to establish that Woolcomb is not being attacked for his colour, but for his character, ring very hollow. Similarly, Philip's disdain for his vulgar but kindly employer, Mugford, and the way in which he quarrels with his bread-and-butter, are shown to be unwise, but completely understandable. Perhaps this, as well as the Paris scenes in which Philip is first the accepted and then the excluded wooer of Charlotte, is taken from life, and is an attempt at a self-justification of the young Thackeray's relationship with James Fraser. Certainly Mugford shows himself generous and forgiving to the young man, as Fraser was to his sometimes haughty contributor.

Something seems to have gone badly wrong with the ideal of the gentleman in *Philip*. There is a shrewd article in the *Cornhill* for September 1861, 'Keeping up Appearances' by Fitzjames Stephen, which hits at Thackeray's sentimentality about poverty and rash early marriages, though without ever naming him. Stephen points out that though the qualities which entitle a man to be considered a gentleman are personal and moral, 'their retention depends to a great extent upon the external conditions under which people live'. Gentlemanliness is predominantly an aesthetic quality, and, 'it does cost a great deal of money to be a gentleman, and a great deal more to be a lady'.[18] This is close to Thackeray's earlier hard-headedness about the rarity of 'nature's gentlemen', and the efficacy of a decent income as a gentleman-maker. But Philip glories in his rags, marries on nothing a year, and takes a pride in being rude to those who are in a position to help him.

It is not only his circumstances that are not those of a gentleman; his behaviour is that of a rude and quarrelsome snob. This adds to his realism as a character, but alienates the reader's sympathy too effectively from him as the central character, who dominates the novel as no other of Thackeray's 'heroes' does, with the exception of Pendennis and the anti-hero Barry Lyndon. Since the narrator, who is Pendennis again grown even more fogey-like since his last appearance in *The Newcomes*, deplores his young friend's behaviour only on the practical grounds that it will harm his career, the reader is left to assume that Thackeray means his hero to be admired and sympathized with. His boorishness makes an effective contrast with his father's devious but inept financial corruption, but it is a contrast of two unlikeable people, each thinking himself superior to those around him.

Philip is at its liveliest in the chapters set in Paris, in which there is one character, the boarding house owner Mme Smolensk, drawn with all Thackeray's old skill in conveying the complexities and ambiguities of a woman who may be dubious in conventionally moralistic terms, but whose courage and good-heartedness are beyond question. The further Thackeray goes back into his own past, the more convincing the characters become; if Mme Smolensk is possibly the phoney-sounding Mme la Baronne de Vaud of his undergraduate trip to Paris, the Reverend Tufton Hunt, Dr Firmin's seedy blackmailing incubus, is surely based on Henry Matthew, the evil genius of Thackeray's days at Trinity, who became such an unconvincing clergyman. Mrs Baynes,

Thackeray's final stab at mothers-in-law, is probably a fairer portrait of Mrs Shawe than Mrs Mackenzie, albeit a less rivetingly awful one. Though Mrs Shawe had repudiated the responsibility for Isabella, she did take charge of the child of her hopelessly alcoholic son Henry. Mrs Baynes is granted some minor virtues. 'Mrs General B. was an early riser. She was a frugal woman; fond of her young, or, let us say, anxious to provide for their maintenance; and here, with my best compliments, I think the catalogue of her good qualities is ended.'[19] It is a grudging enough acknowledgement, but an indication of some lessening of Thackeray's hatred. Philip's journalistic hackwork as a Paris correspondent, able to 'smash Louis Philippe or Messieurs Guizot and Thiers in a few easily turned paragraphs, which cost but a very few hours labour to that bold and rapid pen'[20] is recognizably Thackeray's own for the *Constitutional*. As usual, characters from earlier novels reappear: not only those from *A Shabby Genteel Story*, but, as well as Pendennis and Laura, J. J. Ridley, who, in an attenuated version of the story Whitwell Elwin begged Thackeray not to write, has a pure and undeclared passion for Charlotte, after her marriage to Philip.

Thackeray finished *Philip* at the beginning of July 1862, with 'rather a lame ending'[21] and wrote a Roundabout Paper, 'De Finibus', about the pang of parting with his characters, which reads like a farewell to more than this one book. He felt that the novel writing vein was used up; FitzGerald commented sharply that 'it is a pity he was not convinced of this before'.[22] Certainly he had said as much often enough, but he does sound increasingly weary in his letters, worn out by the frequent attacks of illness. The projected history of the reign of Queen Anne, which he had hoped to write in the new house, receded ever further from him. The sustained effort of a long narrative was almost too much for him now, and he took an unusually long time, almost a year, off work, apart from writing the monthly *Roundabout Papers*.

Readers of Thackeray find the *Roundabout Papers* either charming or infuriating. As the title suggests, they are rambling, leisurely, digressive, using the techniques which he had earlier employed for satiric purposes, but without satiric intent. Their closest ancestor is Lamb's *Essays of Elia*, though they also owe something to Montaigne, Thackeray's habitual bedside reading. Like Lamb and Montaigne, Thackeray creates an 'I' who, if not always to be entirely identified with the author, is extremely close to him, and communicates, in a conversational tone, confidences and personal anecdotes. Thackeray himself said, apologizing for not writing more often to his mother, 'I am writing through the printer all day long and the song is always Ego, Ego, God bless us all.'[23] As they came out in the *Cornhill*, once a

The printer's devil still waiting

month, they must have been pleasant, diverting, and not too demanding reading, but they are emphatically not designed to be read one after another. Some of them – particularly those concerned with a nostalgic look back at Thackeray's own childhood and youth, such as 'De Juventute', or 'Tonbridge Toys', have lasted better than those on more topical issues, but all transmit, quite deliberately, a powerful flavour of an 'old codger' of the 1860s, looking back over a half-century which has seen tremendous and only half-understood changes. He is unabashed about airing his prejudices; the incident of the bearded lady on the Mississippi steamer is pressed into service in an attack on women in public life.

> You would like admiration? Consider the tax you pay for it. You would be alone were you eminent. Were you so distinguished from your neighbours – I will not say by a beard and whiskers, that were odious – but by a great and remarkable intellectual superiority – would you, do you think be any the happier? . . . Ah, Chloe! To be good, to be simple, to be modest, to be loved, be thy lot. ('A Mississippi Bubble', *Works*, 17, p. 544.)

In the summer of 1863 he had to set to work again on another novel, feeling that, like Scott at Abbotsford, he had spent far too much on furnishing the new house. He described himself as 'almost *non compos mentis*. When I am in labour with a book . . . I sit for hours before my paper, not doing my book, but incapable of doing anything else, and thinking upon that subject always, waking with it, walking about with it, and going to bed with it.'[24] *Denis Duval*, of which only eight chapters had been completed at Thackeray's death, was another return to his favourite eighteenth century, this time in a form closer to the kind of adventure story for boys Thackeray had always wanted to write. He wanted to give his readers the unsophisticated pleasure that he had found himself in the stories of Dumas. The hero and narrator is the son of a French Huguenot, born at Winchelsea in 1764, and according to the plan of the book, was to become an Admiral. Thackeray was worried, with reason, that he wouldn't be able to cope with the research needed on the technicalities of life at sea a century earlier. As far as it goes, it is a lively, straightforward tale, full of action, and with almost no digressive commentary to hold things up. It is impossible to judge whether he would have managed to continue with this uncharacteristic narration. The chief interest it still retains is in the description of the Countess de Saverne, who goes mad following the birth of her daughter. It is the only time that Thackeray ever brought himself to confront and describe directly in print Isabella's state after Minny's birth, and, in a slightly disguised form, her attempt to drown Anny; for the Countess abandons her baby by the seashore, where she is only rescued from the incoming tide by the boy Denis. He could even joke about it to his daughters, with characteristically reductive imagery. ' "The Countess is growing very mad," he said one night; "last night St Sebastian appeared to her stuck all over with arrows – *looking like a fricandeau*," he added gravely, though with a mock shudder.'[25]

Thackeray's health continued to deteriorate throughout the last year of his life. 'Life at this purchase is not worth having,' he told Anny. 'If it were not for you children I should be quite ready to go.'[26] An American visitor who saw him a month before his death was shocked at the 'signs of impending apoplexy so apparent to the unprofessional eye',[27] and his child friend Edith Story remembered being present at Palace Green when he had a sudden attack of pain, and how, as soon as the worst had passed, his first thought was to reassure the anxious child.[28] The old life of clubs and dinners was more often disrupted by his attacks, and he often had to refuse invitations at the last minute, but he was present at a *Punch* dinner on 16 December. On the last Sunday in Advent he went to the evening service at the Temple church with Anny and Minny. Bishop Ken's evening hymn – one of his favourites – was sung, with its well-known lines:

> Teach me to live, that I may dread
> The grave as little as my bed.

Writing in bed

Afterwards he praised it, saying 'it was simple and unaffected, and
entirely to the purpose, expressing just what was needful, and no
more'.[29] On 23 December, when he should have gone out to a dinner,
he was unwell and stayed at home. By evening he was so ill, with the
familiar spasms and retching, that his servant suggested he should stay
with him. But Thackeray dismissed him, and at some time during the
night he died of a stroke. He was found in the morning. 'The features
were much distorted, and discoloured by the bursting of the blood-
vessel . . . Moreover both arms were bent, the hands clutching at the
collar of his night-shirt, and were so rigidly fixed that he was buried in
that position.'[30] After years of suffering, he was not granted an easy
death.

Thackeray had always insisted that he wanted a small and unpretentious funeral. 'A drive to the cemetery, followed by a coach, with four
acquaintances dressed in decorous black, who separate and go to their
homes or clubs, and wear your crape for a few days after – can most of
us expect much more?'[31] In fact his funeral, on 30 December, brought a
huge gathering of literary men and artists and a great crowd of curious
women strangers wearing inappropriately bright colours, though there
were few of the 'great folks' whom he had alternately scorned and
cultivated: most of them were out of town for Christmas and the New
Year.

Thackeray's death at the age of fifty-two, and the manner and
suddenness of it, affected many of his friends deeply; perhaps more
deeply than some of them had expected. Henry Silver, one of the
younger men to whom Thackeray was almost invariably kind, had the
news kept from him by his relatives until Christmas was over, for they
knew how much he would feel it. Many in the literary world had a sense
of personal loss. Even the public obituaries reflect this feeling of
affectionate regard for the man, as well as respect for the writer; but
perhaps the best summing-up came privately from Carlyle, whose

relationship with Thackeray had not been an easy one for many years. He wrote to their mutual friend Richard Monckton Milnes: 'He had many fine qualities, no guile or malice against any mortal: a big mass of soul, but not strong in proportion: a beautiful vein of genius lay struggling about him – Poor Thackeray, adieu, adieu!'[32]

Selected Bibliography

Altick, R. D., 'Topicality as Technique', in *Carlyle and his Contemporaries*, ed. J. Clubbe, North Carolina, 1976.

Aspinall, A., 'The Social Status of Journalists at the beginning of the Nineteenth Century', *Review of English Studies*, **XXI** (83), July 1945.

Bedingfield, R., 'Personal Recollections of Thackeray', *Cassells Magazine*, New Series **II**, 1870.

Boyes, J. F., 'A Memorial of Thackeray's Schooldays', *Cornhill Magazine*, **XI**, January 1865.

Brookfield, C. and Brookfield, F., *Mrs Brookfield and her Circle*, London, 1906, 2 volumes.

Buchanan-Brown, J., *The Illustrations of William Makepeace Thackeray*, Newton Abbot, 1979.

Canham, S., 'Art and the Illustrations of *Vanity Fair* and *The Newcomes*', *Modern Language Quarterly*, **43** (1), March 1982.

Carey, J., *Thackeray: Prodigal Genius*, London, 1977.

Carlyle, T., *On Heroes, Hero-Worship and the Heroic in History*, London, 1897.

Carlyle, T., 'Biography', in *Critical and Miscellaneous Essays*, vol. 3, London, 1899.

Colby, R. A., *Thackeray's Canvass of Humanity*, Ohio, 1979.

Collins, P., *Thackeray: Interviews and Recollections*, London, 1983, 2 volumes.

Crowe, E., *With Thackeray in America*, London, 1893.

Crowe, E., *Thackeray's Haunts and Homes*, London, 1897.

Davies, J. A., *John Forster: A Literary Life*, Leicester, 1983.

Dickens, C., *The Letters of Charles Dickens*, ed. G. Storey and K. J. Fielding, vol. 5, Oxford, 1981.

Dodds, J. W., *Thackeray, a Critical Portrait*, New York, 1941.

Elwin, M., *Thackeray, a Personality*, London, 1932.

Fisher, J. L., 'The Aesthetics of the Mediocre: Thackeray and the Visual Arts', *Victorian Studies*, **26** (1), Autumn 1982.

FitzGerald, E., *The Letters of Edward FitzGerald*, ed. A. McK. Terhune and A. B. Terhune, Princeton, N.J., 1980.

Flamm, D., *Thackeray's Critics: An Annotated Bibliography of British and American Criticism 1836–1901*, North Carolina, 1967.

Fuller, H. and Hammersley, V., *Thackeray's Daughter, Some Recollections of Anne Thackeray Ritchie*, Dublin, 1951.

Gérin, W., *Anne Thackeray Ritchie*, Oxford, 1981.

Gilmour, R., *The Idea of the Gentleman in the Victorian Novel*, London, 1981.

Grego, J., *Thackerayana, Notes and Anecdotes Illustrated by nearly Six Hundred Sketches*, London, 1875.

Guest, I., 'Thackeray and the Ballet', *Dancing Times*, **LXII**, 73b, January 1972.

Hannay, J., *A Brief Memoir of the Late Mr Thackeray*, Edinburgh, 1864.

Hardy, B., *The Exposure of Luxury: Radical Themes in Thackeray*, London, 1972.

Harvey, J. R., *Victorian Novelists and their Illustrators*, London, 1970.

Hotten, J. C. ('Theodore Taylor'), *Thackeray; the Humourist and the Man of Letters*, London, 1864.

Johnson, E., *Charles Dickens: his Tragedy and Triumph*, London, 1953.

Lerner, L., 'Thackeray and Marriage', *Essays in Criticism*, **25** (iii), July 1975.

Loofbourow, J., *Thackeray and the Form of Fiction*, Princeton, N.J., 1964.

McMaster, J., *Thackeray: the Major Novels*, Toronto, 1971.

Merivale, H. and Marzials, F. T., *Life of W. M. Thackeray*, London, 1891.

Moers, E., *The Dandy: Brummell to Beerbohm*, London, 1960.

Phillips, K. C., *The Language of Thackeray*, London, 1978.

Price, R. G. G., *A History of 'Punch'*, London, 1957.

Ray, G. N. (ed.), *The Letters and Private Papers of W. M. Thackeray*, London, 1945–6, 4 volumes.

Ray, G. N., *The Buried Life: A Study of the Relation between Thackeray's Fiction and his Personal History*, Cambridge, Mass., 1952.

Ray, G. N. (ed.), *Thackeray's Contributions to the 'Morning Chronicle'*, Urbana, Ill., 1955.

Ray, G. N., *Thackeray: The Uses of Adversity*, London, 1955.

Ray, G. N., *Thackeray: The Age of Wisdom*, London, 1958.

Ritchie, A. T., *The Orphan of Pimlico*, London, 1876.

Ritchie, A. T., *Chapters from some Unwritten Memoirs*, London, 1894.

Ritchie, A. T. (ed.), *The Biographical Edition of the Works of W. M. Thackeray*, London, 1898–9, 13 volumes.

Saintsbury, G. (ed.), *The Collected.Works of W. M. Thackeray*, Oxford, 1908, 17 volumes.

Shillingsburg, P. L. (ed.), *Thackeray, Costerus* N.S. vol. 2, supplementary vol. 1, Amsterdam, 1974.

Sutherland, J., *Thackeray at Work*, London, 1974.

Sutherland, J. (ed.), *The Book of Snobs*, Queensland, 1978.

Thrall, M. M. H., *Rebellious Fraser's: Nol Yorke's Magazine in the Days of Maginn, Thackeray and Carlyle*, New York, 1934.

Tillotson, G., *Thackeray the Novelist*, Cambridge, 1954.

Tillotson, G. and Hawes, D., *Thackeray: The Critical Heritage*, London, 1968.

Trollope, A., *Autobiography*, Oxford, 1950.

Trudgill, E., *Madonnas and Magdalens: The Origins and Development of Victorian Sexual Attitudes*, London, 1976.

Wilson, J. G., *Thackeray in the United States*, London, 1904, 2 volumes.

Yates, E., *Mr Thackeray, Mr Yates, and the Garrick Club*, London, 1859.

Notes

The following short titles have been used in the notes:

Biographical Introductions: Ritchie, Anne Thackeray, *The Works of William Makepeace Thackeray: with Biographical Introductions by his daughter, Anne Ritchie*, London, 1898–9, 13 volumes

L.P.P.: Ray, Gordon N. (ed.), *The Letters and Private Papers of W. M. Thackeray*, Oxford, 1945–6, 4 volumes

Works: Saintsbury, George, (ed.), *The Collected Works of W. M. Thackeray*, Oxford, 1908, 17 volumes

PREFACE

1. *Biographical Introductions*, 8, p. xvi.
2. *L.P.P.*, II, p. 309.
3. *L.P.P.*, II, p. 772.
4. *L.P.P.*, III, p. 13.
5. Gérin, Winifred, *Anne Thackeray Ritchie*, Oxford, 1981, pp. 261–2.

CHAPTER I

1. Thompson, H. L., *Memoir of H. G. Liddell*, London, 1899, p. 9.
2. Lowell, James Russell, *Letters*, ed. Charles Eliot Norton, New Haven, 1894, p. 266.
3. *Biographical Introductions*, 8, p. xiv.
4. Ray, Gordon, *Thackeray: The Uses of Adversity*, London, 1955, p. 58.
5. Ritchie, Anne Thackeray, *Chapters from some Unwritten Memoirs*, London, 1894, p. 15.
6. Fuller, Hester, and Hamersley, Violet, *Thackeray's Daughter, Some Recollections of Anne*
   Thackeray Ritchie, Dublin, 1951, p. 28.
7. Bedingfield, Richard, 'Personal Recollections of Thackeray', *Cassells Magazine*, II, 26 March 1870, p. 12.
8. Hunter, Sir William, *The Thackerays in India*, London, 1897, p. 156.
9. Ray, *Adversity*, p. 48.
10. Ray, *Adversity*, p. 63.
11. *L.P.P.*, II, p. 609.
12. Ritchie, Gerald, *The Ritchies in India*, London, 1920, p. 11.
13. *L.P.P.*, I, p. 4.
14. Bedingfield, p. 29.
15. *Works*, 10, p. 202.
16. *L.P.P.*, I, pp. 9–10.
17. *L.P.P.*, I, p. 10.
18. Ray, *Adversity*, p. 80.
19. Thompson, *Liddell*, p. 6.
20. Thompson, *Liddell*, p. 8.
21. Silver, Henry, unpublished *Punch* Diary, 21 October 1858 entry.
22. Tupper, Martin, *My Life as an Author*, London, 1886, pp. 20–1.
23. *L.P.P.*, II, p. 123.

24. *L.P.P.*, IV, p. 223.
25. Boyes, John Frederick, 'A Memorial of Thackeray's Schooldays', *Cornhill Magazine*, **XI**, 1865, p. 119.
26. *L.P.P.*, I, p. 14.
27. Flamm, Dudley, *Thackeray's Critics: An Annotated Bibliography of British and American Criticism 1836–1901*, North Carolina, 1966, p. 96.
28. *L.P.P.*, I, p. 25.
29. Boyes, p. 120.
30. *Works*, 17, p. 430.
31. Ritchie, G., *Ritchies*, p. 11.
32. Merivale, Herman and Marzials, Frank T., *Life of W. M. Thackeray*, London, 1891, p. 56.
33. *L.P.P.*, I, p. 9.
34. Bedingfield, p. 29.

CHAPTER 2

1. *L.P.P.*, I, p. 25.
2. Unpublished letter, Berg Collection, New York Public Library.
3. Ray, Gordon, *Thackeray: The Uses of Adversity*, London, 1955, p. 128.
4. *L.P.P.*, I, p. 31.
5. *L.P.P.*, I, p. 44.
6. *L.P.P.*, I, p. 37.
7. *L.P.P.*, I, p. 50.
8. *L.P.P.*, I, p. 47.
9. *L.P.P.*, I, p. 58.
10. Stephen, Leslie, *Sketches from Cambridge*, London, 1865, p. 102.
11. Wright, J. M., *Alma Mater*, London, 1827, p. 30.
12.. *Works*, 1, pp. 1–3.
13. *L.P.P.*, I, p. 76.
14. *L.P.P.*, I, p. 77.
15. *L.P.P.*, I, p. 90.

16. *L.P.P.*, I, p. 93.
17. *L.P.P.*, I, p. 91.
18. *L.P.P.*, I, pp. 85–6.
19. *L.P.P.*, I, p. 266.
20. *Works*, 4, p. 285.
21. *L.P.P.*, I, p. 95.
22. *L.P.P.*, I, p. 84.
23. *L.P.P.*, I, p. 87.
24. *L.P.P.*, I, p. 99.
25. *L.P.P.*, I, pp. 96–7.
26. FitzGerald, Edward, *Works*, vol. 1, New York, 1887, p. 264.
27. *L.P.P.*, II, p. 542.
28. *L.P.P.*, II, pp. 541–2.
29. *Works*, 17, p. 617.
30. FitzGerald, Edward, *The Letters of Edward FitzGerald*, ed. A. McK. Terhune and A. B. Terhune, vol. I, Princeton, 1980, p. 84.
31. *L.P.P.*, I, p. 138.
32. *L.P.P.*, I, p. 137.
33. *L.P.P.*, I, p. 112.
34. *L.P.P.*, I, p. 116.
35. *L.P.P.*, I, p. 123.
36. *L.P.P.*, I, p. 119.
37. *L.P.P.*, I, p. 123.
38. *L.P.P.*, I, p. 130.
39. *L.P.P.*, I, p. 141.
40. *Works*, 11, p. 794.
41. *L.P.P.*, I, p. 133.
42. *L.P.P.*, I, p. 147.
43. *L.P.P.*, I, p. 148.
44. *L.P.P.*, I, p. 133.
45. *Works*, 7, p. 71.
46. *Works*, 10, p. 633.
47. *L.P.P.*, I, p. 121.
48. *L.P.P.*, I, p. 126.
49. *L.P.P.*, I, p. 131.
50. *Works*, 7, p. 382.
51. *L.P.P.*, I, p. 130.
52. *L.P.P.*, I, p. 133.
53. *L.P.P.*, I, p. 135.
54. *L.P.P.*, I, p. 142.
55. *L.P.P.*, I, p. 146.
56. *L.P.P.*, I, p. 142.

57. Braun, Lily, *Im Schatten der Titanen*, Braunschweig, 1909, p. 105.
58. *L.P.P.*, I, p. 146.
59. *Works*, 4, pp. 201–314.
60. Unpublished letter, Bodleian Library (Ms Eng. Lett. d. 398).
61. Weimar Sketchbook, Berg Collection, New York Public Library.
62. *L.P.P.*, I, p. 146.
63. *L.P.P.*, II, p. 11.
64. *L.P.P.*, I, pp. 137–140.
65. *L.P.P.*, I, p. 144.
66. *L.P.P.*, I, p. 147.

CHAPTER 3

1. *Works*, 13, p. 626.
2. *L.P.P.*, I, p. 243.
3. *L.P.P.*, I, p. 176.
4. *L.P.P.*, I, p. 152.
5. *L.P.P.*, I, p. 200.
6. *L.P.P.*, I, p. 182.
7. *L.P.P.*, I, p. 199.
8. Aspinall, A., 'The Social Status of Journalists at the beginning of the Nineteenth Century', *Review of English Studies*, XXI, 1945, pp. 216–32.
9. *L.P.P.*, I, p. 226.
10. *L.P.P.*, I, p. 241.
11. *L.P.P.*, I, p. 237.
12. *L.P.P.*, I, p. 182.
13. *L.P.P.*, I, p. 160.
14. *Works*, 1, pp. 539–60.
15. *L.P.P.*, I, p. 504.
16. *L.P.P.*, I, p. 230.
17. *L.P.P.*, I, p. 244.
18. Martineau, Harriet, *Autobiography*, London, 1877, p. 375.
19. *L.P.P.*, I, p. 196.
20. *L.P.P.*, I, p. 207.
21. *L.P.P.*, I, p. 190.
22. *L.P.P.*, II, p. 292.
23. FitzGerald, Edward, *The Letters of Edward FitzGerald*, ed. A. McK. Terhune and A. B. Terhune, vol. 1, Princeton, 1980, p. 15.
24. FitzGerald, *Letters*, vol. 1, p. 668.
25. *L.P.P.*, III, p. 98.
26. *L.P.P.*, I, pp. 167–8.
27. *L.P.P.*, III, p. 114.
28. *L.P.P.*, I, p. 166.
29. *L.P.P.*, I, p. 198.
30. *L.P.P.*, I, p. 208.
31. *L.P.P.*, I, p. 206.
32. *L.P.P.*, I, p. 163.
33. *L.P.P.*, I, p. 190.
34. Jerrold, Blanchard, *The Final Reliques of Father Prout*, London, 1876, p. 141.
35. *L.P.P.*, IV, p. 252.
36. Thrall, Miriam, *Rebellious Fraser's: Nol Yorke's Magazine in the Days of Maginn, Thackeray and Carlyle*, New York, 1934, p. 180.
37. *L.P.P.*, I, p. 197.
38. *L.P.P.*, I, p. 209.
39. Thrall, *Rebellious Fraser's*, p. 190.
40. *L.P.P.*, I, p. 262.
41. *L.P.P.*, I, p. 264.
42. *L.P.P.*, I, p. 264.
43. *Works*, 2, pp. 43, 44.
44. *L.P.P.*, I, p. 273.
45. *L.P.P.*, I, p. 279.
46. Wilson, James Grant, *Thackeray in the United States*, vol 1, New York, 1904, p. 118.
47. *L.P.P.*, II, p. 118.
48.. *Works*, 10, p. 13.
49. *Works*, 1, pp. 55–65.
50. *L.P.P.*, I, p. 291.

CHAPTER 4

1. *L.P.P.*, I, p. 267.
2. *L.P.P.*, I, pp. 266–7.
3. *L.P.P.*, I, p. 293.

4. *L.P.P.*, I, p. 295.
5. *Works*, 1, p. 559.
6. *L.P.P.*, I, p. 229.
7. *Works*, 2, p. 13.
8. Cornish, Blanche Warre, *Some Family Letters of W. M. Thackeray: Together with Recollections by his Kinswoman*, Boston, 1911, p. 20.
9. Laughton, J. K., *Memoirs of the Life and Correspondence of Henry Reeve*, London, 1898, p. 59.
10. *L.P.P.*, I, p. 321.
11. Ritchie, Anne Thackeray, *Chapters from some Unwritten Memoirs*, London, 1894, p. 20.
12. *L.P.P.*, I, p. 303–4.
13. *L.P.P.*, I, p. 316.
14. *L.P.P.*, I, p. 320.
15. *L.P.P.*, I, p. 320.
16. *L.P.P.*, I, p. 317.
17. *Works*, 4, p. 390.
18. *Works*, 5, p. 345.
19. *L.P.P.*, II, p. 431.
20. *Works*, 3, p. 328.
21.. *L.P.P.*, I, p. 328.
22. *L.P.P.*, I, p. 328.
23. Carlyle, Thomas, *Letters to his Youngest Sister*, London, 1899, p. 86.
24. *L.P.P.*, I, p. 348.
25. *L.P.P.*, II, p. 210.
26. *Works*, 1, p. 231.
27. *Works*, 1, p. 190.
28. *Works*, 1, p. 311.
29. *L.P.P.*, I, p. 433.
30. *L.P.P.*, I, p. 354.
31. *L.P.P.*, I, p. 366.
32. *L.P.P.*, I, p. 382.
33. Ray, Gordon, *Thackeray: The Uses of Adversity*, London, 1955, p. 204.
34. *L.P.P.*, I, p. 435.
35. *L.P.P.*, I, p. 395.
36. *L.P.P.*, I, pp. 419–20.

37. *L.P.P.*, I, p. 421.
38. *L.P.P.*, I, p. 429.
39. *L.P.P.*, I, p. 432.
40. *Works*, 3, pp. 189–205.
41. Ray, *Adversity*, p. 254.
42. *L.P.P.*, I, p. 469.
43. *L.P.P.*, I, p. 467.
44. *L.P.P.*, I, p. 471.
45. *L.P.P.*, I, p. 473.
46. *L.P.P.*, I, p. 468.
47. *L.P.P.*, I, p. 472.
48. *L.P.P.*, I, p. 476.
49. *L.P.P.*, I, p. 479.
50. *L.P.P.*, I, p. 479.
51. *L.P.P.*, I, p. 478.
52. *Biographical Introductions*, IV, pp. xxix–xxx.

CHAPTER 5

1. *L.P.P.*, II, p. 81.
2. *L.P.P.*, II, p. 15.
3. *L.P.P.*, II, p. 36.
4. *L.P.P.*, II, p. 23.
5. *L.P.P.*, II, p. 217.
6. *L.P.P.*, II, p. 43.
7. Unpublished letter, Fales Library, New York University.
8. *L.P.P.*, II, p. 440.
9. *L.P.P.*, II, p. 50.
10. *L.P.P.*, II, p. 47.
11. *L.P.P.*, II, p. 53.
12. *L.P.P.*, II, p. 137.
13. Carlyle, Thomas, *On Heroes, Hero-Worship and the Heroic in History*, London, 1897, p. 241.
14. *Works*, 3, p. 398.
15. *Works*, 3, p. 445.
16. *Works*, 3, p. 436.
17. *Works*, 3, p. 437.
18. *Works*, 3, p. 441.
19. *L.P.P.*, II, p. 10.
20. Reid, T. Wemyss, *The Life of Lord Houghton*, vol. 1, London, 1890, p. 167.

21. *Works*, 4, pp. 342–462.
22. *L.P.P.*, II, p. 88.
23. Lever, Charles, *Roland Cashel*, London, 1850, pp. 200–1.
24. FitzGerald, Edward, *The Letters of Edward FitzGerald*, ed. A. McK. Terhune and A. B. Terhune, vol. 1, Princeton, 1980, p. 329.
25. *L.P.P.*, II, p. 78.
26. *The Tablet*, 13 May 1843, pp. 291–2.
27. *Works*, 5, pp. 86–7.
28. *Works*, 5, p. 78.
29. *Works*, 5, p. 326.
30. Lever, *Cashel*, p. 200.
31. *L.P.P.*, II, p. 78.
32. Vizetelly, Henry, *Glances back through Seventy Years*, London, 1893, p. 250.
33. *Works*, 3, pp. 509–36.
34. *Works*, 8, pp. 194–207.
35. *Works*, 7, p. 30.
36. Ray, Gordon, *Thackeray: The Uses of Adversity*, p. 301.
37. *L.P.P.*, II, p. 193.
38. *Works*, 6, p. 70.
39. *L.P.P.*, II, p. 197.
40. *L.P.P.*, II, p. 240.

CHAPTER 6

1. *L.P.P.*, II, p. 82.
2. *L.P.P.*, II, p. 135.
3. *L.P.P.*, II, p. 172.
4. Jerrold, Walter, *Douglas Jerrold and 'Punch'*, London, 1910, p. 27.
5. Price, R. G. G., *A History of 'Punch'*, London, 1957, p. 51.
6. Cundall, H. M., *Birket Foster*, London, 1906, p. 36.
7. Jerrold, *Jerrold*, p. 28.
8. *Works*, 3, p. 204.
9. *L.P.P.*, II, p. 681.
10. Ruskin, John, *The Art of England* (1884), in *The Works of John Ruskin*, vol. 33, London, 1908, p. 360.
11. *Works*, 8, p. 38.
12. *Works*, 9, p. 127.
13. *The Thackeray Alphabet*, London, 1929.
14. Clough, Arthur Hugh, *Correspondence*, ed. Frederick L. Mulhauser, Oxford, 1957, vol. 2, p. 512.
15. *L.P.P.*, II, p. 97.
16. Gilbert, W. S., *The Bab Ballads*, ed. James Ellis, Harvard, 1970, p. 126.
17. *Works*, 9, p. 386.
18. *Works*, 9, p. 493.
19. *Works*, 7, pp. 439–70.
20. *L.P.P.*, II, p. 418.
21. James, Henry, *A Small Boy and Others*, London, 1913, pp. 93–4.
22. James, *Small Boy*, p. 94.
23. *Works*, 9, p. 269.
24. *Works*, 9, p. 461.
25. Bagehot, Walter, *Collected Works*, vol. 2, London, 1965, p. 308.
26. *Works*, 8, p. 155.
27. *Works*, 8, pp. 83–166.
28. *Works*, 6, p. 507.
29. *L.P.P.*, II, pp. 240–1.
30. *L.P.P.*, II, p. 110.
31. *L.P.P.*, II, p. 231.
32. *Works*, 6, p. 442.
33. Brookfield, Charles and Brookfield, Frances, *Mrs Brookfield and her Circle*, London, 1906, vol. 1, p. 163.
34. Brookfield, *Mrs Brookfield*, vol. 1, p. 174.
35. Brookfield, *Mrs Brookfield*, vol. 1, p. 191.
36. *L.P.P.*, II, pp. 255–6.
37. *L.P.P.*, IV, p. 437.
38. Unpublished letter, Morgan Library.

39. Corkran, Henriette, *Celebrities and I*, London, 1902, p. 28.
40. *L.P.P.*, II, p. 284.
41. *L.P.P.*, II, p. 233.
42. *L.P.P.*, II, pp. 242–3.
43. Carlyle, Jane Welsh, *Letters to her Family*, ed. Leonard Huxley, London, 1924, p. 279.
44. *L.P.P.*, II, p. 286.
45. *L.P.P.*, II, p. 335.
46. *L.P.P.*, II, p. 382.
47. Stephen, Leslie, *Mausoleum Book*, ed. Alan Bell, Oxford, 1977, p. xxiii.
48. *L.P.P.*, II, p. 240.
49. Stephen, *Mausoleum Book*, p. 17.
50. Corkran, *Celebrities*, p. 24.
51. Corkran, *Celebrities*, pp. 21–3.
52. *Works*, 12, p. 35.

CHAPTER 7

For a detailed analysis of the composition of *Vanity Fair*, and a discussion of Carlyle's influence on the novel, see John Sutherland, *Thackeray at Work*, London, 1974, Chapter 1, 'The art of improvisation'.
1. *L.P.P.*, II, p. 261.
2. *L.P.P.*, II, p. 318.
3. *L.P.P.*, II, p. 242.
4. *L.P.P.*, II, p. 247.
5. *L.P.P.*, II, p. 423.
6. Fitzpatrick, W. J., *Life of Charles Lever*, vol. 2, London, 1879, p. 405.
7. Sutherland, *Thackeray*, pp. 23–5.
8. Carlyle, Thomas, 'Biography', in *Critical and Miscellaneous Essays*, vol. III, London, 1899, pp. 45, 49.
9. Stevens, Joan, '*Vanity Fair* and the London Skyline', *Costerus*

N.S. II, supplementary vol I: *Thackeray*, Amsterdam, 1974, pp. 13–41.
10. Carlyle, Thomas, *On Heroes, Hero-Worship and the Heroic in History*, London, 1897, p. 183.
11. *Cornhill to Cairo*, *Works*, 9, p. 127.
12. *Biographical Introductions*, 1, p. xxviii.
13. *A Collection of Letters of W. M. Thackeray*, ed. Jane Brookfield, London, 1887, p. 178.
14. Booth, Wayne, *The Rhetoric of Fiction*, Chicago, 1961, pp. 71–7.
15. *L.P.P.*, II, p. 772.
16. Martineau, Harriet, *Autobiography*, London, 1877, p. 376.
17. *L.P.P.*, II, p. 375.
18. *L.P.P.*, II, p. 309.
19. *Works*, 11, p. 406.
20. *Works*, 11, p. 356.
21. *Works*, 11, p. 871.
22. *L.P.P.*, II, p. 394.
23. *L.P.P.*, II, p. 276.
24. *L.P.P.*, II, p. 380.
25. *L.P.P.*, II, p. 439.
26. *L.P.P.*, II, p. 309.
27. *L.P.P.*, I, p. 311.
28. Bedingfield, Richard, 'Personal Recollections of Thackeray', *Cassells Magazine*, II, 26 March 1870, p. 74.
29. *L.P.P.*, II, p. 243.
30. *L.P.P.*, I, p. 460.
31. Carlyle, 'Biography', p. 58.
32. *L.P.P.*, II, p. 378.
33. In Morgan Library, New York.
34. *L.P.P.*, II, p. 393.
35. *L.P.P.*, II, p. 401.
36. *L.P.P.*, II, p. 407.
37. *L.P.P.*, II, p. 409.

CHAPTER 8

1. *L.P.P.*, II, p. 533.
2. *L.P.P.*, II, p. 531.
3. Dickens, Charles, *The Letters of Charles Dickens*, ed. G. Storey and K. J. Fielding, vol. 5, Oxford, 1981, p. 569.
4. Ritchie, Anne Thackeray, *Chapters from some Unwritten Memoirs*, London, 1894, p. 167.
5. *L.P.P.*, II, p. 437.
6. *L.P.P.*, II, pp. 140–1.
7. *Works*, 13, p. 689.
8. *L.P.P.*, III, p. 13.
9. Unpublished letter, Fales Library, New York University.
10. Burnand, F. C., *Records and Reminiscences*, vol. 1, London, 1904, p. 237.
11. *L.P.P.*, II, p. 566.
12. *L.P.P.*, II, p. 272.
13. *L.P.P.*, II, p. 380.
14. ALS in Morgan Library, New York.
15. *L.P.P.*, II, p. 469.
16. Dickens, Charles, *Collected Works*, vol. 14, Oxford, 1954, p. 396.
17. Corkran, Henriette, *Celebrities and I*, London, 1902, p. 113.
18. Rosenbach Museum and Library, Philadelphia.
19. Rosenbach Museum and Library, Philadelphia.
20. *L.P.P.*, II, p. 662.
21. *L.P.P.*, II, p. 650.
22. *Works*, 11, p. 478.
23. *Works*, 12, p. 780.
24. *L.P.P.*, II, p. 587.
25. *L.P.P.*, II, p. 610.
26. *Biographical Introductions*, II, p. xxxvii.
27. *L.P.P.*, II, p. 609.
28. *L.P.P.*, II, p. 701.
29. *L.P.P.*, II, p. 707.
30. *L.P.P.*, II, p. 708.
31. *L.P.P.*, II, p. 719.
32. *L.P.P.*, II, p. 724.
33. *Works*, 10, p. 221.
34. Wise, Thomas J. and Symington, John A., *The Brontës: Their Lives, Friendships and Correspondence*, vol. 3, Oxford, 1932, p. 253.
35. Wise and Symington, *The Brontës*, p. 195.

CHAPTER 9

1. Wise, Thomas J. and Symington, John A., *The Brontës: Their Lives, Friendships and Correspondence*, vol. 3, Oxford, 1932, pp. 240–1.
2. Bagehot, Walter, *Collected Works*, vol. 2, London, 1965, p. 284.
3. *The Correspondence of Emerson and Carlyle*, ed. Joseph Slater, London, 1964, p. 474n.
4. *L.P.P.*, II, p. 781.
5. Wise and Symington, *The Brontës*, vol. 4, p. 67.
6. Wise and Symington, *The Brontes*, vol. 4, p. 63.
7. *L.P.P.*, II, p. 796.
8. *L.P.P.*, II, p. 795.
9. *L.P.P.*, II, p. 815.
10. *L.P.P.*, II, p. 813.
11. Trollope, Anthony, *Thackeray*, London, 1906, p. 126.
12. Rosenbach Museum and Library, Philadelphia; excerpt in *L.P.P.*, IV, p. 430.
13. Rosenbach Museum and Library, Philadelphia; excerpt in *L.P.P.*, IV, p. 428.
14. *L.P.P.*, IV, p. 429.
15. *L.P.P.*, II, p. 807.
16. *L.P.P.*, II, p. 811.

17. *L.P.P.*, IV, p. 431.
18. *L.P.P.*, IV, p. 431.
19. *L.P.P.*, IV, pp. 431–2.
20. *L.P.P.*, IV, p. 432.
21. *L.P.P.*, III, p. 17.
22. *L.P.P.*, II, p. 815.
23. Martineau, Harriet, *Autobiography*, London, 1877, p. 376.
24. Eliot, George, *Letters*, ed. Gordon Haight, vol. 2, Oxford, 1954, p. 67.
25. Wise and Symington, *The Brontës*, vol. 3, p. 315.
26. *L.P.P.*, IV, p. 125.
27. *L.P.P.*, III, p. 407.
28. *Works*, 13, p. 162.
29. *Works*, 13, pp. 17–18.
30. *Works*, 13, p. 106.
31. *Works*, 13, p. 278.
32. *Works*, 13, p. 30.
33. *Works*, 13, p. 117.
34. *Works*, 13, p. 119.
35. *Works*, 13, p. 77.
36. *Works*, 13, p. 310.
37. *Works*, 13, p. 350.
38. *Works*, 13, p. 363.
39. *Works*, 13, p. 250.
40. *L.P.P.*, II, p. 453.
41. *Works*, 13, p. 232.
42. *Works*, 13, p. 153.
43. *Works*, 13, p. 383.
44. *L.P.P.*, III, p. 248.
45. Rosenbach Museum and Library, Philadelphia.
46. Rosenbach Museum and Library, Philadelphia.

CHAPTER 10

1. *L.P.P.*, IV, p. 115.
2. *L.P.P.*, III, p. 288.
3. *The Correspondence of Thomas Carlyle and R. W. Emerson*, London, 1883, p. 207.
4. *L.P.P.*, III, p. 93.

5. *L.P.P.*, III, p. 93.
6. *L.P.P.*, III, p. 153.
7. *L.P.P.*, III, p. 168.
8. Crowe, Eyre, *With Thackeray in America*, London, 1893, p. 13.
9. *L.P.P.*, III, p. 108.
10. Auden, W. H., 'On the Circuit', *Collected Poems*, London, 1976, p. 549.
11. *L.P.P.*, III, p. 228.
12. *L.P.P.*, III, p. 123.
13. *L.P.P.*, III, p. 149.
14. *L.P.P.*, III, p. 183.
15. *L.P.P.*, IV, p. 265.
16. *Works*, 16, p. 415.
17. *L.P.P.*, III, p. 199.
18. *L.P.P.*, III, p. 229.
19. *L.P.P.*, III, p. 199.
20. *L.P.P.*, III, p. 227.
21. *L.P.P.*, III, p. 245.
22. *L.P.P.*, III, p. 260.
23. *L.P.P.*, III, p. 269.
24. *L.P.P.*, III, p. 269.
25. *L.P.P.*, III, p. 280.
26. *L.P.P.*, III, p. 283.
27. *L.P.P.*, III, p. 287.
28. *L.P.P.*, III, p. 306.
29. *L.P.P.*, III, p. 333.
30. *L.P.P.*, IV, p. 438.
31. Peruzzi de' Medici, Marchesa, 'Thackeray My Childhood's Friend', *Cornhill Magazine*, 31, 1911, pp. 178–81.
32. *L.P.P.*, III, p. 355.
33. James, Henry, *The Art of the Novel*, New York & London, 1934, p. 84.
34. *L.P.P.*, IV, p. 436.
35. Elwin, Whitwell, *Quarterly Review*, xcvii, Sept. 1855, pp. 350–78.
36. *L.P.P.*, III, p. 469.
37. Trollope, Anthony, *Autobiography*, Oxford, 1950, p. 243.
38. *L.P.P.*, III, p. 350.

39. Ray, Gordon, *The Buried Life: A Study of the Relation between Thackeray's Fiction and his Personal History*, London, 1952, p. 105.
40. *Works*, 14, p. 935.
41. *Works*, 14, p. 775.
42. Wilson, James, G., *Thackeray in the United States*, vol. 2, London, 1904, p. 90.

CHAPTER 11

1. *L.P.P.*, III, p. 415.
2. *L.P.P.*, IV, p. 30.
3. Trollope, Anthony, *Letters*, ed. N. John Hall, vol. 2, Stanford, 1983, p. 247.
4. *L.P.P.*, III, p. 364.
5. *L.P.P.*, III, p. 617.
6. *Works*, 2, p. 713.
7. *L.P.P.*, III, p. 404.
8. Pope, Alexander, *Poems*, vol. 6, London, 1964, p. 250.
9. *Works*, 15, p. 175.
10. *L.P.P.*, III, p. 645.
11. Collins, Philip, *Thackeray: Interviews and Recollections*, vol. 1, London, 1983, p. 182.
12. *L.P.P.*, IV, p. 5.
13. *L.P.P.*, III, pp. 589–90.
14. *L.P.P.*, III, p. 555.
15. *L.P.P.*, III, p. 588.
16. *L.P.P.*, III, p. 524.
17. *L.P.P.*, III, p. 642.
18. *L.P.P.*, III, p. 617.
19. *Works*, 15, p. 425.
20. Elwin, Whitwell, *Some XVIIIth Century Men of Letters*, vol. 1, London, 1902, p. 157.
21. *Works*, 15, p. 592.
22. *Works*, 15, p. 427.
23. *L.P.P.*, IV, p. 86.
24. Collins, *Thackeray*, vol. 2, p. 290.
25. *Works*, 15, p. 361.

26. *Works*, 6, p. 507.
27. Trollope, *Letters*, vol. 2, p. 671.
28. Sala, George Augustus, *Things I Have Seen and People I Have Known*, London, 1894, p. 41.
29. *Correspondence of Carlyle and Emerson*, London, 1883, vol. 2, p. 230.
30. Collins, *Thackeray*, vol. 2, p. 276.
31. Merivale, Herman and Marzials, Frank, *Life of W. M. Thackeray*, London, 1891, p. 12.

CHAPTER 12

1. Martineau, Harriet, *Letters to Fanny Wedgwood*, ed. Elisabeth Sanders Arbuckle, Stanford, 1983, p. 182.
2. Collins, Philip, *Thackeray: Interviews and Recollections*, vol. 2, London, 1983, p. 344.
3. *L.P.P.*, IV, p. 152.
4. *L.P.P.*, IV, p. 227.
5. *L.P.P.*, IV, p. 207.
6. *Works*, 17, p. 60.
7. *L.P.P.*, IV, p. 236.
8. *L.P.P.*, IV, p. 213.
9. *L.P.P.*, IV, p. 271.
10. Collins, *Thackeray*, vol. 2, p. 349.
11. Elwin, Whitwell, *Some XVIIIth century Men of Letters*, vol. 1, London, 1902, p. 245.
12. *L.P.P.*, IV, p. 272.
13. *L.P.P.*, IV, p. 230.
14. Ritchie, Anne Thackeray, *From the Porch*, London, 1913, p. 227.
15. Collins, *Thackeray*, vol. 2, p. 345.
16. Collins, *Thackeray*, vol. 2, p. 298.

17. Collins, *Thackeray*, vol. 2, p. 152.
18. *Cornhill Magazine*, 4, 1861, p. 309.
19. *Works*, 16, p. 283.
20. *Works*, 16, p. 281.
21. *L.P.P.*, IV, p. 270.
22. FitzGerald, Edward, *The Letters of Edward FitzGerald*, ed. A. McK. Terhune and A. B. Terhune, vol. 2, Princeton, 1980, p. 393.
23. *L.P.P.*, IV, p. 273.
24. *L.P.P.*, IV, p. 292.
25. *Biographical Introductions*, 12, p. xxvii.
26. Collins, *Thackeray*, vol. 2, pp. 371–2.
27. Collins, *Thackeray*, vol. 1, p. 183.
28. Peruzzi de' Medici, Marchesa, 'Thackeray My Childhood's Friend', *Cornhill Magazine*, 31, 1911, pp. 181.
29. *Biographical Introductions*, 12, p. xxxii.
30. Collins, *Thackeray*, vol. 2, p. 306.
31. *Works*, 16, p. 443.
32. Reid, T. Wemyss, *The Life of Lord Houghton*, vol. 2, London, 1890, p. 113.

Illustrations

CHAPTER II

CHAPTER I2

Index

À Beckett, Gilbert, 118, 234
Addison, Joseph, 197
Age, The, 118
Ainsworth, Harrison, 199
  Crighton, 80; *Jack Sheppard*, 86
Albert (ballet dancer), 66
Albert, Prince Consort, 122, 237, 251
Alexander, Miss, 139, 170
Allen, John, 24, 26, 33, 144
Arcedeckne, Andrew, 249
Arthur, Mr, 7, 8
Ashburton, Lady, 200, 201
Athenaeum, 260
Athenaeum Club, 260
Aytoun, William, 143

Baden, 198, 220
Badger, Albert, 24–5
Bagehot, Walter, 130, 196
Bakewell, Mrs, 97
Barnum, James T., 216
Baxter, Mrs George, 200, 217, 218
Baxter, Lucy, 217
Baxter, Sally (Mrs Hampton), 217,
  229, 241, 246, 260
Bayley, F. W. N., 61
Bayne, Alicia

Memorials of the Thackeray Family,
  225
Becher, Miss Anne, 3, 6, 226, 238
Becher, Harriet, 3
Becher, John Harmon, 2
Becher, Mrs John, 3, 227, 238
Bedingfield, Richard, 4, 20, 99, 163
Beethoven, Ludwig van: *Fidelio*, 34;
  Vittoria, 35
Bell, Laura, 179
Bell, Robert, 144
Bellows, Reverend, 217
Bentley's Miscellany, 81, 86
Beranger, Pierre-Jean
  'Le Roi d'Yvetot', 59
Berry, Agnes, 237
Berry, Mary, 237–8
Blackwood, John, 203
Blackwood's Magazine, 59, 60, 143
Blanchard, Laman, 234
Bölte, Amely, 138
Booth, Wayne, 150
Boppard am Rhein, 96–7
Boston, Massachusetts, 215
Boyes, Frederick, 14, 15, 18
Boyes, Mrs, 14
Bradbury and Evans, Messrs, 118,